The Bible and Epistemology

Biblical Soundings on the Knowledge of God

Sometimes a book, like this one, fulfils a need that is so clear and obvious one wonders why it has not already been done. But it has not. In all the fine work in epistemology done by contemporary Christian philosophers, there has been little attention paid to what the Bible itself says about epistemological questions, and biblical scholars themselves have barely scratched the surface in these matters. This book gives us a series of essays by biblical scholars who are experts in their own fields while being conversant with contemporary work in epistemology by philosophers and theologians. The questions raised are not always the ones western philosophers since the Enlightenment have raised, and that is all to the good. Let us hope that this book will be the start of a profound conversation between biblical scholars, theologians, and philosophers about knowledge and belief. It is a provocative and worthy beginning, one that points us not merely to important New Testament themes found in Paul, John, and Luke-Acts, but helps us see what the Old Testament has to contribute to an understanding of knowledge.'
C. Stephen Evans, University Professor of Philosophy and Humanities, Baylor University, USA

'If it seems unlikely that the Bible offers anything so intellectually refined as an epistemology, this book gives ample evidence to the contrary. Sensitive to both the diversity of the biblical literature and the unity of the canon, these essays show how the interest of the biblical writers in questions about knowledge – above all, naturally, the knowledge of God – is at once pervasive, complex, and coherent. Here biblical scholarship makes a needed and important contribution to closing the gaps, damaging for all, between biblical studies, theology, and philosophy.'
Bruce D. Marshall, Professor of Historical Theology, Southern Methodist University, Dallas, USA

'These essays show how the Bible gives understanding to those who read it in faith. The book examines the new meaning that wisdom, knowledge, information, and belief take on when they occur in response to the Word of God, whether in the Old or the New Testament, whether spoken by the Psalmist or the Prophet, by the Evangelist or St. Paul. It shows that God's revelation of himself can be received only by those who are "attentive" under the guidance of the Holy Spirit. The epistemology it discusses is not sceptical, distrustful, or anxious but contemplative. The book is a superb expression of both faith and reason.'
Robert S. Sokolowski, The Elizabeth Breckenridge Caldwell Professor of Philosophy, Catholic University of America, USA

'Robin Parry and Mary Healy are to be commended for providing a welcome, and long overdue, biblical voice to scholarly debates about the nature of Christian belief. In *The Bible and Epistemology* epistemic issues such as the roles played by faith, reason, empirical experience and the Holy Spirit in forming and justifying Christian belief are examined in terms of how they function within specific biblical texts themselves. What emerges is a timely collection of critical essays from a number of top-notch biblical scholars and Christian thinkers from Protestant and Roman Catholic positions that push the debate about the Bible and epistemology back to the text of Scripture, reminding us first to listen to what it is has to say about issues of belief and faith.'
Myron B. Penner, Professor of Philosophy and Theology, Prairie Bible College, Canada

The Bible and Epistemology

Biblical Soundings on the Knowledge of God

Mary Healy and Robin Parry

MILTON KEYNES ● COLORADO SPRINGS ● HYDERABAD

Paternoster is an imprint of Authentic Media
9 Holdom Avenue, Bletchley, Milton Keynes, MK1 1QR, U.K.
1820 Jet Stream Drive, Colorado Springs, CO 80921, USA
OM Authentic Media, Medchal Road, Jeedimetla Village,
Secunderabad 500 055, A.P., India

www.authenticmedia.co.uk
Authentic Media is a division of IBS-STL U.K., a company limited by
guarantee (registered charity no. 270162)

British Library Cataloguing in Publication Data
A catalogue record for this book is available from the British Library

ISBN 978-1-84227-540-5

Typeset by Anthony Cross
Design by fourninezero design
Print Management by Adare
Printed in Great Britain by J.H. Haynes & Co., Sparkford

For Craig Bartholomew

Contents

Contributors

Cornelis Bennema is Associate Professor of New Testament and Department Head at SAIACS, a postgraduate seminary in Bangalore, India (www.saiacs.org). Among his publications are *The Power of Saving Wisdom: An Investigation of Spirit and Wisdom in Relation to the Soteriology of the Fourth Gospel* (WUNT II/148) and *Excavating John's Gospel: A Commentary for Today.*

Mary Healy is Adjunct Professor of Scripture at Ave Maria University's Institute for Pastoral Theology, and serves as leader of Mother of God Community, a lay Catholic community in Gaithersburg, Maryland. She is the author of *Men and Women Are from Eden: A Study Guide to Pope John Paul II's Theology of the Body* and co-editor of *Behind the Text: History and Biblical Interpretation* and *Out of Egypt: Biblical Theology and Biblical Interpretation.*

Francis Martin holds the Cardinal Adam Maida Chair for Graduate Scripture Studies at the Sacred Heart Major Seminary in Detroit and is also Senior Fellow at the John Paul II Cultural Center in Washington D.C. Among Fr. Martin's many books are: *Sacred Scripture*, *The Disclosure of the Word* and *Acts* in the Ancient Christian Commentary Series.

Ryan P. O'Dowd is Assistant Professor of Old Testament at Briercrest College in Canada. His PhD thesis was on *The Wisdom of Torah: Epistemology in Deuteronomy and the Wisdom Literature.* He has published several essays on creation theology, wisdom and poetry in the Old Testament.

Robin Parry is Editorial Director for Paternoster. He is author of *Old Testament Story and Christian Ethics* and *Worshipping Trinity* as well as several academic articles. He co-edited *The Futures of Evangelicalism, Universal Salvation?, Out of Egypt* and *Canon and Biblical Interpretation.* His current project is the Two Horizons commentary on Lamentations.

Murray Rae is Senior Lecturer in Theology and Ethics at the University of Otago, New Zealand. His most recent book, *History and Hermeneutics,* adds to a range of publications on biblical theology and hermeneutics. He has also published extensively on the thought of Søren Kierkegaard, and on theological ethics.

Thomas D. Stegman is Assistant Professor of New Testament at the Weston Jesuit School of Theology in Cambridge, Massachusetts. A Jesuit since 1985, he earned a PhD in New Testament studies from Emory University. He is the author of *The Character of Jesus: The Linchpin to Paul's Argument in 2 Corinthians* (Analecta Biblica).

D.C. Schindler is an Assistant Professor of Philosophy in the Department of Humanities at Villanova University. He is the author of *Hans Urs von Balthasar and the Dramatic Structure of Truth: A Philosophical Investigation* and *Plato's Critique of Impure Reason: On Truth and Goodness in Plato's* Republic (forthcoming), as well as numerous articles in journals of philosophy and theology.

Gregory Vall is Associate Professor of Theology at Ave Maria University in Naples, Florida, where he teaches courses in Sacred Scripture and biblical languages. He has published articles in *Vetus Testamentum, Biblica, Catholic Biblical Quarterly, Journal of Biblical Literature, The Thomist, Nova et Vetera*, and *The Bible Today*.

Introduction

Mary Healy and Robin Parry

'Let us know, let us press on to know the LORD.' (Hosea 6:3)

Issues surrounding 'belief' and 'knowledge' have been central to philosophical inquiry for as long as human beings have been reflecting philosophically. What is 'knowledge'? Can we know anything, and if so, what, and how? What are the sources of our knowing (e.g., perception, memory, consciousness, reason, testimony, divine revelation), and can they actually support something as robust as 'knowledge'? What is the structure of knowledge? Can doubt ever be eliminated? How might different modes of 'knowing' be distinguished from each other? Is there an ethic of belief such that certain kinds of epistemic practice are to be considered not merely unreliable (if truth is one's goal) but also substandard, irresponsible and perhaps even 'immoral'? Does one need evidence for one's beliefs and, if so, why, what kinds of evidence and how much of it? These and a myriad of other questions clamor for the attention of the philosopher. Epistemology is not merely academic theorizing unrelated to the gritty reality of life – it deals with matters at the heart of all our human engagement with the world, with other people, and with God. This is why it has been, and will ever remain, central to the task of the philosopher.

Less often appreciated is the importance of epistemology for a biblical Christian faith. Christians believe certain things and claim to know certain things. More than that, Christians claim to know and to be known by God. Living in the modern world one cannot be a Christian and escape epistemological questions: Is it rational to believe in God? Is tradition a valid source for belief? Does faith in the resurrection of Jesus, say, require evidence? Can religious experiences be trustworthy grounds for religious faith? How can conflicting religious truth claims be tested? Can one know *God*? Or, in more postmodern mode, are religious claims to knowledge merely power plays or thinly disguised acts of intolerance?

Christian theologians and Christian philosophers have spilled much ink on matters epistemological. They always have and, no doubt, always will. Nevertheless, it would be true to say that in the past thirty years there has been something of an explosion of serious Christian epistemological reflection. There is certainly no unanimity, with believers taking some quite diverse positions, but there is some very healthy work being done within faith and for faith. In these exciting times, faith is continuing to seek understanding.

In the midst of this renewal of Christian epistemological reflection, however, lies a curious black hole. The unaccountable void to which we refer lies in the world of biblical studies. If one seeks to discover what the Bible reveals about matters epistemological it would be natural to think we could turn for an answer to biblical scholars. But amazingly, there has been very little work done by biblical scholars on what various biblical texts may contribute to the wider discussion on knowledge in general and knowledge of God in particular. Certainly, Christian theologians and philosophers have sought to develop accounts of knowledge that are true to Scripture, but in most cases their training is not biblical studies, and so their engagement with the text can lack rigor and nuance. This is no fault of the theologians and philosophers – it is difficult to be an expert in even one field in this age of over-specialization. What is surprising is that, with few exceptions, biblical scholars have not sought to mine the texts to see what, if anything, they may contribute to the discussion. Why is this the case? Is it because biblical scholars do not feel that the texts address matters in any way that would contribute to systematic reflections on epistemology? Perhaps that is part of it. Is it because biblical scholars feel ill-equipped to handle philosophical and theological questions given that their own specialization is in biblical exegesis? That is most certainly part of the reason (as evidenced by our struggle to find biblical scholars both able and willing to contribute to this volume). Could it be that the catastrophic chasm between theology (which, in some contemporary manifestations, is remarkably uninterested in the Bible) and biblical studies (which often aspires to a mythical theological neutrality) has meant that many Christian biblical scholars are not even aware that their theological and philosophical colleagues are asking such questions? Perhaps that too accounts for part of the lacuna. Whatever the reasons, it is clear that biblical scholars have not paid very much attention to what the biblical texts may have to contribute to discussions on epistemology. This means that when theologians and philosophers look for guidance on what Scripture has to say on such matters, there is little of substance to turn to.

The aim of this volume is to begin to fill in this conspicuous and perilous hole in Christian reflection. If issues of knowledge are critical to our faith and discipleship, and if thinking through such questions in the light of Scripture is non-negotiable, then we need biblical scholars to look at the texts afresh, armed with epistemological questions. Even if this book should fail to achieve our goals – and we trust that it will not – and merely inspires other scholars to go and do the job better, then the effort will have been worthwhile. But we trust that readers will find much in the pages that follow that is both inspiring and insightful. The writers are all competent scholars who have a living faith in the triune God and a desire to bridge any gaps between academic biblical studies and the life of the Church. Although they may not agree on everything, the common insights that appear in these diverse essays are telling, and suggest that there is a genuine unity in what Scripture has to say on the issues at hand. What is exciting is the prominent role played in biblical epistemologies by matters that are atypical of many philosophical discussions – for instance, revelation, the Holy Spirit, personal relationship, obedience to God, a life of worship and prayer, community, tradition and engagement with the Scriptures. The very strangeness of some of these biblical conditions for knowledge of God is a challenge to us: Have we been guilty of allowing our agenda to be set by presuppositions foreign to Christian faith? Might biblical revelation have real philosophical wisdom to contribute even to those beyond the Church? For instance, the thought that perhaps certain kinds of knowledge depend on ethical living or prayer seems quite out of place in many contemporary philosophical works, but precisely for that reason it presents a distinctive contribution and offers fuel for reflection and praxis. The complex relationship between knowing God and holy living is suggestive and full of potential for systematic exploration.

It is worth mentioning one crucial clarification at this point. The Bible never presents a systematic or philosophical theory of knowledge. So the place of the Bible in Christian reflections on epistemic issues is not that of providing a comprehensive account. The Bible is not going to settle all our questions. But it does not follow that the Bible has nothing to contribute to theoretical analyses of knowledge. The Bible has much to say that needs to be fed into Christian discussions of faith, reason, belief, trust, knowledge and the like. Its contributions to epistemology are in part explicit and in part implicit, but either way, the Bible provides fundamental insights that Christian thinkers need to accommodate. Any Christian account of knowledge that runs against those biblical rocks will eventually find itself shipwrecked. If scriptural teachings are ignored by an account of knowledge then it is not true to the faith and (false epistemic modesty notwithstanding) not true to reality.

Two observations about the subtitle of the book are in order. First, the goal of the book is to provide 'biblical *soundings*' and not an exhaustive biblical survey. We have not tried to cover all the ground, and there are some obvious gaps. However, we have chosen to drill our shafts in strategic places, with the aim of giving some sense of the breadth of the biblical material. There are explorations in the Pentateuch, Prophetic Literature (including some narrative texts), Psalms, Wisdom Literature, a Synoptic gospel and Acts, John, and Paul. Although not every biblical genre, author, or book is covered, the intention has been to 'take the temperature' at various key locations. The upshot is that readers will come away with a fairly detailed understanding of certain key texts and a broad grasp of the Bible's epistemology as a whole. Clearly, further investigation is required on other biblical texts as well as on the ones already surveyed in this book. We make no claim to present the last word. This book is about opening up new avenues on an old conversation, but much more work is needed to take the project further.

Second, this volume is concerned almost exclusively with 'the knowledge of God' rather than with knowledge in general. Consequently, many of the usual questions philosophers ask about faith, reason and knowledge are not directly addressed here. This is not because the Bible has nothing to contribute to a general epistemology, but because much of its distinctive contribution is found in the area of religious knowledge. And even in this limited area it will leave many matters open for further reflection. We would not wish to suggest that Scripture resolves more questions than it actually does.

The Content of This Volume

Our exploration begins with Ryan O'Dowd's analysis of the sophisticated epistemological strategy of Deuteronomy, the 'book of memory'. As O'Dowd shows, Deuteronomy concludes the Pentateuch – the initial phase of Yahweh's self-revelation in the history of Israel – by ensuring that the knowledge gained will endure in present and future generations. Israel's knowledge is grounded in its historical experience of God's ontological presence and activity, uniquely mediated through his theophanies to Moses. But that knowledge cannot be confined to the past; it must be continually 'actualized' in the present through a corporate memory, rooted in obedience to the torah. Deuteronomy thus teaches that Israel's access to knowledge of God is renewed in successive generations by *living* the redemptive story in accord with the torah.

Gregory Vall brings us forward to a later period of Israelite history, the time of the monarchy, where he finds a 'nascent epistemology of faith'. The narratives of the pre-classical prophets in Samuel and Kings witness to a knowledge of God that is inseparable from the historical particularity of land and people. Access to authentic knowledge entails a life-transforming encounter with Yahweh through one of his true prophets, leading to a confession of faith. Epistemological issues are explored in further depth by the early classical prophet Hosea, for whom knowledge is fundamentally 'an interpersonal relationship between a free and righteous God and free human moral agents'. As such, knowledge includes both a practical-ethical dimension and an emotional-mystical dimension, without sacrificing an objective, propositional content. Ultimately, epistemic certitude only comes through the historical drama by which Israel experiences, first, God's just punishment for sin, and ultimately, his merciful restoration. The prophetic tradition thus affirms the 'epistemologically decisive' role of repentance.

A different and complementary approach is taken by Francis Martin in his exposition of the epistemology of the Psalms, as exemplified by Psalm 86. Martin first briefly traces the progressive loss of transcendence and 'epistemological estrangement' in modern Western thought, where knowledge as assimilation gave way to knowledge as domination, ending in the pervasive hermeneutics of suspicion. He then turns to an analysis of Psalm 86, showing how the retrieval of a biblical view of knowledge as an implicit invitation to communion with God can heal our 'carefully constructed isolation' and recover our intrinsic orientation to transcendence. The prayer of the psalmist reveals that the most fundamental aspect of epistemology is founded in the human capacity to relate to God. Knowledge resides in the 'heart', the centre of human decision and place of encounter where we are addressed by God whom we must answer.

O'Dowd picks up the thread again with an investigation of the complex epistemology of the wisdom literature. Focusing on Proverbs, Job and Ecclesiastes, O'Dowd untangles the 'sometimes atonal and conflicting' themes in these ancient reflections on wisdom. The book of Proverbs, with its repeated refrain of 'the fear of Yahweh', refutes an idea of wisdom as the autonomous accumulation of information, in favour of wisdom as a 'divinely initiated and guided interpretation of reality', founded on a religious encounter with Yahweh. The book of Job explores the epistemological quandary created by the apparent conflict between the suffering of the righteous and the just order found in the created world. Struggling with this dilemma in confrontation with God leads to wisdom as a 'reinterpretation of the whole' in recognition of the limits of human knowledge. Finally, Ecclesiastes at first seems to adopt an unqualifiedly empiricist and rationalistic view of knowledge, resulting in skepticism. But ultimately Qohelet's own misguided search for an unbounded accumulation of worldly knowledge deliberately deconstructs itself. Forming a frame with Proverbs, the author concludes that 'the end of the matter is to fear God'.

The New Testament's witness to the fulfillment of divine revelation in Christ brings to the foreground themes that were only implicit in the earlier biblical tradition. Thomas Stegman begins by analyzing the epistemology of Luke-Acts in terms set by the evangelist himself: that is, his expressed aim of instilling 'certainty' in his reader (Lk 1:4). As Stegman shows, for Luke 'certainty' entails not only knowledge of persons, things and events, but a recognition of their significance within God's plan of salvation. Such knowledge is inculcated by demonstrating how Scripture is fulfilled in Jesus and in the early Church. But only the Holy Spirit can guarantee the correct interpretation of Scripture. Stegman thus finds two unifying threads in a Lukan epistemology. First, the prominence of the Holy Spirit, who both directs the course of events and assures a proper understanding of God's saving actions in history. Second, the necessity of prayer as the means by which the human spirit is opened to the presence and activity of the Spirit. The knowledge thus gained is *transformative* of individuals and communities as they become protagonists and agents in the unfolding story of salvation'.

Cornelis Bennema sheds light on the rich landscape of Johannine epistemology. For John, the human condition is characterized by epistemic darkness: people are unable to 'see', 'hear' or 'know' God. This darkness is overcome by the divine revelation given in Jesus' person and teaching, mediated by the Spirit. The Spirit acts as an epistemic agent, facilitating perception, unlocking the truth revealed in Jesus and enabling the proper human response of belief. Belief includes both a cognitive aspect (perceiving the truth) and a volitional aspect (accepting that truth and committing oneself to Jesus). Through the human response of belief the Spirit brings a person into a life-giving relationship with the Father and the Son, which gives access to further knowledge. John thus asserts a cyclical or spiral relationship between knowledge and belief, such that each stimulates and informs the other.

Mary Healy takes up the often-neglected complex of epistemological themes in the letters of St Paul. As Healy shows, Pauline epistemology involves a two-way dynamic, where knowing is the human act that follows and corresponds to God's act of revelation. Revelation is an irreducibly personal act by which God discloses his own inmost mystery through his interventions in human history, culminating in the crucifixion of his Son. Faith-informed knowledge of God, in response, involves a personal engagement whereby the believer existentially appropriates the reality of God's redemptive self-gift. Pauline knowledge of God thus has an inescapably ethical dimension, since experiential knowledge of God's saving power cannot but lead to inner transformation, resulting in a perceptible change in one's outward conduct. Paul affirms the essential role of the Holy Spirit in this relational dynamic, empowering the human mind to probe 'the depths of God' and to comprehend the immeasurable scope of divine love.

Finally, to set the ball rolling on a broader discussion, we invited one theologian and one philosopher to gather up the insights gleaned from the biblical essays and comment on how they interface with their own discipline. First, Murray Rae offers a theological reflection, noting the 'striking consistency' he finds in the epistemology of the biblical authors. He traces the prominent features of the biblical understanding of knowledge as 'attentiveness', which challenges many of the assumptions of the culture of modernity and is fraught with theological implications. Then D.C. Schindler reflects on the philosophical issues raised by the biblical insights – not least of which is the very possibility of a 'biblical' epistemology, given the irreducible concreteness and singularity of biblical revelation. He explores both the convergences and the novelties of biblical epistemology with respect to the philosophical tradition, both classical and postmodern – leading to some profoundly suggestive conclusions.

There is no intention of suggesting that these are the definitive or only philosophical and theological responses to the biblical material – the goal is simply to provoke further conversation. As mentioned above, much work remains to be done on issues of 'Bible and epistemology'. For a start, there are other texts that would merit closer scrutiny. The book of Jeremiah, for instance, raises the issue of how Israel is to know who is the true prophet and who is the false prophet. How does one know who has 'stood in the council of the Lord' and can thus speak for God? This is both a practical and a profoundly epistemological question. The book of Revelation and other apocalyptic literature, littered with revelations of God through words and visions, would make for an interesting study. Narrative texts, particularly central narratives such as the Sinai stories, have much to teach about what enables and what obscures the knowledge of God. The Adam and Eve story would, under examination, bear interesting fruit. And what of the strange Isaianic theme of God blinding people to the truth so that they do not turn and be healed (Is 6:8-10), which Jesus himself appropriates as an explanation of why he speaks in parables (Mt 13:10-17) and why some people do not believe in him (Jn 12:36-43)? What of Paul's teaching on God's hardening the majority of Israel so that they would not believe the message of the gospel (Rom 9-11)? The outcome of such studies must not be prejudged, but the task is certainly worthy.

It would also be interesting to examine the epistemological impact of the very form of the biblical texts themselves and the kind of reading experience they engender. One will find some discussion of that issue in this volume (see, for instance, O'Dowd on Deuteronomy and Martin on the Psalms). It would be worthwhile to explore the implications of the 'epistemological playfulness' of biblical narrative – the way in which biblical narrators exploit the tensions between what they know, what the readers know and what the characters know. The narrator controls the information flow to readers with various effects and to various ends, and the very way in which readers are engaged is fundamentally an epistemological journey full of twists and turns. Discussions on Bible and epistemology cannot focus merely on the content of the texts to the exclusion of their form. In sum, this book is a start and not an end to the exploration of the contribution of Scripture to Christian reflection on epistemology.

Right from the start this project was conceived as an ecumenical and international effort. Having one Catholic editor (Mary Healy) and one evangelical editor (Robin Parry) ensured that the balance of essays reflected this goal and that each individual essay was scrutinized by both a pair of Catholic and a pair of Protestant eyes. It is our conviction that what unites us is more fundamental than what divides us – which is not to suggest that we see eye-to-eye on everything. It is our conviction that we can explore the wonders of the Scriptures better together than we can apart.

We would like to dedicate this book to Professor Craig Bartholomew in gratitude for his encouragement in the project, his long-term appreciation of the importance of enriching epistemological reflection with biblical scholarship, and his work in bringing Protestant and Catholic scholars together in the hermeneutical engagement with Scripture as the Church's Book. Indeed, it was at one such gathering, at Gordon College in New England in 2002, that we met and this project was dreamed up. So we dedicate this book to Craig and offer it to the Church catholic in its ongoing pursuit of God.

Part I

Biblical Soundings on the Knowledge of God

CHAPTER 1

Memory on the Boundary:
Epistemology in Deuteronomy

Ryan P. O'Dowd

But men remembered little of all that, though some still sang old songs of the dwarf-kings of the Mountain, Thror ... Some sang too that Thror would come back one day and gold would flow in the rivers ... But this pleasant legend did not much affect their daily business. (J.R.R. Tolkien, *The Hobbit*)

Introduction

Deuteronomy is the Old Testament book of memory, par excellence. But Deuteronomy's memory is decisively not a 'recollection' of the old, but rather a 'repetition' which renews the past in the present.[1] In other words, Deuteronomy uses every rhetorical, linguistic and theological tool in its power to 'actualize' the realities of Israel's past in new times and new places. In this chapter, I will demonstrate how Deuteronomy's demand for actualization is meant to shape and protect Israel's knowledge by grounding it in the ontological realities of her history with her God.

Deuteronomy as Story

Before considering the details of Deuteronomy's actualising strategy, it is first necessary to understand how Deuteronomy's meaning is shaped by its place and function in the canon. Sternberg aptly notes, 'Narrative order, event order, world order, hang all together in proper hierarchy, each reflecting its superior to the gain of its own coherence and their joint impact.'[2] When the majority of scholars remove Deuteronomy from its place in the Pentateuch and interpret it in the context of a late

---

[1] Cf. Kirkegaard's similar distinctions between these terms, *Fear and Trembling/Repetition*, H.V. Hong and E.H. Hong (trs. and eds.) (Princeton, NJ: Princeton University Press, 1983), 131ff.

[2] M. Sternberg, 'Time and Space in Biblical (Hi)Story Telling: The Grand Chronology', in *The Book and the Text: The Bible and Literary Theory*, Regina Schwartz (ed.) (Oxford: Blackwell, 1990), 89.

monarchical setting, they (unknowingly) change the narrative order and therefore distort the 'represented' world and the meaning of the book.[3] Because we are interested in the epistemology (and ontology) in Deuteronomy, this simply will not do. As such, the following analysis seeks to describe Deuteronomy's epistemological nature through a canonical and literary reading of the Pentateuch.[4]

We can, therefore, make special note of the strategic functions of *structure*, *rhetoric* and *theology* in Deuteronomy as they form several concentric and framing patterns in the book. Among these are: the commanding presence of Moses' four speeches (1:6ff; 5:1ff; 29:2ff; 33:2ff); the concentric frame of the narrator's speeches (1:1; 4:44f; 28:69; 33:1);[5] the spatial frame of travel from past (Deut 1-3), to present (4:1; 5:3 etc.) to future (Deut 31-34);[6] and the theological and legal wordplay between *tôrâ* (law/teaching) and *dābār* (word) which moves Deuteronomy from speech to writing – from words of torah (1:1-5) to a book of the torah (17:19; 31:24-26).[7] Together, we will see that these framing devices serve Deuteronomy's overall goal of demanding that future generations actualize past realities. Our study will follow the book's natural division into three parts:[8]

From Horeb to Moab: The Past in the Present (Deut 1-11)
Time and Place: The Past in the Future (Deut 12-26)
From Moab to Shechem: Covenant Ceremonies Past, Present and Future (Deut 27-34)

---

[3] M. Sternberg, *The Poetics of Biblical Narrative* (Bloomington, Indiana: Indiana University Press, 1987), 36f says, '... the Bible then falls squarely under the universal rule of representation, whereby the represented and the real world always interrelate.' Cf. O. O'Donovan, *Resurrection and Moral Order; An Outline for Evangelical Ethics* (Leicester, England: Inter-Varsity Press, 1986), 19f.

[4] On the necessity for synchronic reading see P.D. Miller, *Deuteronomy*, Interpretation (Louisville, KY: John Knox Press, 1990), 22f and Jean-Pierre Sonnet, *The Book Within the Book: Writing in Deuteronomy* (Leiden, New York: Brill, 1997), 23f.

[5] See Sonnet, *Book*, 17f, but cf. D.T. Olson, *Deuteronomy and the Death of Moses: A Theological Reading* (Minneapolis, Minnesota: Fortress, 1994), 14f, who adds a similar phrase at 6:1. This, however, is not part of the narrator's speech.

[6] See C.J.H. Wright, *Deuteronomy*, NIBC (Peabody, MA: Hendrickson Publishers/Carlisle: Paternoster, 1996), 4f, and D.L. Christensen, *Deuteronomy 1:1–21:9*, WBC (Dallas, TX: Thomas Nelson, 2001), 4f. Christensen also shows how the book has a concentric Menorah structure ideal for the eleven weekly divisions for Jewish recitations of the book (xciii-xciv).

[7] See Sonnet, *Book* and S.D. McBride, 'Polity of the Covenant People; The Book of Deuteronomy', in *Song of Power*, D.L. Christensen (ed.) (Winona Lake: Eisenbrauns, 1993), 64f.

[8] Speaking to Deuteronomy's structure, Christensen warns that no single structure can capture a work of art and too much attention on the form can detract from the effects of the plot. In the end one should 'enjoy the music'. 'Form and Structure in Deuteronomy 1–11', in *Das Deuteronomium*, Norbert Lohfink (ed.) (Leuven, 1985), 139.

The existence and synthetic force of this structure will be demonstrated in the material that follows. Suffice it to say for now that the book envisions geographical, historical and ethical progress as communicated at a stationary point in time: 'Today'; 'And now'.[9] Rhetorically, this repeated call to 'today' at Moab in fact extends trans-generationally to all readers: 'today is always today'.[10] The past can and should be brought to life in each generation.

From Horeb to Moab: The Past in the Present

Deuteronomy begins with a narrator telling about the past. His first phrase, 'These are the words of Moses' (1:1), shifts the momentum of the previous four books (Genesis to Numbers) away from divine and toward human speech. In Exodus, Moses receives the ten *dĕbārîm* (words) of Yahweh at Sinai (Ex 24:3f; 31;18; 34:27f), and both Leviticus and Numbers begin with God's voice calling to Moses. In Numbers alone the phrase 'Yahweh spoke to Moses' occurs 44 times. Deuteronomy, on the other hand, is the last and abiding words of Moses, Yahweh's mediator (cf. Num 12–17), which begins in the past and is brought to life again by the narrator in the present.

Chapters 1-3 give a concise account of Israel's desert wandering, already recorded in Numbers, not only to position Israel at the end (and new beginning) of their journey toward their entrance into the Promised Land, but also to situate a dying Moses between Yahweh and the nation for his final words (cf. Deut 5:4). In these chapters, a pattern begins – continuing in Deuteronomy 4-5 – whereby Deuteronomy commandeers the Pentateuchal history and turns it into an oral and written tradition for actualization in future generations.

In the larger Pentateuchal story, Yahweh's main purpose for Israel is to begin a process of worldwide redemption. This emerges most clearly in Genesis 12:1-3 and 18:17-19 where Yahweh institutes his re-creative intention for the faith and obedience of Abraham's offspring to result in a blessing and witness to the nations.[11]

---

[9] Depending on how one interprets the various contexts, 'today' (*hayyôm*) occurs 62-74 times in Deuteronomy while 'now' and 'and now' (*wĕʿattâ*) appears strategically in 4:1; 6:1; 10:12, 22; 26:10; 27:1; 31:19 and 32:39. See especially the discussion on Israel's view of history in S.J. DeVries, *Yesterday, Today and Tomorrow: Time and History in the Old Testament* (London: SPCK, 1975), 173f.; J. van Goudoever, 'The Liturgical Significance of the Date in Dt 1,3', in *Das Deuteronomium*, Norbert Lohfink (ed.) (Leuven: Brill, 1985), 148; in addition to the references in note 10.

[10] Cf. J.G. Millar, 'Living at the Place of Decision: Time and Place in the Framework of Deuteronomy', in *Time and Place*, J.G. McConville and J.G. Millar (Sheffield: Sheffield Academic Press, 1994), 43-49; and Olson, *Deuteronomy*, 41f.

[11] See D.J.A. Clines, *The Theme of the Pentateuch*, JSOTSup 10 (Sheffield: Sheffield Academic Press, 1978); Gordon Wenham *Story as Torah: Reading the Old Testament Ethically* (Edinburgh: T. & T. Clark, 2000), 23f; and Richard Bauckham, *Bible and Mission: Christian Witness in a Postmodern World* (Carlisle: Paternoster, 2003).

Genesis thus begins a story of Israel's creational vocation in her covenant relationship with Yahweh which is continued in Exodus and beyond.

The exodus narrative (Ex 1-15) is pivotal in this process as it creates a redemptive and epistemological foundation for the Deuteronomic torah. Zimmerli and Eslinger draw our attention to the unique collocation of *yd‘* (to know) and *Yahweh* in Exodus 1-15 which are combined 'that you (he, they) might know that I am Yahweh.'[12] Not only does this phrase appear for the first time in Pharaoh's question in Exodus 5:2, but its frequency in these chapters is unmatched in the Old Testament aside from Ezekiel 1-40 – passages which hold forth the same epistemological intentions.[13] This leads Eslinger to conclude, correctly, that 'Freeing Israel from Egypt's power seems the point of the whole affair, but a careful look at the overall shape of the events ... leads me to believe that liberation is subordinate to the *manifestation of the divine name* through the miraculous interventions.'[14] The use of 'knowledge of Yahweh' phrases peaks in contexts surrounding the exodus events and Moses' theophanic meetings with Yahweh at Sinai (Ex 5-14, 18, 29-31). The effect is to portray three sets of theophanic revelations to Moses (Ex 3, 6 and 19-24; 29-34) which are in turn mediated to Pharaoh, Egypt and Israel through miraculous signs (Ex 4-12) and the giving of a law (or ten *dĕbārîm*, Ex 19-34). The nature of the divine manifestation, too, is central to this revelation. It shows Pharaoh that Yahweh's glory is greater than his own (Ex 14:18) and, ultimately, for Israel, that Yahweh is 'a God merciful and gracious, slow to anger, and abounding in steadfast love and faithfulness ...' (Ex 34:6).

We find then that the Pentateuch relates a redemptive or re-creative story which is centered upon the presence and knowledge of Yahweh. By the time we come to Deuteronomy, Moses' unique role in experiencing the theophany and receiving the law acts as a sanction for his own 'words' (1:1). These words, alluded to in verse 1, anticipate the material that follows, especially as they enter into a wordplay with torah in verse 5. This verse ends the narrator's introduction by placing Moses at

---

[12] See W. Zimmerli, 'I Am Yahweh', in *Yahweh*, W. Brueggemann (ed.) (Atlanta, GA: Westminster John Knox Press, 1982), 1-28; 'Knowledge of God According to the Book of Ezekiel', in *Yahweh*, W. Brueggemann (ed.) (Atlanta, GA: Westminster John Knox Press, 1982), 29-98 (47) and L. Eslinger, 'Exod 6:3 in the Context of Genesis 1-Exodus 15', in *Literary Structure and Rhetorical Strategies in the Hebrew Bible*, L.J. Regt, J. de Waard, and J.P. Fokkelman (eds.) (Assen: Van Gorcum, 1996), 188–98 and 'Freedom or Knowledge? Perspective and Purpose in the Exodus Narrative (Exodus 1–15)', *JSOT* 52 (1991): 43–60. Although the root *yd‘* and *Yhwh* occur together variously throughout the Old Testament (e.g., 'I know says Yahweh'), what is at issue here is the combination of forms in a way that implies 'knowing Yahweh'. I have not included the phrase 'to know the name' in my analysis, though its use is surely significant.

[13] Eslinger, 'Exod 6:3' counts nine collocations of *yd‘* and *Yhwh* outside of Exodus and Ezekiel (Deut 29:5 [6]; 1 Kgs 20:13, 28; Is 45:3; 49:23, 26; 60:16; Hos 2:22 [20]; Joel 2:27; 4:17 [3:17]. Nine are found in Ex 1-15 alone and six more in Ex 16-33). Zimmerli, 'Knowledge', 30, 47 counts 86 (or 78) uses of the 'monotonous turn of phrase' in Ezekiel!

[14] 'Exod 6:3', 189, emphasis added.

Moab where he 'began to explain carefully all this *torah*'. As the introduction in vv. 1-5 closes, readers begin to understand that Moses' 'words' (1:1) are an explanation of the 'this torah' (1:5).

In the next three chapters, Moses retells Israel her own history, not merely as 'folklore', but to position her hearing in 'the corporate experience of the one people of God'.[15] All generations of Israelite readers are addressed as a people on a journey and this torah promises to prepare them for their own Jordan River crossings. We also see the transitional principle at work as Moses alludes to his own imminent death (Deut 1:37; 3:23-27) which signals to Israel the end of one era and the beginning of a new one. In Deuteronomy, this death raises an urgent question: 'How will the presence and revelation of Yahweh continue after Moses is gone? (i.e., How will Yahweh be known?)' The next thirty chapters answer this suspenseful question.

Teaching and Learning (Deuteronomy 4-11)

Chapter 4 makes a decisive move from past to present: 'And *now* Israel, listen to the statutes and rules I am teaching you ...' (4:1). Here Moses turns from a description of the events in the desert to a close account of Israel's experience at Horeb (Sinai). As we will see, Yahweh's words and fiery presence at Horeb mark the centre of Deuteronomy's ontological continuity with past generations. The fire, revelation and glory on that day are meant to come alive in each generation, and the teaching and memory devices in these chapters are the means to bring that to pass.

In order to see how Deuteronomy creates this Horeb-actualizing imagery in Chapters 4-11, we must remember the wordplay between 'word', 'words' and 'torah' in 1:1 and 1:5. This wordplay creates a rhetorical ambiguity that undergirds Deuteronomy's use of 'actualization' as a means to access knowledge. That is, Israel's history is not just a story, but the place where, in present obedience to the torah, God's redemptive history in Egypt and at Sinai become fully and powerfully realized. This union of story and law can be seen in the extraordinary density of epistemological themes which will be examined briefly here.

THE ONTOLOGY OF YAHWEH'S ACTS AND ESSENCE AT THE HEART OF ISRAEL'S KNOWLEDGE (DEUTERONOMY 4)

To begin with, Deuteronomy 4 uses the convergence of several intertextual themes to continue bridging the past with the present and future. Most significantly, Deuteronomy makes explicit reference to both sides of the double theophany pattern in Exodus: (a) Yahweh's activity in creation and history is confirmed dramatically by a series of questions posed to Israel about their purpose (Deut 4:32-34; cf. 6:20-24; 32:1-14). Referring to Exodus 1-15, these texts remind Israel that Yahweh's

---

[15] Millar, 'Place', 48. Cf. also what Christensen, 'Form', 140, describes as the 'Janus-like feature' in Deuteronomy which looks back to the exodus in order to the present and future (conquest).

redemptive acts have no comparison in the history of the world.[16] (b) Deuteronomy recalls the powerful theophany Israel witnessed at Horeb (4:33; 4:36f; 5:22-27). In an expansion of the Exodus account, Deuteronomy emphasizes Israel's fearful experience of the voice and fire at Horeb (5:22-28). The fear of death moves Israel to retreat to their tents and leave Moses to continue the experience with Yahweh alone: 'you approach (*qrb*)[17] and hear all that Yahweh our God will say and speak to us, then speak to us all that Yahweh our God speaks to you and we will hear and do it' (5:27). Moses receives the torah and teaches it to Israel as a direct expression of his exclusive ability to withstand the danger that comes from the fiery theophany and the voice of Yahweh (cf. 2 Cor 3:7-18).[18]

The entire thrust of Deuteronomy 4, in fact, pivots around this double theophany pattern recorded in Exodus and exists within several 'frames'. The divine knowledge that Israel gained in Egypt and the desert takes on a universal distinctiveness as expressed in the 'inner frame' of Deuteronomy 4:5-8 and 4:32-39 (where the 'outer frame' is 4:1-4 and 4:40-49).[19] The opening of the frame (4:5-8) promises Israel that if she keeps these commandments it will be her 'wisdom' and 'understanding' in the sight of the nations (v. 6, twice). Obedience also communicates the 'nearness' (*qrb*) of Israel's God whenever she calls upon him: 'For what great nation is there that has a god so *qrb* to it as Yahweh our God is to us ...' (v. 7). Finally obedience confirms the 'righteousness' of the rules and statutes (4:8b) and torah (4:8c) which Moses sets before them 'this day'. Israel's obedience communicates to the nations the supremacy of her God and of his law. Deuteronomy thus continues to build upon this insistence that *how* and *what* one knows is tied to the ethics of obedience. There is an inherent virtue required to 'know' this God.

The close of the inner frame in chapter 4 (4:32-39) rejoins these motifs of Yahweh's uniqueness and his revealed law. As already discussed, vv. 32-34 and 36 recall the events of the exodus and the Sinai theophany in order to draw the particular conclusion repeated at the beginning and end of the subsection:

From Creation – uniqueness of Sinai and deliverance (4:32-34)

---

[16] N. Lohfink, 'Verküngkigung Des Hauptgebots in der Jüngsten Schicht Des Deuteronomiums (Dt 4, 1-40)', in *Studien Zum Deuteronomium und Zur Deuteronomistischen Literatur 1, idem.* (Stuttgart: Katholisches Bibelwerk, 1990), 187–91, says, 'Die spielt auf alle Ereignisse an, die wir in Ex 1-15 lesen, zuerst die Plagen, dann den Sieg am Schilfmeer. Der Forschungsauftrag gibt auch sogleich an ... daß diesen Ereignissen in der gesamten Menschheitsgeschichte nichts Vergleichbares an die Seite gestellt werden könnte: 4, 35' (188).

[17] The use of the Hebrew *qārab* is significant, as seen in Deut 4:7 and 30:14 below.

[18] I. Wilson, *Out of the Midst of the Fire: Divine Presence in Deuteronomy*, SBL.DS (Atlanta: Scholars Press, 1995), 56–66, shows that Deuteronomy adds the phrase 'out of the midst of the fire' to the Exodus accounts of Sinai. Deuteronomy's purpose is to solidify not only Moses reception of the words, but the people's objective and almost fatal experience of the fire which testifies to the divine source behind Moses' words.

[19] Olson, *Deuteronomy*, 33ff.

Conclusion – 'To you it was shown that you might know that Yahweh is God and there is no other besides (him)' (4:35).
Promise to Fathers – uniqueness of Sinai and deliverance (4:36-38)
Conclusion – 'Know today and consider it in your heart that Yahweh he is God in heaven above and on earth beneath, there is none besides' (4:39).[20]

These passages declare to Israel that her unique 'election, redemption, covenant and inheritance' testify to her unique knowledge of the one true God.[21] Furthermore, the knowledge (and memory) of the divine, of his activity in history, and of his universal uniqueness are the essential prerequisite to receiving his laws.[22] That this same union of creation and salvation events is used to justify Yahweh's uniqueness in 32:39-43 strengthens the notion that epistemology is grounded in the ontology of Yahweh's divine presence and power and in the ethics of obedience.

Furthermore, this careful juxtaposition of theophany (divine presence) with torah constitutes the first instance of a transcendence/immanence motif that is sustained throughout Deuteronomy.[23] It is Israel's obedience to the rules and statutes of *torah* that demonstrates to the nations the *nearness* of Yahweh and the righteousness of the law (4:6-8). Yet it is also the *words* of this *torah* which express both the reality and the content of Yahweh speaking 'out of heaven' and acting 'on earth' (4:36). Torah provides the means for Israel to experience the nearness and transcendence of Yahweh[24] and this is the first sign that torah will function as a partial replacement of Moses' ministry in Israel – a truth applied to the Messiah by both John and Paul in the New Testament (Jn 1:1ff; Col 1:15-29).

ACTUALIZATION THROUGH FUTURE TEACHING AND REMEMBRANCE (DEUTERONOMY 6-8)

---

[20] Though most translations assume a 'monotheistic' sense to the Hebrew *'yn 'd mlbdw* (v. 35) and *'yn 'd* (v. 39) – 'there is no other besides him' – Nathan MacDonald argues against these renderings, *Deuteronomy and the Meaning of 'Monotheism'* (Tübingen: Mohr Siebeck, 2003), 81–85. While his grammatical reading may be correct, I do not find his argument against theological monotheism in Deuteronomy persuasive.

[21] See C.J.H. Wright, *Knowing Jesus Through the Old Testament* (Downers Grove, IL: InterVarsity, 1992), 40.

[22] See J.J. Niehaus, *God at Sinai: Covenant and Theophany in the Bible and Ancient Near East* (Grand Rapids: Zondervan/ Carlisle: Paternoster, 1995), 21ff.

[23] In this way Deuteronomy 4 parallels Deuteronomy 12, communicating both the place where Yahweh meets his people and the transcendent nature of Yahweh which stands over Israel. See Millar, 'Place', 35f, and J.G. McConville, 'Time and Place and the Deuteronomic Altar-Law', in *Time and Place*, J.G. McConville and J.G. Millar (eds.) (Sheffield: Sheffield Academic Press, 1994), 130–36. Cf. also Nanette Stahl, *Law and Liminality in the Bible*, JSOTSup (Sheffield: JSOT Press, 1995), 53f.

[24] See J.G. McConville, *Grace in the End: A Study in Deuteronomic Theology* (Grand Rapids: Zondervan/ Carlisle: Paternoster, 1993), 125f.

As we have seen in the first four chapters, Moses' unparalleled access to divine knowledge through his relationship with Yahweh undergirds the entire Deuteronomic narrative. Moses' torah ('words') is what will make actualization possible for future generations as Israel continues this story of history by her own obedience to the laws revealed in the past.[25]

At the heart of actualization is the need to restore the loving nature of her ontological union with Yahweh (6:4-9). Here we are introduced to a passage which represents the heart of actualizing and 'performing' the torah. The family and community laws in this passage reaffirm that Israel's knowledge of Yahweh is distinctly relational. Most commentators recognize the Shema (Deut 4:6-9) as the centre of Deuteronomy 4-11, especially as it resonates with the responsibility enjoined in 6:20-25.[26] Commenting on the unity in Deuteronomy 6-12, Nathan MacDonald says:

> The sort of knowledge that Israel is to acquire is more than purely intellectual, for it is a knowledge that, correctly acquired, results in obedience of the commandments ... Whatever may or may not be said about the extent of divine knowledge, there is a basic congruence between the knowledge YHWH seeks and the knowledge he desires for Israel, for both may be described as relational.[27]

This relational knowledge cascades across past, present and future generations as parents 'teach' children through continuous cycles of life in the land. Loving Yahweh means 'knowing' and embracing the relationship initiated by God in his loving redemptive work (cf. 7:6-9) by keeping the torah. Obeying the torah means loving Yahweh and thereby actualizing those experiences perpetually in Israel.[28] In sum, Deuteronomy brings every individual and each community of readers and hearers to Horeb through their own 'boundaries'. The power and promises at Horeb give these readers confidence in the presence of Yahweh needed to cross boundaries towards life in a new land at a new time and in a new place.[29] In this way Deuteronomy uses memory to *realize* the liminal boundaries and thresholds of the past in order to interpret and respond to each new set of challenges. Childs explains this through the Deuteronomic concept of 'remembrance':

> To remember was to call to mind a past event or situation, with the purpose of evoking some action ... To remember was to actualize the past, to bridge the gap of time and to form a solidarity with the fathers. Israel's remembrance became a technical term to

---

[25] O'Donovan *Resurrection*, 87, argues that 'participation' is necessary to perceive the transcendent knowledge of God.

[26] See Miller, *Deuteronomy*, 10, 97, 107.

[27] MacDonald, *Deuteronomy*, 136.

[28] In this way, Sonnet, *Book*, 10, recognizes the rhetorical effect of Moses' address to create an image of a trans-generational Israel.

[29] See variously, B.S. Childs, *Memory and Tradition in Israel* (London: SCM Press, 1962), 53; MacDonald, *Deuteronomy*, 155; Millar, 'Place', 32, 43, 60f; Olson, *Deuteronomy*, 89-112; Wright, *Deuteronomy*, 8f; etc..

express the process by which later Israel made relevant the great redemptive acts which she recited in her tradition. The question of how to overcome the separation in time and space from the great events of the past became the paramount issue.[30]

Furthermore, this process of actualization assumes a past-present-future continuum which we find strikingly visualized when Moses places the (younger) second generation at Horeb to 'remind' them of what they saw and heard:[31] 'Only take care and watch your soul diligently lest you forget the things (*debārîm*) which your eyes have seen and lest they depart from your heart all the days of your life. Make them known to your children and your children's children (Deut 4:9; cf. also 5:22-27; 6:20; 11:2-7).' Moses' fourfold repetition of this anachronistic move reinforces the actualization of the past that is taking place in each new generation. Each generation must prepare for what lies ahead by remembering the past in a way that it becomes present, powerful and real.[32] Actualization is the goal of Deuteronomy's injunctions to 'teach' and 'remember'.[33]

As Deuteronomy actualizes theophany in the context of torah, it enjoins the community to teach the next generation, here indicated by the Hebrew *lāmad*, 'to teach', 'to learn'. The word *lāmad* is used more than 80 times in the Old Testament; yet, in the Pentateuch, it is found only in Deuteronomy and its occurrences are not incidental.[34] While Olson goes a bit too far in saying that *torah* in Deuteronomy is 'catechesis',[35] his point is not far off; Moses is transformed from a prophet slow of speech (Ex 4:10) into the fountain of a teaching pattern that will flow in all future

---

[30] *Memory*, 74f. Cf. also DeVries, *Yesterday*, 347 and Millar, 'Place', 15.

[31] Most of the second generation would have been children or unborn almost forty years before when Israel built the golden calf at Sinai. The subsequent curse of dying in the desert belonged to their fathers. Few interpreters make note of this oddity, but see McConville, *Grace*, 126-33; DeVries, *Yesterday*, 176f; and S.A. Geller, 'Fiery Wisdom: The Deuteronomic Tradition', in *Sacred Enigmas, idem.* (London: Routledge, 1996), 47.

[32] Sonnet, *Book*, 142f, says that the Horeb event is reproduced by reading the torah; cf. Stahl, *Law*, 92. On the combined effect of 'Today' (4:1) in this context, see G. Braulik, 'Wisdom, Divine Presence and Law: Reflections on the Kerygma of Deut 4:5–8 (1977)', in *idem.*, *Theology* (North Richland Hills, TX: BIBAL Press, 1994), 24; and Olson, *Deuteronomy*, 37.

[33] Cf. N. Wolterstorff, 'The Remembrance of Things (Not) Past: Philosophical Reflections on Christian Liturgy', in T.P. Flint (ed.), *Christian Philosophy* (Notre Dame, IN: UNDP, 1990), 118-61, affirms a 'reality interpretation' of past events which allow us to say that the unique reality and experience of the original audience can become our own through the memorials and liturgies.

[34] Deut 4:1, 5, 10, 14; 5:1, 31; 6:1; 11:19; 14:23; 17:19; 18:9; 20:18; 31:12, 13, 19, 22. MacDonald, *Deuteronomy*, 134, observes that only the book of Psalms uses the term more frequently (27 times) and most of these uses are in Ps 119. Cf. also the synonymous and emphatic use of the piel *šnn* in 6:7, 'teach your children diligently'. The piel of *šnn* is hapax but confirmed by Arabic, Targum and Peshitta, see M. Weinfeld, *Deuteronomy 1–11*, AB (New York: Doubleday, 1991), 332f.

[35] *Deuteronomy*, 6, 9-16; cf. however C.J.H. Wright, *God's People in God's Land: Family, Land, and Property in the Old Testament* (Exeter: Paternoster, 1990), 83.

generations. Significantly, God is never said to teach in Deuteronomy;[36] Moses' access to Yahweh is prophetically mediated, via this torah, to be apportioned for teaching throughout the Israelite society: family (Dt 4:9f; 6:4-9, 20-25; 11:19), king (17:19), priests (31:12f), and people (31:19-22). By parents and leaders teaching obedience to the torah, the lines between successive generations are blurred, giving Israel trans-generational access to the power in Egypt and the voice and fire at Horeb.

Between Moses' two major injunctions to teach (Deut 6, 11), he frames another motivational command to remember (Deut 8). This command is contextually situated between two parallel (historical) chapters which remind Israel that she is a rebellious recipient of Yahweh's grace and election (Deut 7, 9). Chapter 8 sustains the rebellion with a sophisticated chiasm[37] which recalls two parallel incidents of rebellion where Yahweh provided manna and water despite Israel's unfaithful, grumbling attitude (Num 11, 21). The doubling structure in the chapter balances three elements:

- Two references to the desert (vv. 2-5; 14-16)
- A twofold injunction to remember (*zkr*, vv. 2, 18) and not forget (*škḥ*, 8:11, 14)
- A play between 'commandment', 'command' (*miṣwôtāyw*, 8:1, 2, 6, 11) 'what proceeds out' (*môṣā'*, vv. 3, 14) and 'thirsty ground' (*ṣimmā'ôn*, 8:15).

This wordplay between 'command' and 'comes out' is similar to the ongoing play between *tôrâ* and *dābār*, yet this play equates what God *gives* in the exodus (vv. 2-5) and what he does in nature (with water, vv. 14-16) with 'all that comes' ('*al-kol-môṣā'*) out of his mouth.[38] In the context of past failure, Israel is meant to learn that just as Yahweh supplies food and water (past), land and victory (future), he supplies the life-giving commands that sustain Israel in her relationship with her God.[39] His commands are grounded in the physical realities and the physical gifts that surround and sustain Israel as God surrounded Adam and Eve in the garden. Creation and torah are corresponding witnesses to Yahweh's covenant faithfulness (cf. Pss 1, 19, 78, 104, etc.).

Thus, in Chapters 6-11 alone, Deuteronomy can be seen to blend history, teaching, memory and laws in an exposition of the special relationship between Israel and her redeeming God. What Israel knows and how she knows is grounded in – and renewed through – references to her history with Yahweh. It is not insignificant that such a dense and lengthy discourse is used to introduce the main

---

[36] Sonnet, *Book*, 37f.

[37] R.C. Van Leeuwen, 'What Comes Out of God's Mouth: Theological Wordplay in Deuteronomy 8', *CBQ* 47 (1985): 55–57 and J.G. McConville, *Deuteronomy*, AOTC (Leicester, Downer's Grove, IL.: InterVarsity Press, 2002), 166f.

[38] Here I am closely following Van Leeuwen, 'Mouth'.

[39] Consider Jesus' use of this passage in Israel's place (Mt 4, Lk 4) which shows his victory over the powers and his identity with Yahweh.

body of laws in Deuteronomy 12-26. One cannot understand these laws, or Yahweh their giver, apart from this story of history.

Time and Place: The Past in the Future (Deuteronomy 12-26)

At the centre of Deuteronomy (Deut 12-26) Moses delivers the 'statutes and ordinances' which are distinguished by their participation in the wordplay between *tôrâ* and *dĕbārîm*. The terms *haḥuqqîm* (the statutes) and *hammišpāṭîm* (the ordinances) are only found between 4:1 and 26:16, and Braulik's work demonstrates a twofold purpose in the use of these words.[40] First, because the material in Deuteronomy 4-11 is primarily didactic, the ten uses there suggest that they introduce the main body of the law in 12-26. This relies on the fact that the repetition of *haḥuqqîm wĕhammišpāṭîm* at 11:32; 12:1 and 26:16 – and nowhere in between – indicate a frame and label for material contained within (Deut 12-26). Further, the repetition of *dābār* (word) at 4:1 and 26:16 draws out the rough parallel between Moses' words and the content in Deuteronomy 12-26.[41] Thus the statutes and ordinances (12-26), while distinct in a sense from the parenetic material in Chapters 4-11, are connected with it in that they represent the constitutional, social and ceremonial means for Israel to actualize Yahweh's presence in the land.

In Deuteronomy 12 we find the trans-generational and parenetic nature of these laws reinforced by some conspicuous features. The thrust of the chapter is to regulate the future nature and place of worship. Whereas the majority of recent interpretation has focused on Jerusalem, McConville offers several challenges to this line of interpretation. Two observations bear mentioning here: (1) not only is Jerusalem never mentioned in Deuteronomy, but several future places of worship are imagined apart from Jerusalem (e.g., Shechem in Deut 27), and (2) this chapter begins using the 'place formula', which will continue through Deuteronomy 16, in order to emphasize *Yahweh's choice*: 'Yahweh's prerogative in choosing the place is more important than any identification of it.'[42] When we consider this in the context and function of history and actualization for Israel, McConville's point of view contributes remarkably: 'As the "today" of Moses' exhortation is made a model for Israel's response to Yahweh in all future times, so the encounter at Horeb is given an entry into all future time through Israel's worship at the chosen place – wherever and whenever that might be.'[43] The ambiguous reference to future times and places gives the law a hermeneutical character that must be applied according to the circumstances of future settings (cf. Deut 18 below).

---

[40] G. Braulik, 'Die Ausdrücke Für 'Gesetz' Im Buch Deuteronomium', in *Studien Zur Theologie Des Deuteronomiums*, *idem.* (Stuttgart: Katolisches Bibelwerk, 1988), 11–38, demonstrates the often synonymous use of these terms.

[41] Braulik, 'Ausdrücke', 34 labels this the 'paränetischen Teil und das Gesetzkorpus als das ganze von Moses promulgierte 'Gesetz' ...'

[42] McConville, *Deuteronomy*, 220; cf. 225.

[43] McConville, *Deuteronomy*, 223.

LEADERSHIP AT THE CENTRE: DEUTERONOMY 16-19

Having introduced the intentionally ambiguous future contexts of the laws in Chapter 12, Chapters 13-26 demonstrate Deuteronomy's intention to preserve and protect Israel's knowledge from ideological and idolatrous temptations in future settings. On the whole, chapters 16-19 demarcate Israel's social and political offices, yet these offices are intuitively always in service to Yahweh, Israel's ultimate king and judge.[44]

Paralleling 1:9-18, the passage in 16:18-20 commands Israel to appoint judges and officers for their towns to judge the cases Moses had previously handled alone. It should not be overlooked that these leaders require *wisdom* and understanding (1:13, 15) to carry out their obligation and bring about righteous judgment. Administering the laws is a circumstantial and interpretive function, and many have exceptions or ranges of application which is also apparent in the other offices.

Whereas the judges are appointed by the people, the priest finds his office through descent from Levi and Aaron. Yahweh alone, however, reserves the right to choose a king (17:15).

The king's office is established by a threefold warning not to multiply horses, wives or riches (vv. 16-17), and a positive decree to live by the torah (vv. 18-20). These constraints, according to Olson, aim at the heart Israel's idolatrous temptations: '*militaristic power, materialism, and self-righteous moralism*', which were emphasized already in Deuteronomy 7-10,[45] and serve to keep the king on the level of the people. The king's responsibility toward the torah is embedded in the thematic progression throughout Deuteronomy which moves from speech to writing. In the presence of the priests, each king must write for himself a copy of the torah and 'speak' it all the days of his life. His obligation parallels the family responsibility to take 'this torah' (4:8) and these 'words' (6:6) and 'teach them', 'talk of them' (6:7) and 'write them' (6:9) as an expression of whole-hearted obedience. And reading the torah reminds the king not to lift his heart above his brothers (17:20). In this way, the king is the torah's 'arch-reader', setting the exemplary pattern for Israel's faithfulness to Yahweh and his laws.[46] In direct contrast to most ancient and modern conceptions of political authority, O'Donovan also observes that the law here stands over the king.[47] In this way, the kingship laws protect Israel from the temptations and ideological vices of foreign kings. As we will see, the role of the prophet serves this same function.

The prophet's role is outlined in 13:1-5 and 18:15-22. According to Chapter 18, the prophet is *raised up by Yahweh* (v. 15) and *recognized by Israel* as one whose word (prediction) comes to pass in history; the prophet's word must be tested against

---

[44] See O'Donovan, *Desire*, 66ff.

[45] Olson, *Deuteronomy*, 82.

[46] Sonnet, *Book*, 71. Cf. J.A. Grant, *The King Exemplar: The Function of Deuteronomy's Kingship Law in the Shaping of the Book of Psalms* (Atlanta: Society of Biblical Literature, 2004).

[47] See O'Donovan, *Desire*, 61-65.

the standard of torah. The earlier passage (13:1-5) gives a more complicated set of instructions regarding the interpretation of prophets or dreamers whose predictions come to pass but whose message is to be rejected if it counsels disloyalty or apostasy. The prophet thus adds both elements of expectation and of uncertainty to the office of the king. He is what Olson calls a 'wild card who often arises from the margins ...'[48] Olson goes on to describe the 'problem inherent in charismatic prophecy':

> How does one tell a true prophet like Moses from a false prophet claiming to speak a word from God? The criteria are set forth, but they leave room for ambiguity ... The reality is that sometimes such tests of truth will be ambiguous and may require the hearer to wait and see, remaining open to the new truth that may be revealed through the prophets. Even with the prophets as guides, the Deuteronomic community of faith is not removed from the ambiguities and struggles of real human existence in a broken world.[49]

In these passages the 'ambiguities and struggles' of Israel's future will come primarily from the idolatrous influence of the surrounding nations (13:2, 6ff; 18:20). The prophet comes in fulfillment of the torah, is recognized by the standards in the torah, and ultimately serves to protect Israel in her faithfulness to the torah. In other words, Deuteronomy is well aware of the distorting and corrupting ideologies of these foreign nations[50] and demands that the direction of influence be 'one-way'. Israel's religion should inspire the nations (4:5ff) but their religions must not be allowed to pollute Israel's worship or inhibit her created vocation.

Our short review of these chapters exhibits the inherent contingency of knowledge and the corporate commitments which torah requires to sustain access to Yahweh's truth. Furthermore, the application of the torah to life requires a breadth of gifts across the Israelite culture. Knowledge is learned and applied in community, where uncertainties and ambiguities abound and where humility and devotion are essential. The laws in this book are anything but temporary or simplistic. They are dangerous and stand under the threat of future prophets, and Yahweh himself, to illumine distorting and idolatrous interpretations.

From Moab to Shechem: Covenant Ceremonies Past, Present and Future (Deuteronomy 27-34)

The prominent feature of these final chapters is not just their shift away from the legal material in 12-26, but more specifically their focus on the continuities and uncertainties of the future. The first eleven chapters prepared Israel for the statutes

---

[48] Olson, *Deuteronomy*, 84.

[49] Olson, *Deuteronomy*, 85f.

[50] On the identification of ideologies as idolatry, see D.T. Koyzis, *Political Visions and Illusions: A Survey and Christian Critique of Contemporary Ideologies* (Downers Grove, IL: InterVarsity Press, 2003), 27f.

and ordinances based upon the events of the past and the needs of the future. With law in hand, the narration now turns to a motivation for keeping the torah in the land.

Deuteronomy returns from distant future to immediate future in Chapter 27 as Moses proscribes instructions for a coming Jordan-crossing ceremony. The passage begins by telling Israel to keep the whole 'commandment' (27:1), introducing another term into the *tôrâ-dābār* wordplay and thereby indicating the whole of Moses' teaching.[51] The wordplay is confirmed by verse 3 when Moses commands Israel to 'write *all the words of this torah*' on the ceremonial stones. 'Writing' also picks up the thematic progression from speech to writing: families (6:5-9), kings (17:18-20) and now corporate Israel write the torah as an expression of its centrality in their future life and its ability to renew the past throughout the community. This ceremony on the mountain (Ebal) also recalls the significance of the covenant Yahweh made with Israel at Horeb (Sinai).[52] In this way, mountains, torah and writing together reinforce Israel's continual need to actualize the realities of Yahweh's covenant promises and covenant demands. Deuteronomy is not an accumulation of historical facts, but rather the interrelated demands to remember God's mercy, obey the laws and observe the traditions and ceremonies that renew the special divine presence.

Chapters 27-28 also relate the blessings and curses which stand over Yahweh's covenant with Israel. The certainty of the curses in the future parallels the past failures in Deuteronomy 1-3 and 9-10. The goodness and Horeb-actualizing potential in the torah now increasingly stand in contrast to the pessimistic overtones of past and future unfaithfulness.

The covenant ceremony at Moab in Chapter 29 utilizes a host of these developing themes and motives, once again, to unite Israel with previous and future generations. The Moab covenant is added to the covenant at Horeb (29:1) to renew what Israel 'saw' and 'heard' there. The choice of perception language here is epistemologically significant, echoing Israel's moral failures in chapters 1-3 and 9-10, and her future failure recorded in chapters 27-28. Here Moses reveals that at Horeb, Yahweh did not give them a 'heart to understand, or eyes to see or ears to hear' (29:4-5), thereby reversing the proverbial motto that 'seeing is believing'. Israel did not have eyes to see in the past because of her rebellious and stubborn nature (Deut 1-3; 9-10). And even though this generation enters the land in a state of renewed grace, the recitation of past, present and future failures (29:18-28) emphatically warns her that disobedience to the torah has epistemological consequences. Israel's access to knowledge is morally conditioned, and Israel appears unable to overcome her stiff-necked condition.[53] The emerging problem between merely seeing and seeing with faith climaxes in chapters 29-30, where the 'secret things' belong to Yahweh and

---

[51] Braulik, 'Ausdrücke', 28.

[52] See Millar, 'Place', 71-73.

[53] See M. Westphal, 'Taking St. Paul Seriously: Sin as an Epistemological Category', in *Christian Philosophy*, T.P. Flint (ed.) (Notre Dame, IN: University of Notre Dame, 1990), 200-26.

'revealed things [belong] to us and to our sons forever that we might do all the words of this torah' (29:29).

The end of Moses' last speech brings this moral problem into striking relief. In an ironic declaration, 30:11-14 proclaims the 'nearness' (*qrb*) of this 'commandment' and Israel's ability to obey it (30:11-14). This echoes the 'revealed things' which have been plainly given to Israel that she might obey (29:29). The 'commandment' (30:11) and 'word' (*dābār*, 30:14) continue the ongoing legal wordplay which captures the entirety of Moses' words. Already we have seen that this *dābār* which Moses *commanded* (6:5) was to be on the heart and taught in families (6:6-9), and now Moses assures Israel that the *dābār* in the mouth and on the heart (30:14) envisions a nearness by which Israel 'can' obey. Like the seed of Abraham (Gen 18:17ff), Israel's faith and obedience are meant to project her righteousness to the nations (Deut 6:20-25).

Yet the past and future record Israel's 'stiff-necked' tendency to choose her own way despite the ease, goodness and nearness of this torah. Thus, in line with Genesis, Deuteronomy envisions law-keeping of 'this torah' as righteousness which blesses and impresses the nations, yet it also upholds the need to continue faithful trust at the heart of righteousness itself.[54] The goodness of the law and Israel's downward moral trajectory stand in a mysterious and eschatological tension. Torah is a provisional means to reproduce the divine presence and enable obedient righteousness. It demands a faith distinguished by its righteous acts.[55] The Psalmists uphold this optimistic side of the torah as the means to righteousness (Pss 1, 19, 50, 119).[56] The undercurrent of pessimism in Deuteronomy's prophetic rhetoric is not to cast doubt on the torah but rather to highlight Israel's tendency toward idolatry and self-deception despite Yahweh's goodness. This distinction returns in Deuteronomy 32 below.

Meanwhile it is necessary to recognise the way this language not only evokes legal obedience but anticipates divine incarnation. The nearness (*qrb*) of the *dābār* (word) corresponds to Yahweh's nearness (*qrb*) when the law is obeyed (4:6-8) and Moses' nearness (*qrb*) to Yahweh when he received the law at Horeb (5:27). In these parallels, we find a most remarkable display of literary skill as Deuteronomy draws together Moses' access to theophany, the torah, and the continuing presence of Yahweh for Israel. The effect is to announce the actualizing potential of the Yahweh-Horeb-presence *if the law is obeyed*. Because the law will not be obeyed by this sinful nation, a law-keeper is needed to return epistemological surety to Yahweh's redemptive plan – a fact reinforced in the following chapters.

Chapter 31 draws together the theophany, legal wordplay and the writing motif in a series of alternating settings. First, a brief succession narrative signals the end of

---

[54] McConville, *Deuteronomy*, 116; Wright, *Deuteronomy*, 291.

[55] Miller, *Deuteronomy*, 56, says, 'The righteous laws being written on the heart and being kept are in some sense a manifestation of the presence of God. God draws near in the law that God gives.'

[56] See Wright, *Deuteronomy*, 291.

Moses' life as he calls Joshua and commissions him for leadership (31:1-8). Then Moses is said to 'write this torah' (31:9) as Yahweh wrote the ten words at Horeb (5:22).[57] Then the narrative turns back to succession where Yahweh calls Joshua and Moses into the tent of meeting and appears 'in the tent in a pillar of cloud' (31:15). This confirms the notion that Moses' leadership carries with it a solidarity in the theophanic power and presence of Yahweh.[58] Joshua will assume part of this role and the rest of the responsibility will be dispersed throughout the community.

At the end of the chapter, the narrative turns back to Moses' writing and the Levites' role: 'When Moses finished writing the words of this book to the very end he commanded the Levites, who carry the ark of the covenant, saying: "take this book of the torah and set it next to the ark of the covenant of Yahweh your God and it shall be there as a witness against you"' (31:24-26). Israel thus has a pair of theophanic images crossing the Jordan before them: the ark, which contains Yahweh's ten words from Horeb, and the book of Moses, which is replacing the prophet's access to Yahweh. The death of Moses will not impede the continuing revelation of the knowledge of God to Israel. Miller summarizes:

> If the law in some way embodies the presence or nearness of God, then the ark continues to function in some fashion as the vehicle for God's presence in the midst of the people ... God can be, and is, near – in a way that is true of no other gods – in this law. And Israel will demonstrate its wisdom above all others in the careful attention it gives to keeping this law of God.[59]

In the future reading of this torah-book we have a clear picture of the actualization by which Israel continues her ongoing story with Yahweh her redeemer. In Chapter 32, the song of Moses acts as a climax to the moral and performative nature of Israel's knowledge in the torah. The 'things revealed' (29:29) are now clearly threatened by Israel's future disobedience. In keeping with Israel's nature, Yahweh calls three witnesses against her:

> 30:19 'I call heaven and earth to witness against you today'
>   31:19, 21 Song as witness
>   31:26 Book as witness
> 31:28 '(I) call heaven and earth as witness' (cf. 32:1, 40, 43)

Witnesses testify to truth, but Deuteronomy's witnesses do more. They are embedded in the structure of Israel's torah which lives on the hearts and in the mouths of her people. They testify to history, failure, need and the certainty of their judgment and restoration. Motivated by his love, forgiveness and faithfulness, Yahweh intends to fulfill and renew his covenant promises, and his witnesses perform double duty both for and against Israel.

---

[57] See Sonnet, *Book*, 142f.

[58] Cf. Sonnet, *Book*, 157.

[59] Miller, *Deuteronomy*, 56.

Unlike any other Old Testament hymn of Israel's history, Moses' song identifies Israel in creation and the primordial design for the nations (32:1-7).[60] This gives a universal dimension to the ontology of Yahweh's purpose for Israel and therefore reassures the nation of her unique identity and God's sovereign vocation for her.[61] After detailing Israel's future unfaithfulness (32:4-38), Yahweh promises to restore Israel with this climactic summary to his actions: 'See now that I, I am he and there is no other God besides me. I kill and I give life. I wound and I heal and there is none who can deliver from my hand' (32:39). This echoes 4:32-39, which offers a similar course of history – from creation to redemption to apostasy to restoration – and the same purpose: the revelation of Yahweh's supreme glory.

The extraordinary feature of this lengthy text is its poetic and performative function amidst the people. Music enhances the memory and weaves this song into Israel's permanent corporate memory to accompany and recollect the torah-book, the ark and the special presence of Yahweh with this people. As Fisch has observed, this song is not mere nostalgia but memory.

> Nostalgia for the Golden Age is not what Moses means by 'witness,' but rather memory weighted with obligation. Nostalgia does not obligate; it fills the mind with a rosy image tinged with sadness. In that sadness we take a kind of consolation; we hide ourselves in 'the soft vestments' ... Memory is something else, not the ever-returning spring, coming to us again with the perennially blooming lilac, but a naked confrontation with a past that is terribly present in spite of the passage of years.[62]

This song is a small summary for Deuteronomy – a tradition-creating agent in trans-generational Israel which provokes a response to rejoin the story in light of Yahweh's decisive creative and redemptive activity in history. The rest of the Old Testament confirms the continuing power of this song as witness (cf. Ps 50; Is 1:2; 41:4; 48:12; Jer 23:14-15; Ezek; Hos 2:20; 4:1; 5:4; 6:1-6). Meanwhile, Deuteronomy ends on an ambiguous note, with the goodness of torah giving Israel the ability to retain the knowledge of God, and Israel's innate pride which chooses self-deception over truth.

Conclusion

I have provided a brief overview of Deuteronomy's use of a highly crafted narrative to continue the Pentateuchal story of redemption. Yahweh's desire for self-revelation

---

[60] H. Fisch, *Poetry With a Purpose: Biblical Poetics and Interpretation* (Bloomington: Indiana University Press, 1988), 68-72, demonstrates the motifs in Genesis 1-18 in Deuteronomy 32 and Isaiah 1-6.

[61] Cf. T.E. Fretheim, 'Law in the Service of Life: A Dynamic Understanding of Law in Deuteronomy', in B.A. Strawn and N.R. Bowen (eds.), *A God So Near* (Winona Lake, IN: Eisenbrauns, 2003), 184-88.

[62] Fisch, *Poetry*, 58, 60. Cf. Kierkegaard's *Fear/Repetition*, which makes a similar distinction between 'repetition' and 'recollection'.

forms the foundation of this drama, and Deuteronomy highlights Moses as Yahweh's foremost prophet (34:10ff). Moses' impending death creates a gap in future access to Yahweh. Deuteronomy is specifically fashioned to fill this gap, and our attention to the theological, rhetorical and literary qualities of the final form illuminate the nature of the book's epistemology as it does so.

In one way the epistemology in Deuteronomy is grounded in the *ontology* and *ethics* of Yahweh's created world. Knowledge is a product of living in the redemptive story in accordance with the torah. This torah is a living memorial of Yahweh's Horeb theophany and thus the moral and orderly means to reproduce his powerful presence in all future generations. At the same time, torah is a witness that Israel cannot (will not) keep the torah on her own.

Second, Israel's access to knowledge is *performative* by virtue of the roles Deuteronomy creates for the community. Reading, hearing, writing, singing, remembering and obeying the torah actualize the ontological realities of Israel's relationship with Yahweh. Furthermore, Deuteronomy devises an *interpretive* approach to knowledge, whereby events, laws, people and even history must be interpreted within the contours, principles and purposes in the drama of history. The actualizing feature in Deuteronomy's rhetoric makes the book ultimately *hermeneutical* as the oral and written future of torah form a trans-generational community which continually closes the distance between past and present, between text and speech.

This eschatological climax of 'torah' is appropriated in John's gospel to give permanent actualization to torah: the 'Word' made flesh. It also underlies Paul's image of Christ at the climax of creation (Col 1:15-20) and the decisive cohesion of Israel's renewed ability and willingness to fulfill her created role, bearing fruit among the nations (1:10) and reconciling the world to its reigning God. After the full history of national Israel, the divine identity in the torah emerges as that agent by which we see the sinfulness of sin (Rom 7:13) and are set free to choose life in this new, redeemed and eschatological place.

Bibliography

Bauckham, R., *Bible and Mission: Christian Witness in a Postmodern World* (Carlisle: Paternoster, 2003)

Braulik, G., 'Die Ausdrücke Für "Gesetz" Im Buch Deuteronomium' in *idem.*, *Studien Zur Theologie Des Deuteronomiums* (Stuttgart: Katolisches Bibelwerk, 1988), 11-38

_____, 'Wisdom, Divine Presence and Law: Reflections on the Kerygma of Deut 4:5-8 (1977)' in *idem.*, *Theology* (North Richland Hills, TX: BIBAL Press, 1994), 1-25, 199-214

Childs, B.S., *Memory and Tradition in Israel* (London: SCM Press, 1962)

Christensen, D.L. *Deuteronomy 1:1–21:9*, WBC (Dallas, TX: Thomas Nelson, 2001)

_____, 'Form and Structure in Deuteronomy 1–11' in Norbert Lohfink (ed.), *Das Deuteronomium* (Leuven: Brill, 1985), 135-44

Clines, D.J.A., *The Theme of the Pentateuch*, JSOTSup 10 (Sheffield: Sheffield Academic Press, 1978)

DeVries, S.J., *Yesterday, Today and Tomorrow: Time and History in the Old Testament* (London: SPCK, 1975)

Eslinger, L., 'Exod 6:3 in the Context of Genesis 1-Exodus 15' in L.J. Regt, J. de Waard, and J.P. Fokkelman (eds.), *Literary Structure and Rhetorical Strategies in the Hebrew Bible* (Assen: Van Gorcum, 1996), 188-98

_____, 'Freedom or Knowledge? Perspective and Purpose in the Exodus Narrative (Exodus 1–15)', *Journal for the Study of the Old Testament* 52 (1991), 43-60

Fisch, H., *Poetry With a Purpose: Biblical Poetics and Interpretation* (Bloomington: Indiana University Press, 1988)

Fretheim, T.E., 'Law in the Service of Life: A Dynamic Understanding of Law in Deuteronomy' in B.A. Strawn and N.R. Bowen (eds.), *A God So Near* (Winona Lake, IN: Eisenbrauns, 2003), 183–200

Geller, S.A. 'Fiery Wisdom: The Deuteronomic Tradition' in *idem.*, *Sacred Enigmas* (London: Routledge, 1996), 30-61

Goudoever, J. van, 'The Liturgical Significance of the Date in Dt 1,3' in Norbert Lohfink (ed.), *Das Deuteronomium* (Leuven: Brill, 1985), 145–48

Grant, J.A., *The King Exemplar: The Function of Deuteronomy's Kingship Law in the Shaping of the Book of Psalms* (Atlanta: Society of Biblical Literature, 2004)

Kirkegaard, S., *Fear and Trembling/Repetition*, H.V. Hong and E.H. Hong (trs. and eds.) (Princeton, NJ: Princeton University Press, 1983)

Koyzis, D.T., *Political Visions and Illusions: A Survey and Christian Critique of Contemporary Ideologies* (Downers Grove, IL: InterVarsity Press, 2003)

Leeuwen, R.C. van, 'What Comes Out of God's Mouth: Theological Wordplay in Deuteronomy 8', *Catholic Biblical Quarterly* 47 (1985), 55–57

Lohfink, N., 'Verküngkigung Des Hauptgebots in der Jüngsten Schicht Des Deuteronomiums (Dt 4, 1–40)' in *idem.*, *Studien Zum Deuteronomium und Zur Deuteronomistischen Literatur 1* (Stuttgart: Katholisches Bibelwerk, 1990), 167-91

MacDonald, N., *Deuteronomy and the Meaning of 'Monotheism'* (Tübingen: Mohr Siebeck, 2003)

McBride, S.D., 'Polity of the Covenant People: The Book of Deuteronomy' in D.L. Christensen (ed.), *Song of Power* (Winona Lake: Eisenbrauns, 1993), 62–77

McConville, J.G., *Deuteronomy*, AOTC (Leicester/Downer's Grove, IL: InterVarsity Press, 2002)

_____, *Grace in the End: A Study in Deuteronomic Theology* (Grand Rapids: Zondervan/ Carlisle: Paternoster, 1993)

_____, 'Time and Place and the Deuteronomic Altar-Law' in J.G. McConville and J.G. Millar (eds.), *Time and Place* (Sheffield: Sheffield Academic Press, 1994), 89–139

Millar, J.G., 'Living at the Place of Decision: Time and Place in the Framework of Deuteronomy' in J.G. McConville and J.G. Millar (eds.), *Time and Place*, (Sheffield: Sheffield Academic Press, 1994), 15–88

Miller, P.D., *Deuteronomy*, Interpretation (Louisville, KY: John Knox Press, 1990)

Niehaus, J.J., *God at Sinai: Covenant and Theophany in the Bible and Ancient Near East* (Grand Rapids: Zondervan/ Carlisle: Paternoster, 1995)

O'Donovan, O., *The Desire of the Nations: Rediscovering the Roots of Political Theology* (Cambridge: Cambridge University Press, 1996)

_____, *Resurrection and Moral Order: An Outline for Evangelical Ethics* (Leicester: Inter-Varsity Press, 1986)

Olson, D.T., *Deuteronomy and the Death of Moses: A Theological Reading* (Minneapolis, Minnesota: Fortress, 1994)

Sonnet, J.-P., *The Book Within the Book: Writing in Deuteronomy* (Leiden/ New York: Brill, 1997)

Stahl, N., *Law and Liminality in the Bible*, JSOTSup (Sheffield: Sheffield Academic Press, 1995)

Sternberg, M., *The Poetics of Biblical Narrative* (Bloomington, IN: Indiana University Press, 1987)

_____, 'Time and Space in Biblical (Hi)Story Telling: The Grand Chronology' in R. Schwartz (ed.), *The Book and the Text: The Bible and Literary Theory* (Oxford: Blackwell, 1990), 81–145

Weinfeld, M., *Deuteronomy 1–11*, Anchor Bible (New York: Doubleday, 1991)

Wenham, G.J., *Story as Torah: Reading the Old Testament Ethically* (Edinburgh: T. & T. Clark, 2000)

Westphal, M., 'Taking St. Paul Seriously: Sin as an Epistemological Category' in T.P. Flint (ed.), *Christian Philosophy* (Notre Dame, IN: University of Notre Dame Press, 1990), 200-26.

Wilson, I., *Out of the Midst of the Fire: Divine Presence in Deuteronomy*, SBL.DS (Atlanta: Scholars Press, 1995)

Wolterstorff, N., 'The Remembrance of Things (Not) Past: Philosophical Reflections on Christian Liturgy' in T.P. Flint (ed.), *Christian Philosophy* (Notre Dame, IN: University of Notre Dame Press, 1990), 118–61

Wright, C.J.H., *Deuteronomy*, NIBC (Peabody, MA: Hendrickson Publishers/ Carlisle: Paternoster, 1996)

_____, *God's People in God's Land: Family, Land, and Property in the Old Testament* (Exeter: Paternoster, 1990)

_____, *Knowing Jesus Through the Old Testament* (Downers Grove, IL: InterVarsity, 1992)

Zimmerli, W., 'I Am Yahweh' in W. Brueggemann (ed. and tr.), *Yahweh* (Atlanta, GA: Westminster John Knox Press, 1982), 1-28

_____, 'Knowledge of God According to the Book of Ezekiel' in W. Brueggemann (ed. and tr.), *Yahweh* (Atlanta, GA: Westminster John Knox Press, 1982), 29-98

CHAPTER 2

An Epistemology of Faith:
The Knowledge of God in Israel's Prophetic Literature

Gregory Vall

The topic of 'knowledge' (*da'at*) is prominent in Israel's prophetic literature, both prose narratives and poetic oracles. Sometimes it is a question of God's own knowledge (e.g., 1 Sam 2:3; Amos 3:2), but more often the concern of these texts is with the knowledge that human beings – Israel and the nations – may come to possess by way of divine revelation. These sacred texts do not pose epistemological questions in an abstract philosophical manner (e.g., What is knowledge? Is certitude possible?). They are concerned, rather, with the concrete possibility of knowing Yahweh 'the God of Israel' and his 'counsel' (i.e., wise plan) for humanity. But insofar as they demonstrate how such knowledge is mediated through the prophetic ministry and may be appropriated through a multifaceted response of faith, we may speak of a nascent epistemology of faith. The Old Testament prophetic literature testifies to – and invites the reader to partake in – a mode of knowledge that is 'whole-hearted', involving intellect, memory, and will in a concrete personal and communal response to God's historical revelation. My hope is that a fresh examination of selected texts and a brief epistemological reflection will deepen our appreciation of this mode of knowledge.[1]

This essay will consist of three sections. The first will consider a selection of five narratives involving three pre-classical prophets: Samuel (1 Samuel 3), Elijah (1 Kings 17 and 18), and Elisha (2 Kings 4 and 5). In these narratives, each of which involves a conversion of one sort or another, the Hebrew verb *yāda'* ('to know') has a programmatic significance. It is found especially in confessions of faith and refers either to the recognition of a true prophet or to the knowledge of the true God that comes through the prophetic word. The second section will examine the leitmotif of 'knowledge of God' (*da'at 'ĕlōhîm*) in the book of the classical prophet Hosea. As space restrictions preclude a more general survey of the classical prophets, Hosea was chosen because of the significant attention he gives to this theme and because of the influence he seems to have had on later prophets, especially Jeremiah. The third section will employ philosophical categories in order to flesh out the epistemology

---

[1] I would like to dedicate this essay to the memory of Monsignor Terry J. Tekippe (1940-2005), a fine scholar and dear friend, who devoted much of his life to the study of epistemology.

that is operative in Hosea's oracles and in the conversion narratives. In particular, I will develop the thesis that the prophetic 'knowledge of God' is a primordial or protological mode of knowledge.

Faith-Knowledge in Selected Narratives from Samuel and Kings

The books of Samuel and Kings, which narrate half a millennium of Israelite history – roughly 1060 to 560 B.C. – from the rise of the monarchy to its fall and immediate aftermath, present Samuel's multifaceted ministry as the dawning of a new age of prophecy and monarchy in Israel. In 1 Samuel 1-4, Eli the priest and his sons, Hophni and Phineas, serve as foils for Samuel. Eli's advanced age (2:22), diminished eyesight (3:2; 4:15), and overweight condition (4:18) symbolize the spiritual obtuseness and lassitude of Israel's leadership as the age of the judges draws to a close. He takes Hannah's fervent prayer to be the babbling of a drunkard (1:12-16) and is remarkably slow to discern that it is Yahweh who is summoning the young Samuel (3:4-8). The narrator explains that 'the [prophetic] word of Yahweh was rare in those days, there being no frequent vision' (3:1).[2] The narrative of Samuel's prophetic call (3:1-21) represents a dramatic development for Israel collectively (cf. vv. 11, 20) and for Samuel personally. He goes to bed as a 'lad' who 'did not yet know Yahweh' (vv. 1, 7) and rises the next morning as a prophet. But whereas Samuel's initial lack of knowledge of Yahweh is due to the fact that 'the word of Yahweh had not yet been revealed to him' (v. 7), the statement that Eli's sons 'did not know Yahweh' (2:12) is expounded in terms of their venality and sexual immorality (vv. 13-17, 22). Thus, at the outset we encounter two complementary dimensions of the knowledge of God that are found throughout the prophetic literature: the intellectual-spiritual understanding of God that comes through the reception of divine revelation, and the practical knowledge of God constituted by righteous moral conduct.[3] The latter dimension, like the former, is present in Samuel, whose conduct is above reproach (12:3-5).

Significantly, the specific oracle that inaugurates the age of prophecy is one of judgment (3:11-14), and the events to which it refers – the defeat at Aphek-Ebenezer and the Philistine captivity of the ark (circa 1050 B.C.) – foreshadow the catastrophe toward which the entire narrative of Samuel and Kings inexorably moves: the destruction of Jerusalem in 586 B.C. and the ensuing Babylonian Captivity. The prophetic word will come to Israel within a specific series of historical events, and, broadly speaking, it is through exile and restoration from exile that Israel will come to 'know' Yahweh (cf. Ezek 39:28). That is, Israel will come to a new depth of

---

[2] The biblical translations throughout this essay are my own.

[3] As will become clear below in my treatment of Hosea, these two aspects are not extrinsic to each other, so that it would be wrong to say that righteous conduct merely 'evidences' the knowledge of God. For the human person, who is a body-soul unity, knowledge of God cannot abide in the intellect if it is not acted upon in the concrete historicity of the body.

theological understanding and a new epistemic certitude of faith when God deals decisively with their sin.

The narrative of Samuel's call concludes on an epistemological note. The text itself embodies a prophetic judgment, narrating the consistent fulfillment of Samuel's oracles as the historical action of Yahweh, who 'did not allow any of [Samuel's] words to fall to the ground' (1 Sam 3:19). By further reporting that, in view of this prophetic success, 'all Israel from Dan to Beersheba *knew* that Samuel had been confirmed as a prophet of Yahweh' (v. 20), the author calls upon the reader to receive the authoritative witness of the inspired text in a corresponding act of epistemic faith.[4] In Samuel and Kings the recognition of the true prophet and the knowledge that Yahweh the God of Israel is the true God constitute, implicitly or explicitly, two halves of a single confession of faith (cf. 1 Kgs 18:36). This confession is made by believers within the narrative, but it is proper to faithful Israelites of all ages, to whom the deeds and words of Yahweh are available through the agency of the inspired text.

Texts that both narrate and invite confessions of knowledge-giving faith in Yahweh and his prophets have a special prominence in the Elijah and Elisha Cycles.[5] The chapter in which Elijah first appears (1 Kgs 17) has as its punch line the widow of Zarephath's confession of faith-knowledge: 'Now I know that you are a man of God and that the word of Yahweh is truly in your mouth!' (v. 24). Though the form-critical classification of this passage as a 'prophetic legitimation narrative' discloses one dimension of the text, by itself such a classification yields a truncated exegesis.[6] A narrative-critical analysis discloses other dimensions, such as characterization, and enables us to read the passage also as a conversion story and to ask what sort of 'knowledge' the non-Israelite widow attains.

Her first words (v. 12) reveal that she is near despair. Elijah immediately offers encouragement ('Do not fear'; v. 13a) and the divine promise of miraculous sustenance throughout the drought (v. 14). But to receive this blessing she must first pass a test of faith: before caring for herself and her son she must use what little she

---

[4] A hermeneutical presupposition operative here is that biblical Israel did not cultivate the memory of such past events in oral tradition and written text merely for the sake of antiquarian interest but precisely as a living witness and with an eye to the situation and needs of the contemporary community.

[5] We are concerned here with 'divine faith', so called because (a) it is the acceptance of divine revelation and (b) it is a divinely infused supernatural virtue. Such faith 'gives' knowledge, not of itself, but in conjunction with divine revelation. Unless revelation is met by faith, no knowledge is imparted. Thus faith can properly be said to produce knowledge.

[6] Cf. S.J. DeVries, *1 Kings* WBC 12 (Waco, TX: Word Books, 1985), 221; similarly, R. Nelson, *First and Second Kings* Interpretation (Louisville: John Knox Press, 1987), 108. Even less satisfying is the bland 'socio-cultural' description of 1 Kings 17 as 'a kind of advertisement for belief in the prophet's ability to provide solutions to problems', in T.H. Rentería, 'The Elijah/Elisha Stories: A Socio-cultural Analysis of Prophets and People in Ninth-Century B.C.E. Israel', in R.B. Coote (ed.), *Elijah and Elisha in Socioliterary Perspective* (Atlanta: Scholars Press, 1992), 101.

has to feed the Israelite prophet (v. 13b), who ironically is the cause of her distress, inasmuch as it was he who called for the drought (v. 1). She passes the test and presumably gains some sense that the God of Israel cares for her and has chosen to provide for her through this 'man of God'. But when a sterner test follows, it is precisely this truth that she begins to doubt. The death of her son brings to the surface her profound sense of guilt and a growing suspicion that Yahweh and his prophet must be out to punish her after all (v. 18). The raising of her son is a sign aimed at healing her of this suspicion and convincing her that God has brought the prophet into her life with good intent. The confession of v. 24 thus expresses more than mere recognition or even acceptance of Elijah's prophetic authority.[7] Already prior to the second miracle the woman believed Elijah to be a 'man of God' with real spiritual influence (v. 18). The 'knowledge' she now possesses is the sort that is acquired only when one's heart has been transformed by a personal experience of the prophetic word.

The docility and faith-knowledge of the non-Israelite widow of Zarephath stand in contrast to the willful ignorance of Israel in the adjacent narrative of the contest on Mount Carmel (1 Kgs 18). Here Elijah accuses the people of 'limping on two crutches' (that is, wavering between two opinions), noting that they must decide the question of whether it is Yahweh or Baal who is the true God and commit themselves wholeheartedly to the one truth (v. 21a). Implicitly, this requires them to exercise reason together with faith in order to come to knowledge of the truth. In other words, they must consider what has been proposed for faith about Yahweh's saving deeds and moral character as well as the counter-claim made for Baal,[8] and 'through an act of choice' they must 'turn voluntarily to one side rather than the other' and 'cleave firmly' to that side.[9] Their silent refusal to respond to this challenge (v. 21b) indicates their unwillingness to come to knowledge of God in this way. But when Elijah proposes a contest that will virtually *prove* who the true God is (thus minimizing the role of faith), they are all in favor (vv. 22-24). Elijah then prays that they would come to knowledge *nolens volens*: 'Yahweh, God of Abraham, Isaac, and Israel, let it be known today that you are God in Israel and that I am your servant' (v. 36). Through the miracle of the fire from heaven their dramatic confession – 'It is Yahweh who is God! It is Yahweh who is God!' (v. 39) – is all but coerced. Their fault lies not in needing a sign but in requiring one 'up front'. The

---

[7] *Pace* J.A. Todd, 'The Pre-Deuteronomistic Elijah Cycle', in Coote, *Elijah and Elisha*, 15.

[8] What is proposed for faith is precisely that 'Yahweh is God' and that Baal is not (v 21). Yahweh's unique identity as the transcendent God and his deeds and moral character are elaborated in many texts in the Deuteronomistic History (e.g., 1 Kgs 8:23-24, 27). The implicit claim for Baal is that he sends lightening and rain, and it is just this claim that Elijah's announcement of the drought (17:1) and the contest on Mount Carmel disprove. The theological difference between Yahweh and Baal is especially clarified by Hosea, whom I shall consider below.

[9] This is how St Thomas Aquinas describes the act of faith in *ST* II-II, q. 1, a. 4 and q. 2, a. 1, as found in A.C. Pegis (ed.), *Basic Writings of Saint Thomas Aquinas*, vol. 2 (New York: Random House, 1945), 1060 and 1075.

widow of Zarephath (like the two figures we shall consider below) acts in faith on the prophetic word prior to receiving a confirmatory sign of God's love and power.

Turning now from the Elijah Cycle to the Elisha Cycle, we find two more conversion stories, both masterpieces of literary art. Superficially, the narrative of the woman of Shunem (2 Kgs 4:8-37) parallels the story of the widow of Zarephath. But in its exploration of the spiritual dynamics of conversion and its epistemology of faith, it picks up where the earlier story left off. The woman of Shunem makes her confession of faith-knowledge not at the end but at the beginning of the story: 'I know that this is a holy man of God who passes our way continually' (v. 9). Whereas the impoverished non-Israelite widow of Zarephath becomes involved with Elijah due to the exigencies of the drought, the woman of Shunem is married and well-to-do and thus has no need of material assistance from Elisha. She is an Israelite of mature faith who eagerly seeks out the spiritual companionship of this 'man of God', even making frequent pilgrimages to Mount Carmel on holy days (v. 23). The narrator labels her a 'great woman' ('iššâ gĕdôlâ [v. 8]), which on one level refers to her wealth and influence, but on another level to her forceful personality and the spiritual desire that leads her to a deeper conversion.

If the woman of Shunem has a character flaw, it is that she is too self-sufficient and does not allow others to repay her kindnesses (v. 13). (To this extent her worldly 'greatness' may even be an obstacle to personal growth.) The underlying spiritual defect seems to be a certain lack of hope, akin to that of the widow of Zarephath but perhaps more deeply submerged in her personality. She has long since given up on ever bearing a child – convinced, no doubt, that God simply does not want her to experience that joy[10] – and is very reluctant to have her hopes raised in this regard, wishing to avoid any further disappointment (vv. 16, 28). In the meantime, her sublimated desire for motherhood has been transferred to her relationship with the prophet, for whom she cooks meals and prepares a bedroom (vv. 8, 10). In accord with the 'double portion' of Elijah's spirit given to Elisha (2 Kgs 2:9), the woman of Shunem is given a twofold sign that God wills her full happiness: the child's miraculous birth (to which there is no parallel in the story of the widow of Zarephath) as well as his resurrection. To the latter she responds, not with a verbal confession of faith (which she has made already at the outset), but with a silent gesture of profound gratitude (v. 37). With this the narrative ends, leaving the reader to ponder the transformation that has taken place in the heart of the 'great woman'.

Forming something of a diptych with the story of the Israelite woman of Shunem is the narrative of the conversion of the non-Israelite Naaman (2 Kgs 5), who is described as a 'great man' ('îš gādôl [v. 1]). Once again the adjective 'great' cuts in two directions. In order to receive a cure for his leprosy and attain spiritual greatness, Naaman must overcome the obstacle of his own worldly status and pride. For in this narrative the great ones of the earth (kings and generals) harbor mistaken

---

[10] Scripture frequently speaks of God's direct involvement both in the of conception of a child and in the failure to conceive (e.g., Gen 4:1; 16:2, 10-11; 18:14; 20:17-18; 25:21; 29:31-33; 30:1-2; 41:51-52; Judg 13:3, 1 Sam 1:5, 11, 19-20).

notions about where God's power lies and how it may be accessed. Naaman is led to conversion by the lowly – a captive slave girl, his own servants, and the self-effacing prophet Elisha – who through their humility possess a proper understanding of the ways of God. Naaman, for his part, needs to approach Elisha in humility, so that, like the Hebrew slave girl, he may 'come to know that there is a prophet in Israel' (v. 8; cf. v. 3). Instead, he arrives at Elisha's house with a large retinue and expects the prophet to join in this ostentation. When Elisha refuses to play the game, pride and anger nearly get the best of Naaman, who is ready to storm off without a cure (vv. 9-12). But at the narrative's climax his servants convince him with simple wisdom to perform the humble gesture called for by the prophet (v. 13). When his newly cleansed flesh is described as like that of a "young lad" (*naʿar qāṭôn* [v. 14]), we recognize that the leprosy had symbolized his pride and that he has now become humble like the 'young lass' (*naʿar qĕṭannâ* [v. 2]).[11] Most importantly, Naaman's conversion from pride to humility is also a conversion from ignorance to knowledge of the true God (v. 15).

This chapter's oft-noted universalism – Yahweh is the one true God, whose influence extends beyond Israel (cf. v. 1) – is combined with an equally striking (and for moderns more difficult to comprehend) accent on particularism. Yahweh reveals himself to the nations *through* Israel. But it is not only the *people* of Israel (i.e., the slave girl and the prophet) who mediate healing and faith-knowledge to the gentile Naaman. Mysteriously, the *land* of Israel itself plays a quasi-sacramental role. The slave girl is twice said to be 'from the land of Israel' (vv. 2, 4), and Elisha is identified as a prophet 'in Samaria' (v. 3). In order to receive his healing, Naaman must go to the land of Israel and dip himself into 'the waters of Israel' – that is, the River Jordan – for which the more beautiful rivers of Damascus are no substitute (v. 12). In this way Naaman not only comes to 'know that there is a prophet *in Israel*' (v. 8), but to 'know that there is no God in all the earth, *except in Israel*' (v. 15). Accordingly, Naaman's request for two mule loads of Israelite soil (v. 17) reflects his new understanding that by choosing to reveal himself in a particular place God has consecrated the land of Israel to his worship.[12] The land itself is thus a tangible sign of the grace of the knowledge of the true God that makes authentic worship possible.

At this point we can take stock of what we have learned from the conversion narratives of Samuel and Kings. Knowledge of the true God entails a life-

---

[11] Naaman's newfound humility is evident both in the way he speaks to Elisha (vv. 15-18) and in the way he deals with Gehazi (vv. 21-23).

[12] Commentators who do not hold a sacramental view of reality are puzzled by this request. John Gray finds it 'naïvely inconsistent' with the monotheistic confession of v. 15 (*I & II Kings: A Commentary* [OTL; Philadelphia: Westminster Press, 1963], 455), overlooking the fact that the confession itself contains the same particularism, insisting as it does that the true God is 'in Israe'l. T.R. Hobbs implausibly suggests that Naaman is motivated by 'sentiment' and is asking for 'a souvenir of Israel' (*2 Kings* [WBC 13; Waco, TX: Word Books, 1985], 60). Apparently unconvinced by his own hypothesis, Hobbs still finds Naaman's request 'strange' and in 'conflict' with the author's statement of universalism in v. 1 (p. 66).

transforming encounter and comes to those who receive a true prophet of Yahweh in humility and faith. Miraculous signs are given to the docile, enabling them to overcome spiritual impediments such as discouragement (the widow of Zarephath), self-sufficiency (the woman of Shunem), and pride (Naaman), but the Israelites present on Mount Carmel in 1 Kings 18 appear to be obstinate and weak in faith by comparison. They witness a great sign and confess Yahweh to be the true God but do not seem to undergo a profound spiritual transformation. Baalism will continue to be a rampant problem in Israel throughout the remainder of the monarchic period. Finally, these narratives are not mere timeless tales but integral parts of sacred history. Knowledge of the true God comes into the world through the mystery of Israel – people and land – and can never be abstracted from this divinely chosen mediation.

'Knowledge of God' in the Book of Hosea

Hosea was among the first of the 'classical' prophets, i.e., those whose oracles are preserved mostly in poetic form. He lived about a century after Elisha and prophesied in the Northern Kingdom during the tumultuous quarter century leading up to its collapse before the advancing Assyrian Empire (746-722 B.C.). Like his older contemporary Amos, Hosea understands this political catastrophe to be divine chastisement for Israel's sins, both cultic and social. Reflecting on a long history of covenantal infidelity, he provides a penetrating theological and spiritual diagnosis of Israel's chronic malady – their persistent apostasy – concluding that his people is 'perishing for lack of knowledge' (Hos 4:6).[13]

There is a consensus among scholars that the concept of 'knowledge of God' (4:1; 6:6) lies near the center of Hosea's thought, but there is less agreement regarding precisely what Hosea means by this expression. According to Vawter, it denotes 'a practical knowledge of Yahweh's moral will',[14] and Blenkinsopp similarly finds evidence of 'an emerging consensual ethic' in Hosea 4:1-2.[15] While granting this practical-moral dimension, Botterweck takes a more romantic view, stressing that for Israel's prophets 'knowledge of God' has to do with 'true religious feeling', a 'subjective attitude', and a 'spontaneous preoccupation with the interests of Yahweh.'[16] Heschel moves even farther in this direction, defining Hosea's *da'at 'ĕlōhîm* as 'sympathy for God' and laying heavy emphasis on its 'emotional

---

[13] I will cite Hosea according the chapter and verse divisions of the Hebrew Masoretic Text, which are also that of the NAB. Some translations (including the RSV) follow the divisions of the Greek Septuagint, which diverges occasionally from the Hebrew.

[14] Bruce Vawter, C.M., *The Conscience of Israel: Pre-Exilic Prophets and Prophecy* (New York: Sheed & Ward, 1961), 115.

[15] J. Blenkinsopp, *A History of Prophecy in Israel* (Louisville: Westminster John Knox, 1996, rev. ed.), 90.

[16] G.J. Botterweck, 'Knowledge of God', in J.B. Bauer (ed.), *Encyclopedia of Biblical Theology* (London: Sheed & Ward, 1970), 473.

component'. What Hosea finds lacking in Israel is 'inwardness'.[17] Steering away from this stress on the subjective and emotional dimension, Gerhard von Rad characteristically identifies 'knowledge of God' as 'familiarity with the historical acts' of Yahweh.[18] Each of these views contains at least a grain of truth.

Many interpreters seem eager to downplay, if not deny outright, any 'theoretical' or 'propositional' dimension in Hosea's use of the phrase 'knowledge of God'.[19] As Heschel sees the matter, *daʿat ʾĕlōhîm* 'does not connote a knowledge *about* God, but an awareness *of* God.'[20] Occasionally such judgments are explicitly based on the well-worn dichotomy between 'Hebraic' and 'Greek' conceptions of knowledge, the former taken to be 'practical' and the latter 'purely speculative'.[21] One senses here that certain modern views may be imposing themselves too forcefully on the biblical text. Whether it is a question of the Enlightenment view of 'true religion' as concerned with morals rather than rituals or Romanticism's emphasis on religious feeling and subjective experience, the potential for distortion of Hosea's theology is quite real. While it is true that the Book of Hosea contains few propositional statements of a strictly theological nature (but cf. 11:9), at the very heart of the prophet's concern is the contention that Israel has a deficient *understanding* of who Yahweh is, rendering themselves thus incapable of authentic worship.

One exegete who grasps this point and bucks the scholarly trend is Dentan, who holds that Hosea favors the term 'knowledge of God' (rather than, say, 'the fear of the Lord') precisely to give priority to 'the act of understanding'. Without sacrificing the practical-moral and emotional-subjective dimensions, Dentan takes the phrase *daʿat ʾĕlōhîm* to mean 'knowing who God is and what he expects' and to be thus roughly equivalent to our word 'theology'.[22] While there is some risk of anachronism and overstatement here too, two considerations especially support Dentan's interpretation. First, alongside his frequent use of the words 'know' (*yādaʿ*) and 'knowledge' (*daʿat*), Hosea employs other terms that accent the noetic dimension of what Israel lacks. Israel is 'a people that does not understand [*bîn*]' (4:14). They are 'like a dove, silly and without sense [*lēb*]' (7:11) or 'a son who is not wise [*ḥākām*]' (13:13). Significantly, the book's final verse is loaded with such terms, maintaining as it does that only the reader who is 'wise' (*ḥākām*) and 'discerning' (*nābôn*) will be able to 'understand' (*bîn*) and 'know' (*yādaʿ*) the realities dealt with in Hosea's oracles (14:10).

---

[17] A.J. Heschel, *The Prophets* (New York: Harper & Row, 1962), 59-60.

[18] G. von Rad, *Old Testament Theology, Volume II: The Theology of Israel's Prophetic Traditions* (London: SCM, 1965), 143; similarly, H.W. Wolff, *Hosea: A Commentary on the Book of the Prophet Hosea*, Hermeneia (Philadelphia: Fortress, 1974), 79.

[19] E.g., Botterweck, 'Knowledge of God', 473.

[20] Heschel, *Prophets*, 60 (emphasis in original).

[21] E.g., O.A. Piper, 'Knowledge', *IDB* vol. 3, p. 44; and with more nuance, Vawter, *Conscience of Israel*, 120.

[22] R.C. Dentan, *The Knowledge of God in Ancient Israel* (New York: Seabury Press, 1968), 36.

Second, and even more decisive in this regard, is Hosea's properly theological concern to differentiate clearly between Yahweh and the Baals (the fertility deities of Canaan). An explication of this crucial point will help us grasp not only what he means by 'knowledge of God' but how the various key elements in his theology cohere within a broad prophetic vision of reality. These elements include: (1) frequent allusions to Israel's historical traditions, (2) the presentation of Yahweh as Israel's 'husband' and of Israel's covenant infidelity as 'harlotry', (3) a concern with cultic matters and idolatry, (4) a nascent moral theology, and (5) poetic imagery dominated by references to land, weather, agriculture, and human fertility.

The storm-god Baal and the other Canaanite fertility deities are mythological personifications of meteorological phenomena and the cyclic forces of nature. As such, they are incapable of historical activity, self-revelation, or entering into a covenant relationship. Yahweh, by contrast, is 'the living God' (2:1), who has acted in sovereign freedom within the course of history to claim Israel for himself and who holds them accountable to his moral will. The 'knowledge' to which Israel is called is an interpersonal relationship between a free and righteous God and free human moral agents. Since the exodus from Egypt, Yahweh has 'known' Israel, and Israel is to 'know' Yahweh (5:3; 13:4-5).

Hosea identifies the wilderness as the locus of Yahweh's first espousal of Israel (9:10; 13:5) and of Israel's initially faithful response to Yahweh (2:16-17). Israel's infidelity began when they entered the fertile land of Canaan. Already in the Transjordan they 'consecrated themselves' to the Baal of Peor (9:10), and after crossing the Jordan they committed similar acts of apostasy at Adam (6:7), Gilgal (9:15), and Gibeah (10:9). In the poetic symbolism of Hosea these all represent the same primal defection, and the rest of Israel's history in the land up to the prophet's own day has been merely a further living out of that 'original sin'. Having experienced the fruitfulness of the land (i.e., vegetative, animal, and human fertility), Israel's heart was enticed and led astray to worship the gods who had been associated from time immemorial with that fertility (10:1-2a). Perhaps because Yahweh for his part was associated with the exodus from Egypt and his original home was understood to be the Sinai wilderness, there were – in addition to simple apostasy to 'other gods' (3:1) – syncretistic attempts to assimilate Yahweh to Canaanite fertility religion (2:18; 4:15; 8:5-6; 10:5).

In his attempt to untangle this web of theological confusion, Hosea by no means buys into the notion that Yahweh is properly the god of the wilderness whereas the land of Canaan belongs to the Baals. In fact, he calls Canaan 'the land of Yahweh' (9:3). Still less does the prophet accept a division of labor by which Yahweh is the god of history while the Canaanite deities supply the goods of creation. Israel needs to come to 'know' that it is emphatically Yahweh, and not Baal, who gives them 'the grain, the wine, and the oil' (2:10). And while Hosea speaks nostalgically of Israel's time in the wilderness, he does not accord the wilderness some absolute advantage over the arable land. Although agricultural blessings provide the occasion for Israel's apostasy, this does not mean that there is anything inherently wrong with them.

On the contrary, much as we saw in the narrative of Naaman's conversion (2 Kgs 5), Hosea presents the Holy Land as a sort of sacrament of the knowledge of God. But his teaching in this regard can only be understood within the context of his view of salvation-history. Yahweh delivers Israel from servitude in Egypt so that they will know him and be free to worship him in truth. Israel's residence in the land of Canaan is the goal of this self-revelatory act of God. There they are to enjoy the fruits of the earth as signs of Yahweh's special love for them, and they are to render these blessings back to him via the cultus as an expression of their commitment to him and their clear conviction that it is he who provides for them. In other words, the blessings of the land are intended to promote not sinful idolatry, but authentic worship of the true God.

Israel's sin – which Hosea ascribes in the first place to the priests and prophets – is fundamentally their willful 'rejection' of this revealed 'knowledge' of the true God (4:4-6). Israel has become 'as stubborn as a stubborn heifer' (4:16). They have chosen to regard the blessings of the fruitful land as a 'prostitute's pay' from their 'lovers', the gods of Canaan (2:7, 14; 9:1). The Israelites celebrate many religious festivals (2:13; 5:6; 6:6; 8:11-13; 10:1), but their syncretism and outright idolatry indicate that these cultic acts are devoid of any true understanding of who God is (13:2). In the exuberance of worship they may cry out, 'We know you, O God of Israel!' (8:2), but in fact they do not. Meanwhile, the injustice and decadence of Israelite society reflect the people's failure to appropriate Yahweh's own righteous character.

> There is no truth, no faithful love, no knowledge of God in the land;
> rather cursing, lying, killing, stealing, and adultery abound (4:1b-2).

That Hosea both condemns literal adultery and speaks figuratively of Israel's idolatry as 'adultery' or 'harlotry' (2:4-15; 4:10-19) is significant. It suggests that Israel's moral and cultic failures are symptoms of a single defect of the heart, namely infidelity. When they 'consecrated themselves' to Baal (a god known to have multiple consorts), they became – by a sort of *connaturalitas* with the object known – 'as detestable as that which they loved' (9:10). This was a travesty of what ought to have taken place. Had they drawn close to Yahweh, Israel would have appropriated something of his characteristic fidelity. To imitate his 'faithful love' (*ḥesed*) would have been to possess the 'knowledge of God' that Yahweh desires more than any mere sacrifice or offering (6:6).

Deeply troubled by Israel's apostasy, Hosea offers a profound diagnosis of Israel's defect of the heart that touches on the mystery of human freedom and its abuse. In classical Hebrew thought there is no heart-versus-head dichotomy. The 'heart' (*lēb*) is the seat of intellect, will, conscience, and emotion. When Yahweh 'fed' Israel with the good things of the land, 'they were sated, and their heart was lifted up; therefore they forgot [him]' (13:6). To have a heart that is 'lifted up' is to be self-sufficient and willful and to rely on one's own understanding. To 'forget' God is not merely to experience a memory lapse but to choose to ignore him, to relinquish the knowledge of God (cf. 2:15; 4:6; 8:14). In sum, Israel's heart was drawn to the creature for its own sake and away from the Creator. In this regard, syncretism represents an attempt to have one's cake and eat it too. Israel was fatally attracted to a hybrid of Canaanite fertility worship and Yahweh worship because, on the one hand, it provided the exhilaration of orgiastic rites (4:14; 13:2), the promise of agricultural bounty (2:7), and a sense of devotion to Yahweh (8:2), but on the other hand, left them free to ignore Yahweh's moral requirements (4:1-2) and to construct objects of worship 'according to their own understanding' (13:2).

Like the other classical prophets, Hosea describes Yahweh's jealous love for Israel in rather intense terms (e.g., 2:4-8; 13:7-8). To empathize with Israel just a bit, one gets the impression that the encounter with Yahweh was simply too much for them. Their infidelity might then be viewed as an effort to temper Yahweh's absolute claim over them with an admixture of Baal worship.

> When Israel was a lad, I loved him; and out of Egypt I called my son.
> The more I summoned them, the farther they went from my presence;
> they sacrificed to the Baals, burnt incense to idols (11:1-2).

Such behavior will be intelligible to anyone who, in attempting to draw near to the 'Other' whose freedom qualifies human autonomy, has reached the point where the experience becomes terrifying. In such a case there is an ever-present temptation to attach oneself to almost any created thing rather than abandon oneself into the hands of the Creator. And those created realities that can provide an ersatz elevation of the human spirit (e.g., music, art, sexuality, or the intellectual life) may hold the most powerful allurement.

Hosea speaks in this connection of a 'spirit of harlotry' that has led to Israel's apostasy (4:12). By this striking expression he seems to mean a strong inner susceptibility to any creaturely enticement that may divert one from whole-hearted union with God. The same phrase figures into a succinct articulation of Hosea's diagnosis of Israel's chronic malady.

> Their misdeeds do not allow them to return to their God,
> for a spirit of harlotry is within them, and they do not know Yahweh (5:4).

To paraphrase, sin has become so deeply habitual for Israel that repentance is not within their power. Their fatal attraction to fertility worship has become an interior spiritual principle that holds them in bondage, with the result that they lack the theological understanding, the moral rectitude, and the whole-hearted personal devotion to Yahweh that together constitute the knowledge of God. Implicitly, only a divine act of spiritual deliverance can save Israel.

The initial step in Yahweh's remedy for Israel's defect of the heart is withdrawal. He will take the blessings of the land away from them for a time, first through drought and famine (2:11; 9:2), and then by means of foreign invasion followed by exile to pagan lands such as Assyria and Egypt. There God's people will eat food that is 'unclean ... like mourners' bread' (mourners were defiled by contact with the dead), fit only to satisfy one's hunger and by no means to be offered in sacrifice to the holy God (9:3-5). The bounty of 'Yahweh's land' was meant to be a sign of the covenant and of the spiritual 'fruitfulness' that the true God alone can give to his people (14:9). The sacrificial offering of abundant crops and livestock was to be a sign that the true God was known and worshipped in the land. Instead, the land 'withers' and 'mourns' (the Hebrew verb *ʾābal* in 4:3 denotes both) as a sign that there is 'no knowledge of God *in the land*' (4:1). The land itself bears witness to Israel's idolatry when 'thorns and thistles ... grow up around their altars' at the outdoor shrines, and the land is poetically depicted as the agent of Yahweh's eschatological wrath when Israel is imagined to cry out to the mountains, 'Cover us!' – and to the hills, 'Fall upon us!' (10:8). Through the desolation of the land and Israel's exile from it, Yahweh himself 'withdraws' from Israel until such time as they 'realize their guilt and seek [his] face', saying, 'Come, let us return to Yahweh! ... Let us know, let us strive to know Yahweh!' (5:6, 15; 6:1, 3; cf. 2:9; 3:1-5).

After this repentance, Israel will be ready for the eschatological 'covenant' (2:20). In a remarkable passage that anticipates and closely parallels the famous 'new covenant' oracle of Jeremiah 31:31-34, Hosea poetically describes Yahweh's eschatological 'espousal' of his people in such a way as to suggest the mysterious role that the physical creation will have in mediating the knowledge of God to Israel (Hos 2:16-25). First, Yahweh will 'allure' Israel and 'lead her' once again 'into the wilderness', where he will 'speak to her heart' (2:16). This Hebrew idiom ('speak to her heart') suggests that Yahweh will reveal himself – indeed, *offer* himself – to Israel in a highly personal and intimate manner. Removed temporarily from the distractions and temptations of the fertile land of Canaan, Israel will be able to 'respond' to these overtures, much as she did 'in the days of her youth' following the exodus (2:17b). Yahweh will espouse Israel to himself 'in righteousness and justice, in steadfast love and compassion' – in a word, 'in faithfulness' – with the result that they will 'know Yahweh' (2:21-22). That is, he will communicate something of his own character to his people, so that they will know him through experiencing and imitating his love.[23]

At this point, Yahweh will bestow the gift of the land upon Israel a second time (2:17a). But this time Israel will receive the concomitant grace to call upon Yahweh as 'my husband' with clarity of understanding and purity of devotion, no longer calling him 'my Baal' in syncretistic confusion, nor invoking many 'Baals' in polytheistic idolatry (2:18-19). Yahweh will banish warfare from the land and even draw the land's wild denizens into his covenant with Israel, so that the land may be a place of security and peace (2:20). Yahweh's loving 'response' to Israel's prayer will flow from the heavens to the earth, from the earth to 'the grain, the wine, and the oil', and through these blessings to Israel (2:23-24). Prosaically rendered, this means that Israel will pray for rain and get it. But Hosea's point is that the blessing of rain and the resultant agricultural bounty will now be correctly received by Israel as a

---

[23] Cf. Vawter, *Conscience of Israel*, 120-21.

word of love from her covenant partner, who is the true master of heaven and earth, not as a 'harlot's pay' for services rendered to the fertility deities.

Israel is referred to in this passage as 'Jezreel', which means 'God sows', and in a striking modulation of the oracle's guiding metaphor we find that it is not simply 'the grain, the wine, and the oil', but Israel herself that Yahweh will 'sow' for himself 'in the land' (2:25a). The imagery of Israel as Yahweh's special agricultural project is, of course, an important theological symbol elsewhere in Hosea (10:1; 14:6-9) and throughout Scripture (e.g., Ex 15:17; Is 5:1-7; Ps 80:9-17; Mk 12:1-12; Lk 13:6-9; Jn 15:1-10; Rom 11:16-24; 1 Cor 3:6-9). Here it embodies a poetic insight into the way God's mysterious purpose for Israel will be realized in and through a particular piece of land.

The Knowledge of God as Primordial Knowledge

To this point my analysis has been largely exegetical and theological. In this final section I shall employ epistemological categories in order to consider from a more philosophical angle what sort of 'knowledge of God' is spoken of in the narratives of Samuel and Kings and in the Book of Hosea. My thesis is that the knowledge referred to in these texts has several features in common with what has been called 'primordial knowledge'. This term refers to 'a family of kinds of knowledge' that have in common that they communicate their insights without the aid of discursive reasoning or rigorous conceptual logic.[24] My analysis will be organized by discussing five types of primordial knowledge that often overlap and in fact converge in the 'knowledge of God' spoken of in the Old Testament prophetic literature. These are: (1) knowledge of (and through) concrete particulars, including the contingencies of history; (2) knowledge communicated through a literary work of art; (3) practical knowledge or 'doing-knowing', including the knowledge present in and witnessed to by moral acts; (4) personal and interpersonal knowledge, including the mystical knowledge of God; and (5) knowledge attained through faith, that is, through the acceptance of testimony.

With respect to the first of these, it is clear that the biblical texts we have been examining are concerned first and foremost with concrete particularities and the contingencies of history. Certainly universal truth (above all, the reality of the living and personal God and of his steadfast love and divine mercy) is revealed through these texts, but this revelation takes place in and through particularities of geography, ethnicity, and temporal sequence. We saw this emerge as a theological theme in our narrative analysis of the healing and conversion of Naaman (2 Kgs 5). It is also present in Hosea, whose overriding concern is with historical Israel and its encounter with the 'living God' in the wilderness and in the Holy Land. Prior to the early twentieth century, the Western philosophical tradition was largely concerned with the deductive conceptual knowledge of universals, so that knowledge of the

---

[24] T.J. Tekippe, *Scientific and Primordial Knowing* (Lanham, MD/New York/London: University Press of America, 1996) 451-62 (quote from 458).

concrete particular – and inductive knowledge of universals *through* the contingencies of history – presented something of a problem. Is such knowledge possible? If so, is it genuinely intellectual? That is, does it qualify as 'knowledge' in the full sense? The now well-known 'turn' toward the subjective-personal, the inductive-experiential, and the linguistic-contextual in modernity and post-modernity suggests that more recent philosophies may supply tools for elucidating this dimension of biblical knowledge. At the same time, in my opinion, such contemporary insights will be of little avail in this endeavor unless they are combined with a recovery of the traditional theological notion of 'mystery'. Given the limited scope of this essay, I will attempt in what follows only to offer a few suggestions along these lines.

The second type of primordial knowledge is present in Old Testament prophetic literature insofar as these texts present the knowledge of God to the reader by way of literary art – historical narrative and poetic oracle – rather than through the sort of discursive argument and rigorous deductive reasoning prized by the Western philosophical tradition. To head off any misunderstanding of this fact, three caveats are in order. First, it is necessary to avoid the common mistake of pitting literature against historicity. Though they may not supply the empirically verifiable data that modern historians desire, the narratives of Samuel and Kings do embody an historiographical intentionality that must be respected. And however creative and imaginative Hosea's poetry may be, he is concerned all the same with Iron Age social, political, and religious realities in the Near East. Second, nothing in these texts suggests that the authors employed literary artifice in order to dress up a pre-conceived theological 'message'. It is far too simplistic, for example, to read the narratives of Samuel and Kings looking for 'the moral of the story', as if a universal meaning could be extracted so easily. The Old Testament is not *The Book of Virtues*, and it is doubtful whether the question 'What would Elisha do?' would provide one with a clear moral compass.

One respects the communicative *intentio auctoris et textus* far better by approaching the narrated events of salvation history as *mysteria*. That is, such events do not merely recede into the past (so that they may or may not be retrievable in terms of empirically verifiable data) but live on via Scripture in the *traditio* and liturgy of Israel and the Church. In this way, the people of God in every age experience the efficacy of these saving events through the witness of the sacred text. Moreover, each *mysterium* discloses an aspect of the one Mystery, namely, God's plan for the world as it is revealed and realized in Israel/Christ/Church.[25] If Hosea

---

[25] A mystery is something that can be known only through revelation and even when it is known remains incomprehensible. *The* Mystery is God himself, his inner trinitarian life, and his eternal plan of creation and salvation. This is 'the mystery kept in silence for eternal ages' (Rom 16:25). This Mystery is 'made known' through God's historical act of salvation, which Paul calls the 'economy of the fullness of times' (Eph 1:9-10), or simply, 'the economy of the mystery' (3:9). This act has its center, of course, in the person and action of Christ, but inasmuch as he 'recapitulates all things' (cf. 1:10) it embraces all of creation, all of human history, and in a special manner the history of Israel's encounter with Yahweh. Events in

presents his privileged prophetic glimpse of this Mystery in poetry and symbolic gesture (e.g., his marriage to Gomer), it is presumably because this glimpse came to him in the form and modality of a poetic insight. If, as Michael Polanyi maintains, it is generally the case that, 'In order to describe experiences more fully language must be less precise,'[26] this would be *a fortiori* true of Israel's encounter with God and should caution us not to disparage the Bible's protological literary presentation of that experience.[27]

Finally (and this is my third caveat regarding the second type of primordial knowledge), Romanticism's claim that the meaning of a poem or narrative is untranslatable into an abstract and discursive statement is a half-truth. This assertion represents an overreaction to the simplistic idea that I have just resisted, namely, that the meaning of a literary text is reducible to its 'message'. It is an overreaction because poetry and narrative rarely dispense with abstract concepts altogether and because the biblical texts have shown themselves amenable to the sort of discursive commentary that sends one back to the text for an enhanced rereading. The *via media* here may be found in Kant's happy formulation by which the 'aesthetic idea' embodied in a work of art 'induces much thought' but such that no conceptual articulation 'can be wholly adequate' to it.[28] Biblical interpretation thus has a legitimate and necessary role at various levels of the Church's appropriation of the inspired text's witness (e.g., dogmatic, exegetical, liturgical, and homiletic), but it never renders the text obsolete.

As for the third type of primordial knowledge, Hosea may refer to a sort of practical knowledge or 'doing-knowing' when he seems to imply that moral action itself constitutes the 'knowledge of God' (4:1-2; 6:6). But here we must avoid three reductionistic pitfalls. First, we must not suppose that Hosea has in mind a knowledge that is *merely* practical and thus without any real theological content. As

---

Israel's history in which God's self-revelatory action and plan for his world are especially manifest may be called *mysteria* ('mysteries'). They participate in and prepare for *the* Mystery because the 'Spirit of Christ' was already present to (and active in) Israel prior to the Incarnation (cf. 1 Pet 1:11). The individual events of Christ's life are also called 'mysteries' inasmuch as each of them manifests something of the whole Mystery and anticipates in its own way the Paschal mystery (e.g., the Lord's baptism in the Jordan anticipates the 'baptism' of his passion [cf. Mk 10:38; Lk 12:50]). All of these mystery-events of both testaments are glorified along with the humanity of Christ in his Resurrection and Ascension. They are thus potentially present to all peoples of all times and are actually accessed through the sacramental life of the Church, including in a special manner the spiritual reading of the Sacred Text, which is itself a sort of sacrament.

[26] M. Polanyi, *Personal Knowledge: Towards a Post-Critical Philosophy* (Chicago: University of Chicago Press, 1962), 86.

[27] Biblical thought is 'protological' insofar as it does not conform to Western canons of logical argumentation or consistency and precision of expression but relates to reality via more or less undifferentiated symbols.

[28] I. Kant, *The Critique of Judgment*, J. Meredith (tr.) (Oxford: Clarendon Press, 1952), 175-76; cited in Tekippe, *Scientific and Primordial Knowing*, 293. My aim here is to remove this element from Kant's idealist epistemology and transpose it into a realist 'key'.

we have already seen, the *da'at 'ĕlōhîm* he wishes Israel to possess has a noetic dimension. Second, only a highly selective reading of Hosea would restrict his notion of 'knowledge of God' to the moral realm. Hosea (in contrast to Amos) refers far more often to Israel's cultic aberrations than to their moral shortcomings, and for him the former reflect precisely Israel's deficient understanding of who God is (e.g., 13:2). Third, Hosea's moral doctrine is more profound and more integral to his covenant theology than some scholars seem to appreciate. To act in justice and steadfast love constitutes 'knowledge of God', not simply because it reflects an accurate knowledge of what God requires, but because such human virtues are a true participation in Yahweh's own character and thus actually put one in touch with the living God. The moral demands Yahweh places on Israel are part and parcel of his plan to bind Israel to himself in a covenant relationship.

The fourth type of primordial knowledge is the personal involvement of the knower with the known, especially the interpersonal knowledge of committed love. The widow of Zarephath, the Shunemite woman, and Naaman the Syrian all come to the knowledge of Yahweh through a life-changing personal encounter with a 'man of God' and a profoundly existential conversion experience. The deeply personal dimension of Hosea's own prophetic knowledge of God is hinted at in the enigmatic passages concerning his marriage to Gomer and the symbolic naming of their children (1:2-9; 3:1-5), and one is immediately reminded of the much fuller treatment this dimension of prophecy receives in the Book of Jeremiah. As for Israel's covenant with Yahweh, Hosea presents it in the most personal of terms. Yahweh is portrayed as a jilted lover or an offended father, and Israel's sin is described as infidelity, rebellion, betrayal, and deceit. When in the end Yahweh will 'heal their defection' and 'love them freely' (14:5), the knowledge they will possess of him will have the intimacy of a spousal union (2:21-22).

The fifth type of primordial knowledge is faith-knowledge. The role of faith as a means of attaining knowledge of God pervades Scripture as an epistemological and hermeneutical presupposition, even where it is not an explicit theme. It is hermeneutical in the sense that the Scriptures themselves constitute a testimony to be received by faith. This testimony is offered in a variety of modes, in accordance with the Bible's many genres. For example, a conversion narrative such as 2 Kings 5 calls upon the reader to make an act of faith that is analogous to that made by Naaman and thus to enter into an experiential faith-knowledge of the realities to which the sacred text bears witness. Something similar is operative in the Book of Hosea, the final verse of which challenges the reader to put forth the considerable effort necessary to understand 'these things' (14:10a). The reference, of course, is to Hosea's words, but not merely so. Through understanding the words and accepting their testimony the reader comes to know realities. The same verse thus points to the practical and personal dimensions of a faith-knowledge that attains *adaequatio intellectus et rei* via participation. One must 'walk in' the upright ways of Yahweh through being/becoming righteous oneself (14:10b).

One begins to sense how closely intertwined these five types of primordial knowledge are in the case of the *da'at 'ĕlōhîm* spoken of by Hosea. Indeed, they represent five aspects of a single unified mode of knowledge. The convergence of these aspects will come into still sharper focus if we return to consider a leitmotif in Hosea's prophecy that was touched on briefly above, namely, Israel's 'return' (*šûb*) to Yahweh (2:9; 3:5; 5:4; 6:1; 7:10; 12:7; 14:2-3). Long before the call to repentance was addressed (in the gospel of Christ) to all peoples of all times, repentance was Yahweh's particular requirement for Israel at a decisive moment in her history. We can hardly expect, then, to understand this theme if we attempt to abstract it from the classical prophets' schema of salvation history and turn it into a mere timeless ideal. The political catastrophe that overtook Israel and Judah, beginning with the Assyrian advance in Hosea's day and culminating with the Babylonian exile, was the revelation of Israel's sin and thus of her need for repentance. This 'moment' stretched over two centuries, to be sure, but it was precisely the role of the classical prophets to discern the providential trajectory and significance of this succession of events.

At the same time, a flat, linear view of history will hardly suffice either. Hosea presents Israel's 'return' to Yahweh first as an event in the eschatological future (2:9; 3:5; 5:15-6:3); but after indicating how Israel's sin and pride presently holds them in spiritual bondage, making repentance humanly impossible (5:4; 7:10), Hosea concludes – incongruously, to modern ears – by summoning present Israel to their eschatological repentance and salvation (12:7; 14:2-9). While remaining truly future, the eschatological moment with its grace of repentance is a *mysterium* available to Old Testament Israel in advance. For our purposes, it is especially important to note that, just as the failure to repent keeps one ignorant of God (Hos 5:4), so acceptance of the eschatological grace of repentance is precisely the entry way into Israel's eschatological knowledge of God (2:16-22; 6:1-3). This knowledge, though it certainly arrives at that which is non-contingent and universal (i.e., God himself), is primordial insofar as it is attained through the prophetic vision of God's mysterious plan unfolding in the concrete particularities and contingencies of history, and insofar as this prophetic vision of history is communicated through a poetic mode of thought that defies strict logic.

Knowledge of God by way of repentance is also primordial knowledge in the sense that it is an instance of 'doing-knowing' and is profoundly interpersonal and mystical. However much Israel's 'return' is possible only 'by the help of [their] God' – that is, by grace – it also necessarily entails a free movement of the will expressed in concrete action, and this action involves both the horizontal-moral dimension of 'maintaining steadfast love and justice' and the vertical-spiritual dimension of 'hoping in your God continually' (12:7). Hosea closely associates Israel's repentance with 'seeking' Yahweh (3:5; 5:15) and 'striving to know' him (6:3). He also subtly accents the interpersonal and mystical dimension of the knowledge of God by several references to the words of prayer by which Israel directly addresses Yahweh. In their present ignorance they confusedly call Yahweh 'my Baal' (2:18) and say, 'Our God', to the work of their hands (14:4); they falsely swear, 'As Yahweh lives!' (4:15) and falsely confess, 'We know you, O God of Israel!' (8:2). But 'words' of prayer will also play an essential role in Israel's 'return' to Yahweh (14:3), and through the grace of eschatological repentance they will be enabled to say, 'My husband!' in the authentic intimacy that is possible only through true knowledge (2:18). The new covenant thus takes the form of a dialogue of interpersonal communion: Yahweh will say, 'You are my people,' and Israel will reply, 'My God!' (2:25).

Finally, when we consider how the *da'at 'ĕlōhîm* comes to eighth-century Israel and to the contemporary reader only through the faith-acceptance of prophetic testimony, we see just how epistemologically decisive repentance is. Why, after all, should Israel accept Hosea's witness over that of the contemporary prophets that he condemns (4:5)? And how is Israel really to know that Yahweh is the 'living God' (2:1) but Baal a mere idol, when Hosea offers no miracle of the sort performed by Elijah and Elisha? The 'miraculous sign' offered by Hosea and the other classical prophets lies, I suggest, in the entire historical process by which Israel comes to recognize their guilt and their bondage to sin, experiences deliverance and authentic freedom in repentance and righteous conduct, and comes to know the true God as one who first wounds and then heals (6:1). Yahweh shows himself to be 'God and not man' and 'the Holy One' in Israel's midst first in the jealous love that leads him to punish and then even more so in the mercy by which he relents and restores (11:9). Baal never required Israel to face her sin, never called Israel to rise above the selfish and degrading passions of the fertility cult, and never provided the grace to go out from herself to a spousal union with God through participation in God's own righteous character (2:21-22). In sum, the true God reveals himself to us as the one who cares enough to deal with our sin and is able to do so.

Bibliography

Aquinas, T., *ST* II-II, q. 1, a. 4 and q. 2, a. 1, as found in Anton C. Pegis, ed., *Basic Writings of Saint Thomas Aquinas*, vol. 2 (New York: Random House, 1945), 1060 and 1075

Blenkinsopp, J., *A History of Prophecy in Israel* (Louisville: Westminster John Knox, 1996, rev. ed.)

Botterweck, G.J., 'Knowledge of God', in J.B. Bauer (ed.), *Encyclopedia of Biblical Theology* (London: Sheed & Ward, 1970), 472-75

Dentan, R.C., *The Knowledge of God in Ancient Israel* (New York: Seabury Press, 1968)

DeVries, S.J., *1 Kings*, WBC 12 (Waco, TX: Word Books, 1985)

Gray, J., *I & II Kings: A Commentary*, OTL (Philadelphia: Westminster Press, 1963)

Heschel, A.J., *The Prophets* (New York: Harper & Row, 1962)

Hobbs, T.R., *2 Kings*, WBC 13 (Waco, TX: Word Books, 1985)

Kant, I., *The Critique of Judgment*, J. Meredith (tr.) (Oxford: Clarendon Press, 1952)

Nelson, R. *First and Second Kings*, Interpretation (Louisville: John Knox Press, 1987)

Piper, O.A., 'Knowledge', G.A. Buttrick (ed.), *The Interpreter's Dictionary of the Bible: An Illustrated Encyclopedia*, 4 vols. (New York/Nashville: Abingdon Press, 1962)*,* vol. 3, 42-48

Polanyi, M. *Personal Knowledge: Towards a Post-Critical Philosophy* (Chicago: University of Chicago Press, 1962)

Rentería, T.H., 'The Elijah/Elisha Stories: A Socio-cultural Analysis of Prophets and People in Ninth-Century B.C.E. Israel', in R.B. Coote (ed.), *Elijah and Elisha in Socioliterary Perspective* (Atlanta: Scholars Press, 1992), 75-126

Tekippe, T.J., *Scientific and Primordial Knowing* (Lanham, MD/New York/London: University Press of America, 1996)

Todd, J.A., 'The Pre-Deuteronomistic Elijah Cycle', in R.B. Coote (ed.), *Elijah and Elisha in Socioliterary Perspective* (Atlanta: Scholars Press, 1992), 1-35

Vawter, B., *The Conscience of Israel: Pre-Exilic Prophets and Prophecy* (New York: Sheed & Ward, 1961)

von Rad, G., *Old Testament Theology, Volume II: The Theology of Israel's Prophetic Traditions* (London: SCM, 1965)

Wolff, H.W., *Hosea: A Commentary on the Book of the Prophet Hosea*, Hermeneia (Philadelphia: Fortress, 1974)

CHAPTER 3

The Word at Prayer:
Epistemology in the Psalms

Francis Martin

The effort to describe biblical epistemology is a theological task. It requires transposing, as far as possible, the implicit anthropology of the Bible, in the case of this essay the Psalms, into other categories in order to understand the biblical teaching on humanity in its specificity, namely, the ability to know and love. There is probably no other task as urgent as this in our day, since a large part of the estrangement of the modern mind from the light and teaching of revelation is due to the pervasive view that the thinking subject is dominative in the act of knowing. This is a view which began in its present form with William of Ockham in the fourteenth century and has been consistently orchestrated by Descartes, Kant and others so that it has become, until very recently, the view that underlies nearly all western thought.

The result has been that most modern Christians have been deprived of the profoundly healing experience of having their minds fully participate, as far as possible, in their faith. Though the devout have experienced the realities mediated to us through God's revelation, they are often unable to share in the ancient thrill of rendering these realities at least partially intelligible through a 'faith seeking understanding'. One of the fruits of the essays in this book will surely be to begin an integration of ancient epistemology with what is sound in modern epistemology, mediated precisely by the implicit epistemology in the Sacred Text itself.

This essay will proceed in two steps. First there will be a consideration of traditional western Christian thinking on the theme of man as the image of God. This will be followed by a brief analysis of the successive closing of the mental horizon in the West and an account of the philosophical efforts to open it up again by a deeper appreciation of the nature of the relation between knower and known. In the second part of the essay I will consider Psalm 86 as an example of the power of the word of God to bring us face to face with our own transcendence. I will then reflect on what other aspects of reality, often missed in our individualistic view of our selves and our atomistic view of history, are reopened in the prayer of the psalms.

The Image of God

The Teaching of Former Generations

While much modern thinking, in considering the image of God, concentrates on the relational aspect of man as male and female,[1] the other aspect, that of human beings in their capacity to know and love, especially to know and love God, is still extremely important and will serve us well here.[2] Epistemology is part of anthropology, and the medievals, following the lead of St Augustine, developed their theological anthropology on the basis of Genesis 1:26-27: 'And *ʾĕlohîm* said: "Let us make *ʾādām* in our image, as our likeness, that they may rule over the fish of the sea, and the birds of the heavens, and the tame beasts, and all the earth, and all the creeping things creeping on the earth." And *ʾĕlohîm* created the *ʾādām* in his image, in the image of *ʾĕlohîm* he created him/it, male and female he created them.'

The best summary and development of Augustine's thought is found in the works of Thomas Aquinas. The following texts will suffice for our purposes here

> God's image in man can be considered in three ways. The first way is man's natural aptitude for knowing and loving God, an aptitude which consists in the very nature of the mind which is common to all men. Another way is where man is actually or habitually knowing and loving God, but still imperfectly; and this is through the conformation of grace. The third way is where man is actually knowing and loving God perfectly; and this is the image according to the likeness of glory.[3]

Aquinas holds that the very capacity to know and love makes a human being the image of God, but he also maintains, as in the text just cited, that in the human activity of knowing and loving there is an imitative participation in the procession of the Word and the spiration of the Spirit, though only in a remote form: 'Now since the rational creature also exhibits a word procession as regards the intelligence and a love procession as regards the will, it can be called an image of the Uncreated Trinity by a sort of representation in kind.'[4]

There are two other aspects of this medieval theological epistemology that bear remarking upon. I will use Aquinas again as an example, though he is not alone in this but has much in common with his predecessors and contemporaries. These two aspects are, first, the teaching that in the act of knowing the person knowing is assimilated to what is known: exactly the opposite of our Kantian-influenced thinking. And second, all thinking is both a share in divine light and contains an

---

[1] I have treated of this aspect in previous studies. One may consult F. Martin, 'Male and Female He Created Them: A Summary of the teaching of Genesis Chapter One', *Communio* 20 (1993); F. Martin, 'The New Feminism: A New Humanism?', *JJT* 8:1 (2000).

[2] For an excellent study of this aspect of the divine image in man see D.J. Merriell, *To The Image of the Trinity: A Study in the Development of Aquinas' Teaching*, Studies and Texts 96 (Toronto: Pontifical Institute of Medieval Studies, 1990).

[3] *Summa Theologiae* (hereafter *ST*) 1, 93, 4.

[4] *ST* 1, 93, 6.

implicit knowledge of God. To illustrate the first point I will cite some lines from Aquinas' treatise *De Veritate*.

In the very first article of *De Veritate* Aquinas, who is asking the question "*Quid sit veritas?*" discusses the relation of being to the intellect. He makes the following statement:

> True (*verum*) expresses the correspondence (*convenientia*) of being to the knowing power (*intellectus*), for all knowing is produced by an assimilation of the knower to the thing known, so that assimilation is said to be the cause of knowledge (*assimilatio dicta est causa cognitionis*). Similarly, the sense of sight knows a color by being informed with a species of the color.

> The first reference (*comparatio*) of being to the intellect, therefore, consists in its agreement with the intellect (*ut ens intellectui correspondeat*). This agreement is called 'the conformity of thing and intellect' (*adaequatio rei et intellectus*) and in this conformity is found the formal constituent of the true (*et in hoc formaliter ratio veri perficitur*), and this is what the true adds to being, namely, the conformity or equation of thing and intellect (*conformitatem seu adaequationem rei et intellectus*). As we said the knowledge of a thing is a consequence of this conformity (*ad quam conformitatem, ut dictum est, sequiter cognitio rei*); therefore it is an effect of truth, even though the fact that it is a being is prior to its truth (*Sic ergo entitas rei praecedit rationem veritatis; sed cognitio est quaedam veritatis effectus*).

'Assimilation is the cause of knowledge.' And again, 'knowledge of a thing is a consequence of the conformity of thing and intellect.' And since truth is precisely the 'assimilation of the knower to the thing known', it follows that 'knowledge is a certain effect of truth'. We may call the conformity or assimilation of the knower to what is known 'ontological truth', and the knowledge that follows from this 'epistemological truth'. It is at the ontological level that the act of knowing imitates, in a created manner, the procession of the Word in the Trinity. A person is already modified by being or a being before he can articulate the conformity established through what Maritain calls 'the basic generosity of existence'.[5] Beings give themselves to us and modify us, thus establishing us in truth, whose effect is knowledge.

The second aspect of medieval epistemology is twofold and can be briefly illustrated by the following texts. First, that we know God implicitly in every act of knowing is stated later in *De Veritate*. In answering the question whether all things desire God himself, Aquinas confronts the objection that all things are ordered to God as knowable and desirable, but not all beings capable of knowledge actually know God, therefore neither do they actually desire him. This is his answer: 'All knowing beings implicitly know God in whatever they know. For just as nothing is desirable except as it bears a likeness to the First Goodness, so nothing is knowable

---

[5] J. Maritain, *Existence and the Existent* (New York: Doubleday, 1957), 90.

except as it bears a likeness to the First Truth.'[6] Second, the light by which we know is a created share in God's own light. Thus, the act by which God confers light on the mind is something unique to him, and in this sense only God can teach. Aquinas says of the interior light of reason that it is itself a 'certain participation in divine light' it is, in fact 'nothing else but the imprint of the divine light in us.'[7]

The Loss of Transcendence

Nearly all historians of western thought place the origins of this trajectory in the fourteenth century. Though preparatory stages can be discerned, the move became apparent and productive of consequences with the rise of the *via moderna*, whose most salient characteristic was the search for the intelligibility of the really existing concrete reality, not in a relation to a universal idea but in terms of a network of equally concrete relationships. Western thought had appealed to ideas either as independently existing models for what we experience (Plato), or as intrinsic to what we experience (Aristotle). Still later, Christian antiquity understood that the things of this world are intelligible because they share in the eternal reasons existing in the Word of God through whom all things are made. William of Ockham, by denying that concrete individual things are intelligible because of relation to something greater, cut the human mind off from anything but itself in the search for intelligibility. The mind became the norm of the real, and intelligibility ultimately became identified with utility.

The progress in epistemological sophistication undeniably contributed to a growth in understanding of the universe and history. But the problem lay in the fact that all of these advances of the mind were considered to have a mutually exterior relationship to faith. The 'blindness' of faith no longer lay in the fact that what it considered far exceeded the powers of the mind, it was found rather in the fact that faith had no intelligible content: it could shed no light on what was being learned and could provide no integrating and healing power to the mind. The rising human sciences and theology began, painfully, to agree on this one point: reason and faith were extrinsic to each other in the elaboration of a vision of reality.

While none of what I have recounted above was apparent or even suspected by the original protagonists, the net result of this 'turn to the subject', as it was later to be called, was an increasing mistrust of anything that, since it was not subject, became 'object'. The first trust to be eroded was, as we have seen, trust in God. The

---

[6] *De Veritate* 22, 2, ad 1. The same thing is said in the *ST* (1, 2, 1, ad 1). 'To know that God exists in a certain common and confused way is implanted in us by nature, inasmuch as God is the happiness of man. For man by nature desires happiness. And whatever is naturally desired by man is naturally known by him. But this is not to know in an absolute way (*simpliciter*) that God exists, just as to know that someone is coming is not to know Peter even if it is Peter who is indeed coming." (Translation from Henri de Lubac, *The Discovery of God*, D. Schindler (ed.), M.S.A. Dru, C. Fulsom (trs.), *Ressourcement* (Grand Rapids: Eerdmans, 1996), 75.

[7] *ST* 1, 12, 11, ad 3; and *ST* 1-2, 91, 2.

next trust to be weakened was trust in what was handed down by the Church and by the traditions of society. This began in the Renaissance with its independent and critical access to documents, its reliance on the findings of 'modern science' (especially physics, history and geography), and the resulting divergence between a sophisticated understanding of the world and history and the worldview of the Bible. The intrinsic intelligibility of the universe and of humanity's place in it became rather an independent intelligibility that had no need of revelation. To anticipate a later development, modern atheism arose when, because of a misguided understanding of 'philosophy', religion appeared to need physics to establish its fundamental principle, that is, the existence of God, but physics did not need religion to return the favor. As Michael Buckley puts it: 'Atheism came out of a turn in the road in the development and autonomy of physics.'[8]

Next, trust was lost in the ability of our senses to bring reality's witness to itself into our consciousness, and with this any ability to account for the mystery of human communication. The isolated subject, trapped in a world of uncertain impressions, must have recourse to the immediate presence of individual consciousness (Descartes) and finally to the structures of that consciousness as it confronted an alien and rigidly determined cosmic system. Immanuel Kant's description of the isolated subject which must be determinative in the act of knowing bears eloquent witness to the penultimate stage in the journey toward a complete hermeneutics of suspicion.[9]

There are other aspects equally important to an understanding of the Kantian legacy, particularly the presupposition that what surrounds the tiny island of subjectivity is 'nature', a foreboding, recalcitrant and deceptive environment that refuses to yield to human effort, though it continually invites it. Thus, we know only what we can dominate. The obverse, then, is Kant's image of human freedom: an area of retreat within a world of necessity. From this point there arose, via the immanent thinking of Hegel, the three 'masters of suspicion' – Marx, Freud and Nietzsche – who, each in their own way, continued the movement toward an

---

[8] M. Buckley, 'The Newtonian Settlement and the Origins of Atheism', in W. Stoeger, R. Russell, G. Coyne (eds.), *Physics, Philosophy, and Theology: A Common Quest for Understanding* (Vatican City State: Vatican Observatory, 1988), 81-102, at 96.

[9] 'We have now not merely explored the territory of pure understanding, and carefully surveyed every part of it, but have also measured its extent, and assigned to everything in it its rightful place. This domain is an island, enclosed by nature itself with unalterable limits. It is the land of truth – enchanting name! – surrounded by a wide and stormy ocean, the native home of illusion, where many a fog bank and many a swiftly melting iceberg give the deceptive appearance of farther shores, deluding the adventurous seafarer even anew with empty hopes, and engaging him in enterprises which he can never abandon and yet is unable to carry to completion.' (*Critique of Pure Reason*, N.K. Smith (tr.) (New York: St. Martin's Press, 1929), 257.

autonomous universe, but one that now was subject, at least in the case of Marx and Freud, to forces that are aberrant, unmastered and unintelligible in themselves.[10]

The ultimate stage in the journey is arrived at in the postmodern suspicion of language itself which, rather than being an instrument of inter-subjective communication, becomes the tool of power. While acknowledging the validity of this insight into the abuse of language, it must be borne in mind that an abuse is essentially the distortion of something by using it in a way that is contrary to its nature. In the realm of communication, suspicion becomes the way in which structures of power hidden in language are identified and unmasked. Where these are present, they must be understood for what they are, but this very unmasking presupposes that language is for the communication of truth and for the creation of community, not for the establishment of domination. A thoroughgoing socio-critical hermeneutics destroys, even while it uses, language as a means of communication.[11] A further step in the suspicion of language is taken by the Deconstructionists who, were it not for their inconsistencies, would bring us into a morass of language without meaning, without subjects, without any personal communication: the climax of our path to isolation.

The Move Toward a Theological Epistemology

The complete account of the western pilgrimage back to a sense of transcendence is, of course, beyond the scope of this essay. I wish merely to point to two movements of thought that are relevant to our subject matter and that are important in the effort toward a retrieval of the basic insights of traditional Christian epistemology integrated with the advances in modern philosophy. Both of these movements owe a debt to Phenomenology, though their approach is different.

DISCLOSURE

The first line of thought may be called, in the expression of Robert Sokolowski, a 'theology of disclosure'. It consists in an appreciation of the phenomenological insights of Edmond Husserl and their ability to bypass the dilemmas set up by a subject-dominated understanding of knowledge and its consequent isolation. Sokolowski writes

---

[10] For an enlightening account of what I must treat of rapidly here see L. Dupré, *Passage to Modernity: An Essay in the Hermeneutics of Nature and Culture* (New Haven/ London: Yale University Press, 1993). One may consult also M.P. Gallagher, *Clashing Symbols: An introduction to Faith and Culture* (London: Darton, Longman and Todd, 1997).

[11] '*Socio-critical hermeneutics* may be defined as an approach to texts (or to traditions and institutions) which seeks to penetrate beneath their surface-function *to expose their role as instruments of power, domination, or social manipulation*' A.C. Thiselton, *New Horizons in Hermeneutics: The Theory and Practice of Transforming Biblical Reading* (Grand Rapids: Zondervan/Carlisle: Paternoster, 1992), 379.

[According to modernity i]deas exist in the self-enclosed mind and they are immediately present to it. Ideas come between us and things. We have to get around them and outwit them if we are to reach the things themselves. To do so, we form hypotheses and build models in our minds, and we try to determine, by experiment, which of these hypotheses and models are false and which can be at least provisionally confirmed. In this way we hope to get beyond appearances to the things themselves, to the things that always remain absent and hidden from us.[12]

In another work he states

One of phenomenology's greatest contributions is to have broken out of the egocentric predicament, to have checkmated the Cartesian doctrine. Phenomenology shows that the mind is a public thing, that it acts and manifests itself out in the open, not just inside its own confines ... By discussing intentionality, phenomenology helps us reclaim a public sense of thinking, reasoning, and perception. It helps us reassume our human condition as agents of truth.[13]

Being an 'agent of truth' requires a creative receptivity to the disclosure of being and an intentional presence to being. None of this can come about without a certain spiritual energy, an active dimension of mind: what the ancients called 'intellectual light'. Therefore we are still dealing with what may be understood to be an extension or development of the Augustinian principle: 'Man's eminence lies in this, that God made him after his own image in so far as he gave him an intelligent mind whereby he surpasses the animals.'[14]

TRUST

I mentioned earlier that modern thought on Genesis 1:26-27 looks to relationality, particularly that between man and woman, as the locus of the image of God. This is usually elaborated in terms of man and woman as the basic realizations of ʾādām destined to embody and show forth, in their ineradicable identity and difference, a glimpse of the Trinitarian mystery. Epistemologically, the relational aspect of imaging God can also be seen in the fact that knowing is always a communal reality. As we saw above, 'the mind is a public thing'; so too, the very language we need as a medium of thought is a societal possession, a common good.[15] There is yet another social dimension to imaging God in knowledge, namely that fact that most knowing and acquiring of knowledge takes place in a relation of trust between persons. This is

---

[12] R. Sokolowski, *Eucharistic Presence: A Study in the Theology of Disclosure* (Washington, D.C.: Catholic University of America Press, 1993), Chapter 13, 'The Theology of Disclosure', 86.

[13] R. Sokolowski, *Introduction to Phenomenology* (New York: Cambridge University Press, 1999), 12.

[14] *De Genesi ad Litteram* 6, 12 (*Patrologia Latina* 34, 348). Cited at *ST* 1, 93, 2, *sed contra*.

[15] For a good treatment of the relation between experience and language see J.M. Soskice, *Metaphor and Religious Language* (Oxford: Clarendon Press, 1985).

expressed in a striking manner in certain paragraphs of the encyclical *Fides et Ratio*, one of whose main goals is to restore confidence in our human capacity to think and to arrive at truth. In accenting this dimension, John Paul II points to a way out of the alienation and lack of confidence that, as we have seen, characterize our age.

> Man was not created for a solitary existence ... [I]n human life truths that are simply believed are more numerous than those acquired by means of personal recognition. Who could, strictly speaking, assess the innumerable scientific discoveries which form the basis of modern life? ... Finally, who is able once more to forge anew the paths of experience and thought by whose means so many treasures of wisdom and the religious sense of society have been heaped up? Man, the one who seeks, is therefore *also the one who lives by trusting others* ... But at the same time knowledge that comes through confidence and depends on interpersonal esteem is not given without reference to truth: a man, by believing, is committed to the truth which another has shown him (§§ 31-32).[16]

Our journey back to truth begins by recognizing that truth is most often found in a relationship of trust in another which leads us to a movement of self-giving and of commitment to the truth that the other has shown us. We must be clear about this: thinking is an activity of the *person* and not merely of the mind, and thus the highest form of truth is found as an interpersonal possession. To move from an implicit knowledge of God to an interpersonal knowledge of him requires faith, an entrusting of oneself to him and an acceptance of what he says. What John Paul II said above in regard to interpersonal knowledge among human beings is super-eminently true of our relation to God: 'knowledge that comes through confidence and depends on interpersonal esteem is not given without reference to truth: a man, by believing, is committed to the truth which another has shown him.' This is truth in and through a communion of persons, but this communion with God comes about through prayer. It is in prayer that, even in this life, we image God, we imitate him, by sharing in that act by which he knows and loves himself. This is the basic epistemology of the psalms; they are the word of God that brings us into a relation with God and a communion with each other, thus perfecting our divinely given capacity to know. This power of the psalms not only to actualize our potential for imaging God but also to heal the sickness of our minds was well appreciated in antiquity. Let these passages from St. Athanasius' *Letter to Marcellinus* bear witness to the ancient appreciation of the effective epistemology of the psalms:

> But in the Book of Psalms, the one who hears, in addition to learning these things, also comprehends and is taught in it the emotions of the soul, and, consequently, on the basis of that which affects him and by which he is constrained, he also is enabled by the book to possess the image deriving from the words. Therefore, through hearing, it

---

[16] Translation is from L.P. Heming and S.F. Parsons (eds.), *Restoring Faith in Reason: A New Translation of the Encyclical Letter Faith and Reason of Pope John Paul II Together with a Commentary and Discussion* (London: SCM Press, 2002), 51-53.

teaches not only not to disregard passion, but also how one must heal passion through speaking and acting.[17]

Secondly, we are invited, indeed obliged, to make the words of the psalms our own in order to pray. This means that the word of God becomes our own in a most remarkable way. Again, in the words of Athanasius:

> But contrariwise, remarkably, after the prophecies about the Savior and the nations, he who recites the Psalms is uttering the rest as his own words, and each sings them as they were written concerning him, and he accepts them and recites them not as if another were speaking, nor as if he were speaking of someone else. But he handles them as if he is speaking about himself. And the things spoken are such that he lifts them up to God as himself acting and speaking them from himself.[18]

Psalm 86

I have chosen this psalm for several reasons. First, it is an intensely personal psalm which appropriates the prayer tradition of Israel even while it expresses the suffering of one person. The pronoun 'you', not usually necessary in Hebrew, is addressed to God six times within a tone of direct address sustained throughout the whole psalm. Secondly, though it is personal, it is not individualistic. Not only is God's covenant with Israel evoked by several allusions, but also Israel's role in regard to the nations is set forth with prophetic insight. Finally, by the place assigned to it in the final edition of the Psalter, it acquires an added dimension of meaning that is important for Israel's self-understanding and that of the Church as well. Thus, in paying close attention to this psalm we will be enabled to appreciate most aspects of the epistemology in the Psalter, the aspects of knowing reality that it is able to produce in us.

The mention above of the place of the psalm within a series of 'editions' of the Psalter may strike some as a new notion. Critical scholarship, building on observations as ancient as the rabbinic writings, has shown that the clearly visible editorial work that assembled the Psalter into five 'Books' was only part of the profound and refined organization of the psalms, giving them an enhanced meaning that includes and transcends the meaning each individual psalm had in its own right.[19] Collecting independent works and placing them in mutual context is much

---

[17] Athanasius, *The Life of Anthony and the Letter to Marcellinus*, R.J. Payne (ed.), R.C. Gregg (trs.), *Classics of Western Spirituality* (New York: Paulist, 1980). 108.

[18] *Ibid.* number 11, p. 110.

[19] There are five 'books' which make up our present psalm collection: 1-41, 42-72, 73-89, 90-106, 107-150. These books, perhaps modeled on the five books of the Pentateuch, are clearly delineated by a doxology at the end of each collection: Pss 41:14; 72:18; 89:53; 106:58; Pss 148-150. For an introduction to this aspect of research in the psalms, one may consult G.H. Wilson, *The Editing of the Hebrew Psalter*, SBL.DS 76 (Chico: Scholars Press,

like placing bells or chimes in a carillon in order to create a specific sound effect: collecting psalms and placing then together serves to create a 'meaning effect'.

Commentators usually classify Psalm 86 as an 'individual lament', meaning a prayer that appeals to God for help in time of suffering. The psalm is surely that, but it is also a psalm whose central section (Ps 86:10-13) includes praise and prayer both for the universal reign of YHWH and for deeper personal conversion, as well as an expression of confidence in God's saving help. The title given to the psalm is 'A Prayer of David', or less likely, 'A Prayer for David', thus making it one of approximately 72 psalms which bear his name in its title.[20] The attribution fulfills various functions and is often, as here, an editorial designation meant to evoke the figure of David, the ideal king, the model of prayer, the embodiment of Israel and, as Ezekiel 34:23-24 promises, the king who will be 'prince' and 'shepherd' when God himself reigns over his people.[21]

We may ask the question, then, who is praying this psalm and in what context? Most likely, this prayer was first composed by a person who was able effortlessly to incorporate phrases from other psalms and other places in Scripture in order to express his plight before God, to pray for a universal manifestation of God, 'the worker of wonders', and to ask for the gift of a unified heart. The fact that the psalm ultimately found a place in the Third Book in the collection of 150 psalms may point to a use in the public worship of Israel where the people prayed as one, appropriating the words of the psalm both as individuals and as a corporate group. At one point, the individual was identified editorially as David, in whom all Israel found expression. Thus psalms such as this became the prayer of all Israel in its centuries of suffering during the exile and after. People prayed individually or collectively in union with the prayer of David in whom they saw themselves summed up. This ability to identify with David the king as he prayed in suffering was part of the heritage of Israel which enabled the Christians, seeing in Jesus the new David, to pray in union with him and with one another. This mystery was plain to St. Augustine who, commenting on this very psalm, had this to say

> When we speak to God, praying, we do not separate the Son from him, and when the Body of the Son prays it does not separate its head from itself. Thus it is he, the one Savior of his Body, our Lord Jesus Christ the Son of God, who prays for us and prays in us and is prayed to by us. He prays for us as our priest, he prays in us as our Head, he is prayed to by us as our God. Let us then, recognize our voice in his and his voice in ours.[22]

1985) and J.C. McCann (ed.), *The Shape and Shaping of the Psalter*, JSOTSup 157 (Sheffield: Sheffield Academic Press, 1993).

[20] Some manuscripts omit the title, probably correctly, at Psalm 133 while the Septuagint has the title over fourteen other psalms.

[21] For an early study on this point see J.L. Mays, 'The David of the Psalms', *Interpretation* 40 (1986).

[22] *On Psalm 85*, 1 (*Corpus Christianorum Latinorum* 39, 1176 [Turnholt: Brepols, 1956]).

In what follows, we must try to bear in mind all the levels of the psalm as it comes to us now. There is the level of the suffering poor man, then that of the community identifying itself with him, and then the personification of the community in David, and then in Jesus. Because the first level is the foundation of all the rest, I will devote most of my time to it, allowing the word of God to reveal him as we enter into it, and in this process we will come to understand ourselves in dialogue and in communion.[23]

The First Section of the Psalm: Verses 1-7

1 A prayer of David
   Incline your ear, O YHWH
   for I am poor and needy
2 Preserve my soul
   for I am loyal.
   Save your servant, you are my God,
   save this one who trusts in you.
3 Be gracious to me, my Lord,
   for I call to you all day long.
4 Make the soul of your servant glad,
   for to you, my Lord, I lift up my soul.
5 For you, my Lord, are good and forgiving
   and great in loyal-love to all who call to you.
6 O YHWH, listen to my prayer,
   be attentive to the sound of my pleading.
7 On the day of my distress I call to you
   for you will answer me.

Something mysterious happens when we call to someone: we place ourselves and the other in a new manner of relating. This call activates for the first time, or reactivates and deepens, the transition from relation to relationship – to a mutual presence and attention in love. The psalm begins, as do so many, by a direct call and a plea that the 'Other' turn to me. This interior gesture is so instinctive that even atheists make it; it is an indication of our implicit knowledge of the First Goodness and the First Truth, and of the fact that we know that this 'Other' is personal and capable of response. Here, of course, we are not dealing with a vague and implicit knowledge but a calling to the God of the covenant, YHWH.

The psalmist, with whom we are identified, asks that the Lord 'pay attention' to him because he is poor and needy. A poor man is one who finds confidence in the

---

[23] A good commentary on this psalm, one sensitive to many of its dimensions and competent in discussing its technical aspects can be found in M.E. Tate, *Psalms 51-100*, WBC 20 (Dallas: Word Books, 1990), 374-84.

experience of dependence upon God. He is poor, and therefore has a special right to the care of God who, as the King of Israel, must care for those who cannot assert their own rights, just as he has instructed the earthly kings of Israel to do. Thus, the ideal king to come 'shall rescue the needy when they cry out, and the poor when they have no one to help them' (Ps 72:12). However, even when we wish to place ourselves in such a position of being poor and needy, we find that we have absorbed from our culture a pervading cynicism that fears such vulnerability and intimacy. But this is the word of God, given to us precisely to enable us to move beyond the illusions of our culture to a position of communion and trust. It is also being prayed by 'David' as the embodiment of the people, and as Augustine often remarks, as Christians see it, there is one person praying:

> All the members of Christ, the body of Christ diffused throughout the world, are like a single person asking God's help, one single beggar, one poor suppliant; and this is because Christ himself is that poor man, since he who was rich became poor, as the apostle tells us: *Though he was rich he became poor, so that by his poverty you might be enriched* (2 Cor 8:9).[24]

The original petition of direct address is followed by three more: 'preserve my soul … save your servant … be gracious to me.' And three reasons are given: 'for I am loyal … you are my God, [I am] one who trusts in you … I call to you all the day long.' The word I have translated as 'loyal' here is the famous word, *ḥāsîd,* deriving from the noun, *ḥesed.* The more one encounters this word in the Scriptures the more it yields its secrets, revealing God as affectionately faithful to his promises and covenant, indeed making him present in the very act of 'doing *ḥesed*'. God is faithful even when his people are unfaithful; he does not revoke his choice of them, and this consistency is seen as his mercy. The response to God's *ḥesed* can be described as obedience born of trust, gratitude and praise – all personal actions that lead to intimacy.[25] This word is one of the leitmotifs of the psalm.

The fifth direct address of petition asks: 'Make the soul of your servant glad, for to you, my Lord, I lift up my soul.' In Hebrew the word 'soul' (*nepeš*) evokes the whole *physical* human being, living, desiring, relating, but seen, as it were, from the inside. This is not far from the way 'subjectivity' is used in modern theological anthropology. The interior gesture of lifting up one's soul implies an act of entrustment, of confiding oneself to God, expecting protection and guidance. We

---

[24] *On Psalm 39,* 18. Translation is from Saint Augustine, *Expositions of the Psalms Volume 2,* J.E. Rotelle et al. (eds.), M. Boulding (tr.), *The Works of St. Augustine* (Hyde Park, NY: New City Press, 2000), 221.

[25] H.J. Stoebe describes the reality mediated by the word *ḥesed* in these terms: '… an expression for magnanimity, for a sacrificial, humane willingness to be there for the other … It is a given that *ḥesed* always has to do in some way with the life of the other, and one expects and hopes from the recipient of such *ḥesed* a similar willingness that surpasses the obligatory.' J.H. Stoebe, '*ḥesed*', in E. Jenni and C. Westermann (eds.), *Theological Lexicon of the Old Testament 2* (Peabody, MA: Hendrickson, 1997), 456.

read in Deuteronomy 24:15 that a person who hires a day laborer must not withhold his pay: 'For he is poor and he is lifting up his soul for it.' Just as the poor man lifts his soul for his wages which he needs for his existence, so the one praying directs his whole being towards God who alone is his trust and the object of his longings.[26] Intimately linked with the interior gesture of 'lifting one's soul', of entrusting oneself to the Author of the Covenant, is the prayer for guidance, of needing YHWH'S covenant faithfulness, as the psalm later says: 'Teach me, YHWH, your way; I will walk in your faithfulness.' It is remarkable that this same type of petition for guidance is also found in the only two other psalms that have the phrase, 'To you I lift up my soul.'[27]

After the five requests, the reason for our confidence is expressed: 'For you, my Lord, are good and forgiving and great in *ḥesed* to all who call to you.' There has already been an allusion to the psalmist's covenant relation to God in the phrase 'you are my God', which echoes and individualizes the formula 'I will be to you a God, and you will be to me a people' (Lev 26:12). Now we find the first of two allusions (vv. 5 and 15) to a crucial turning point in Israel's relation to God, one whose narrative, while difficult to piece together on our Western norms, is fraught with an anxious question: Can a broken covenant be renewed? This is a question often pondered in the post-exilic editing of the sacred tradition.

According to Exodus 32:1-29, while Moses was receiving the Law from the Lord, the people rebelled against its very first commandment and persuaded Aaron to make a golden calf which they then considered their god who brought them out of the land of Egypt. On the next day, Moses interceded for them, asking that he himself also be blotted out of the Book of Life if that were how God so intended to punish his people. God answered, 'Him only who has sinned against me will I strike out of my Book' (Ex 32:33), but then added that he would no longer travel with his people 'because you are a stiff-necked people, otherwise I might exterminate you on the way' (Ex 33:3). Moses continues to plead with the Lord, who finally accedes to Moses' request that the Lord continue to go with his people: 'This request which you have made, I will carry out, because you have found favor with me and I know you by name' (Ex 3:17). Moses then goes further and asks for a guarantee that God will keep his promise: 'Do let me see your glory!' (Ex 33:18; compare Jn 14:9). The Lord explains that Moses cannot see his face and live, but that he will make all his beauty pass before him and will pronounce his name. The medieval Jewish commentator, Rashi, echoes a long tradition in holding that God did this in order to teach Moses and others how to call upon him when they intercede for the people:

> The time has arrived when you shall see of My Glory so much as I will allow you to see according as I wish and *therefore* I find it necessary to teach you a set form of prayer.

---

[26] I owe this insight and part of its wording to A.A. Anderson, *Psalms (1-72)*, New Century Bible Commentary (Grand Rapids: Eerdmans, 1972), 207.

[27] Ps 25:1, 4, *et passim*; note the prayer for Israel in the editorial conclusion; Ps 143:8. On the contrary, the man who 'lifts his soul to Fraud' cannot climb the mountain of the Lord (Ps 24:4).

Just now when you felt the need to pray for mercy on Israel's behalf you besought me to remember the merits of the patriarchs and you thought that if the merits of the patriarchs are exhausted there is no more hope – I will therefore cause all the attributes of my goodness to pass before you on the rock whilst you are placed in the cave ... to teach you the formula when praying for mercy even though the merits of the patriarchs should be exhausted.[28]

The Lord instructs Moses to ascend the mountain alone and to cut two stone tablets 'that I may write on them the commandments which were on the former tablets which you broke' (Ex 34:1). When the tablets were cut:

YWHW came down in a cloud and took his stand with him there, and he called on the name of YWHW. And YWHW passed before his face and called out: YWHW, YWHW, compassionate and gracious God, long suffering and great in *hesed* and faithfulness; keeping *hesed* for a thousand generations, lifting off wickedness, rebellion and sin, and not declaring the guilty guiltless, visiting the sins of the fathers on the children and the children's children to the third generation and a fourth (Ex 34:5-7).

This formula, then, appears at a crucial moment – that is, when Moses is pleading for a restoration of the covenant and asking specifically that the Lord give a sign that he will continue with his people. The Lord answers with this self-description. Rashi remarked that YHWH gave Israel this means of calling upon him when the sin of Israel is so great that 'the merits of the patriarchs' appear to be exhausted. This seems to be borne out in Numbers 14:8, the only other occurrence of the full formula, where Moses is pleading for the people who had just openly refused to believe the Lord and enter the Promised Land as he had commanded them.[29]

There is another echo of this formula in our psalm; it is in verse 15 and thus serves to frame the central section: 'And you, my Lord, are a merciful and gracious God, slow to anger and great in *hesed* and faithfulness.' It is certainly true that the psalmist, and any one of us, could evoke these words in an individual appeal for mercy. But there is more. This psalm 'of David' is clearly inserted in the midst of five psalms attributed to 'the sons of Korah'. Preceding our psalm we find Psalm 84, a pilgrim song longing for the presence of God in the temple, and Psalm 85, which expresses a plea for restoration and revival. On the other side of Psalm 86 there are three 'Korah psalms': Psalm 87 celebrates the mystical reality of Zion as the mother of all the nations;[30] Psalm 88 is a bitter prayer of distress offered by Israel; and Psalm 89 expresses an anguished questioning of God's faithfulness to his covenant

---

[28] Translation from *Pentateuch with Targum Onkelos, Haphtaroth,and Rashi's Commentary*, M. Rosenbaum and A.M. Silberman (trs.) (Jerusalem: Silberman Family, 1930), *Exodus* 190.

[29] In addition to the phrases in Psalm 86 which we will discuss now, resonances of this formula can be found in Pss 103:8; 145:8 and in Joel 2:13; Nah 1:3; Neh 9:17; Jonah 4:2.

[30] For a commentary on this psalm and its significance for a grasp of Israel's later self-understanding in regard to the nations see N. Lohfink and E. Zenger, *The God of Israel and the Nations: Studies in Isaiah and the Psalms*, E.R. Kalin (trs.) (Collegeville, MN: Liturgical Press, 2000), Chapter 5.

with David now that the monarchy has disappeared.[31] In our Psalm, therefore, David – that is, an individual and the nation (the 'servant' of YHWH, verses 2, 4, 16) through the mouth of David – is pleading for a restoration of Israel and recalling to the Lord his self-description as 'great in *hesed* to all who call to you' and 'a merciful and gracious God, slow to anger and great in *hesed* and faithfulness.' In our individualistic world such identification with God's people as a whole, such anguish over our communal inability to show to the world the *hesed* of God, is both a challenge and a revelation of God who awaits such prayer from us. It is also a revelation of ourselves as the other dialogue partner who can be enabled by the word of God to say in the last line of this section, 'On the day of my distress I call to you, for you will answer me.'

The Second Section of the Psalm: Verses 8-13

8 There is none like you among the gods, my Lord,
    no deeds like yours.
9 All the nations whom you have made
    will come and bow down before you, my Lord,
    and glorify your name.
10 For you are great, and a worker of wonders;
    you are God, you alone.
11 Teach me, YHWH, your way;
    I will walk in your faithfulness;
    unify my heart for the fearing of your name.
12 I will thank you, my Lord, my God, with all my heart,
    and I will glorify your name forever.
13 Yes, your *hesed* is great in my regard;
    and you will rescue my soul from the depths of *šĕ'ôl.*

It is remarkable that, immediately following a personal and communal plea for the renewal of the covenant (vv. 1-7), we find this section whose first part, in anticipation of the following psalm,[32] is a celebration of the universal role of YHWH to be realized through Israel, embodied in David, the servant. In Psalm 22, also 'of David', we find the same rhythm: a lament which begins with the cry of a suffering servant, 'My God, My God, why have you abandoned me?' and ends by celebrating God's universal reign in words similar to Psalm 86:9: 'All the ends of the earth will

---

[31] Psalm 89 is the concluding psalm of Book III of the present Psalter and it also concludes the 'Messianic Psalter' that extends from Psalm 2, includes Psalm 72 (the last psalm of Book II). For a brief treatment of this see Ibid. p. 159.

[32] Some of the expressions in Psalm 87 are as follows: 'I tell of Egypt and Babylon among those that know the Lord; of Philistia, Tyre, Ethiopia: "This man was born there." And of Zion they shall say: "One and all were born in her."'

remember and turn to YHWH; *all the families of the nations will bow down before him*' (Ps 22:28).

Israel is praying in David, and David in Israel. The rhythm of suffering and exaltation is found throughout Israel's history and is held up for all here to see and enter into by the word of God. Experiencing the time of exile and post-exile when there is 'no prince, prophet or leader' (Dan 3:38), and longing for restoration, Israel remembers the promise of the future when the ideal king will come and 'All kings shall bow down before him, and nations shall serve him' (Ps 72:11). But as these horizons expand through suffering, it becomes clear that the renewal of the covenant for which Israel is praying is somehow going to include all the nations: 'And of Zion they shall say: "One and all were born in her"' (Ps 87:5). That is why: 'There is none like you among the gods, my Lord, no deeds like yours ... For you are great, and a worker of wonders; you are God, you alone.'

As we arrive at the hinge at the center of this section of the psalm, the direction changes again. Closely connected with the statement of universality is a petition whose spiritual depth reaches to the very core of a person and a people: 'unify my heart for the fearing of your name.'[33] The heart is the 'within' of a person. 'In addition to feelings and emotions, the heart contains as well our memories, thoughts and ideas, our plans and our decisions.'[34] Robert Sokolowski, following the lead of Robert Spaemann, speaks of the heart in these terms

> [The heart] 'is the ground for the turning away from the good', and it is also, conversely, the ground for the turn toward the good and toward truth. Furthermore, according to Spaemann, this turning toward or turning against is not just a response to an argument or to an idea, but a response to someone – God, and in the more immediate situation, Christ – who discloses the truth ... This concept of the heart is an ultimate 'explanation' for the turn toward truth or darkness, and it is original in the New Testament: 'The heart is the unfounded foundation in a sense for which there is no thinkable or conceptual equivalent in antiquity.'[35]

It would seem to me that the newness of the New Testament understanding of 'heart' lies rather in uncovering new depths of a reality already known and spoken of clearly in the Old Testament. In this instance, as in so many others, the Old Testament provides the initial understanding which is subsequently taken up in the context of

---

[33] For the reading 'unify', preferred by a majority of commentators, rather then 'rejoice', as read by the Septuagint and some modern translations see Tate, *Psalms 51-100*, 376

[34] J. de Fraine and A. Vanhoye, 'Coeur', in X.L. Dufour (ed.), *Vocabulaire de Théologie Biblique* (Paris: Cerf, 1971).

[35] R. Sokolowski, 'The Autonomy of Philosophy in *Fides et ratio*', in *Restoring Faith in Reason: A New Translation of the Encyclical Faith and Reason of Pope John Paul II together with a Commentary and Discussion*, S.F. Parsons L.P. Hemming (eds.) (London: SCM Press, 2002). Sokolowski is drawing upon R. Spaemann, *Personen: Versuche über den Unterschied zwischen 'etwas' und 'jemand'* (Stuttgart: Klett-Cotta Verlag, 1996), 288.

Christ.[36] To pray that God 'unify' the heart, then, is to pray that this 'unfounded foundation' within us, the center of our personhood, cease to be divided between good and evil and respond instead with integrity to someone, to God. In one movement of prayer, the carefully constructed isolation of modern and post-modern humanity is done away with: we are confronted with our ineluctable orientation to Transcendence and its accompanying responsibility.

The psalmist prays that *God himself* work the change, in keeping with the whole of the biblical understanding that a 'pure', that is, a single or simple heart, is literally the creation of God: 'A pure heart *create* for me, O God, renew in me a steadfast spirit' (Ps 51:12). What Israel is praying for in both Psalm 86 and in Psalm 51 is not only moral integrity, but the new covenant as described in Jeremiah 31:31-34; Ezekiel 11:19-20; 36:25-28 and elsewhere, which will be characterized by an action of God putting within the heart the power to respond wholeheartedly to himself. In this prayer, the allusions to the renewal of the covenant found in the use of YHWH's self-proclamation are made more explicit. Such a renewal will bring about the perfection of the 'fear of God', that is, 'fearing his name' in a deep experience of the presence of God, received in single-hearted submission to the expression of his holiness and glory. Holiness is the inner mystery of God's unique being. Glory is the outer manifestation of that mystery, and the Name is the expression of his being that he shares with us a gift.

At this point the poor man, David/Israel, promises to the God of the covenant (*my* Lord, *my* God) that he will thank him with all his heart, probably alluding to the *šĕmaʿ* of Deuteronomy 6:4-5, calling us to love YHWH 'with all your hear'. He promises further: 'I will glorify your *name* forever.' Is it too much to infer that, in the light of the universalist psalm edited to follow, Israel is here looking forward to that future restoration when the nations, as just described in verse 9, will pray along with Israel for an undivided covenant heart and also 'come and bow down and *glorify your name*'?[37] In any event, there is little doubt that the prayer is moving in that direction.

The Third Section of the Psalm: Verses 14-17

14 O God, those who defy you have risen against me
and a pack of ruthless men seek my soul;
they do not put you before their eyes.

---

[36] This process is aptly described by B. Lonergan, by the term 'sublation', using an insight he attributes not to Hegel but to Rahner: 'What sublates goes beyond what is sublated, introduces something new and distinct, yet so far from interfering with the sublated or destroying it, on the contrary needs it, includes it, preserves all its proper features and properties, and carries them forward to a fuller realization within a richer context.' (B. Lonergan, *Method in Theology* [New York: Herder & Herder, 1972], 241).

[37] I owe this suggestion to Lohfink and Zenger, *The God of Israel*, 158.

15 And you, my Lord, are a merciful and gracious God,
    slow to anger and great in *hesed* and faithfulness:
16 Turn to me and be gracious to me;
    give your strength to your servant,
    and save the son of your handmaid.
17 Work a sign on my behalf
    that those hate me will see and be confounded
    that you, YHWH, have helped me and consoled me.

These concluding verses return to the theme and the tone of the opening section, but they have to be understood in the light of the intervening section. In the opening verse (v. 14), the poor man asks God to look on his plight: the words are almost exactly the same as Psalm 54:5, also a psalm 'of David'. It is difficult to determine whether there is any conscious borrowing and, if so, in what direction it took place, but in both contexts, and especially in Psalm 86, the poor man's suffering has become that of the king and the nation. Those who seek his life are ruthless and godless.

In even stronger terms, v. 15 evokes the covenant gift of God's self-identification as 'merciful, gracious, slow to anger, great in *hesed* and faithfulness.' This is followed by a prayer (vv. 16-17): first that God save his servant, one born in his house, so to speak, and secondly, that he work a sign in the sight of the servant's enemies so that those who hate him will be confounded and see that YHWH has helped and consoled him. What kind of a 'sign' is being asked for? Clearly, some act of God delivering the poor man from his persecutors, but also one that restores kingship to David and to Israel, and perhaps one that draws the nations into the privileges of Israel. This prayer is still echoed in the Catholic liturgy, which prays during the Paschal Vigil: 'grant that the fullness of the whole world pass over to the status of the sons of Abraham and the dignity of Israel.'[38] For Christians, therefore, the looked-for sign in its definitive expression is the resurrection of Jesus Christ. In this event the poor man has been heard (Ps 22:25), David reigns, and Israel has begun its vocation as the gathering place of a new people. As Charles H. Dodd expressed it some fifty years ago

> It is this far-reaching identification of Christ, as Son of Man, as Servant, as the righteous Sufferer, with the people of God in all its vicissitudes that justifies the apparent employment of the early Church of Hos. vi. 1-3 as a prophecy of the resurrection of Christ; for the resurrection of Christ *is* the resurrection of Israel of which the prophet spoke.[39]

---

[38] Prayer after the Third Reading (Ex 14:15-15:1).

[39] C.H. Dodd, *According to the Scriptures: The Substructure of New Testament Theology* (London: James Nisbet & Co., 1952; reprint, 1961), 103.

Conclusion

As the word of God, the psalms bear us along into a dialogue with God as we make their words our own. Our journey towards an openness to dimensions beyond the reach of our instrumental reason is not so much a movement back as it is a movement forward, born along by the word of God which is both ancient and always new. Such a movement, as *Fides et Ratio* reminds us, requires trust and a recognition that all knowledge is an implicit invitation to communion with God. I would like now, by way of conclusion, to recapitulate those dimensions of reality that are mediated to us in and through the implicit epistemology of the psalms, particularly those dimensions prominent in Psalm 86 and the world of revelation of which it is a part. The successive levels of integration that the psalms achieve through the editing process is already the expression of an epistemology. In this way we can see the power of literature to transpose the realities it mediates, and we can also see the mystery of a plan of God working out in the history of his people as they see continuity and relation among God's actions. I wish now to sum up what we have seen by looking at nine aspects of reality appreciated in the light of God and expressed by the psalms.

First, I have linked the capacity to know God and love him with the patristic and medieval teaching about the *image of God*. Actually, the term 'image of God' occurs only five times in the Old Testament,[40] but the basic notion of the Genesis text, that of human dignity and responsibility, as well as the capacity to be addressed by God and to address him, is found throughout the Scriptures. This, as we have seen, forms the basis for the more explicit epistemology of Augustine and Aquinas, and is continued in some aspects of Phenomenology as well as John Paul II's teaching on knowledge and trust. The most fundamental aspect of the epistemology of Psalm 86, as of all biblical prayer, is founded on the fact that we are made in the image of God, that is, in other terms, we have 'hearts' and are thus always being addressed by God whom we must answer. This grounds the vocative function of language as intrinsically relational and ultimately theological.

Secondly, there is the dimension of *temporality*. Someone who addresses God, telling him that there is none like him among all the spiritual and cosmic forces of the universe ('the gods'), and who speaks of a moment in which all the nations of the earth will adore him, is someone who sees the ineffably temporal dimension of God's lordship. This is not a prayer to a local force to aid in a struggle against another nation and its patronal force. It is an understanding of the temporal nature of God's action and the interior and teleological dimension of all historical events. Intimately linked to this is the awareness of God's choice as constitutive of a *people*. Ultimately, the only metaphysical explanation of God's historical choice, and the special kind of activity that this implies, is the *Incarnation*. Flowing from this is the appreciation of the mystery of *participation*, the fact that I embody the people and

---

[40] Three times in what is habitually referred to as the Priestly tradition (Gen 1:26-28; 5:1-3; 9:6) and twice, in dependence upon these texts, in the Wisdom Tradition (Sir 17:3; Wis 2:23).

they are an expression of me. Many terms have been proposed for this reality, but perhaps the least difficult is that of 'Corporate Personality' made famous by H. Wheeler Robinson.[41] The 'David' of this and other psalms is the ancient king, the people he represents, the person and community praying now, and ultimately, the Incarnate Son of God in whom all other figures in the plan of God are anticipated analogical realizations, while still being persons and collectivities in their own right.

Intimately linked with choice, temporality, people, participation and Incarnation is *covenant*, not as contract but as relationship, based on God's initiative and promise. This understanding suffuses the psalms and forms the basis for prayer. It gives personal meaning to terms such as *ḥesed*, *lēbāb* (heart), *kbd* (glory, glorify), *šēm* (name), etc. Covenant is a call expressing both privilege and burden, and the combination of these two makes for the particular nature of the *suffering* of God's people, who bear his name to the world and who bear the weight of their infidelity. To plumb the depths of the prayer of the 'poor and needy' of the psalms is to know without knowing the mystery of suffering and the certitude of intimacy that only the Poor Man knows.

The epistemology or 'science' of knowledge expressed in the psalms can, as we pray them, enter into us. As St. Athanasius promised, the power of their words can heal us and bring us to understanding and to the presence of God. When we pray we are brought to enter more deeply into those acts through the words he gives us. We hear God call to us and teach us to pray: 'Return, Israel to YHWH, your God. Yes, you fell in your own evil. Take words with you and return to YHWH. Say to him: Lift off this guilt, take the good, and we will restore to you the fruit of our lips' (Hos 14:2-3). We learn that the presence of God does not leave us at ease but moves us to call out in our own suffering and that of those bound to us in God. We may be angry, disconsolate, humiliated and frightened by our sins, but somehow we know that the initiative of God, his covenant, is unbreakable from his side. The very words he gives us lead us to become aware of his presence. For when the Holy Spirit anoints the word of God, then God is present and we pronounce his name: YHWH, *Abba*. Little by little we are led to affirm what we have always dimly known: God is to be trusted even when he is silent. In this covenant trust we recover and make more explicit an instinct for his awesome presence and his love that confounds our small expectations and meager thoughts.

But the psalms also reveal us to ourselves. We come to know our poverty and need, and are not afraid to own it. We realize that God has made a covenant and renewed it and that his promises are unalterable. We pray to be guided because we begin to understand the immeasurable consequences of our decisions: we are far greater than we wish to be – we do not want the responsibility that God has placed in our hands. Most importantly, the psalms in general, and Psalm 86 in particular, reveal to us our heart: that ineradicable place that is always open to God and which is the locus of our relation to him. Our heart bears witness: no matter how we twist

---

[41] H. Wheeler Robinson, *Corporate Personality in Ancient Israel*, J. Reumann (ed.), Facet Books, Biblical Series 11 (Philadelphia: Fortress, 1964).

and turn and deny, by our inner decisions we will either move toward God or away from him. We pray to God, the only one who can accomplish such a thing, to unify our heart, to create a pure heart, so that we will worship and obey him and enter into that communion with him that opens up once again the world we have tried to close to him.

Bibliography

Anderson, A.A., *Psalms (1-72), New Century Bible Commentary* (Grand Rapids: Eerdmans, 1972)

Athanasius. *The Life of Anthony and the Letter to Marcellinus.* R.C. Gregg (tr.), R.J. Payne (ed.), *Classics of Western Spirituality* (New York: Paulist Press, 1980)

Augustine, Saint. *Expositions of the Psalms Volume 2.* M. Boulding (tr.), J.E. Rotelle et al. (eds.), *The Works of St. Augustine* (Hyde Park, NY: New City Press, 2000)

de Fraine, J., and Vanhoye, A., 'Coeur' in *Vocabulaire de Théologie Biblique*, X.L. Dufour (ed.) (Paris: Cerf, 1971), 176-79.

de Lubac, H., *The Discovery of God*, M. Sebanc, A. Dru & C. Fulsom (trs.), D. Schindler (ed.), *Ressourcement* (Grand Rapids: Eerdmans, 1996)

Dodd, C.H., *According to the Scriptures: The Substructure of New Testament Theology* (London: James Nisbet & Co., 1952. Reprint, 1961)

Dupré, L., *Passage to Modernity: An Essay in the Hermeneutics of Nature and Culture* (New Haven/ London: Yale University Press, 1993)

Gallagher, M.P., *Clashing Symbols: An introduction to Faith and Culture* (London: Darton, Longman and Todd, 1997)

Heming, L.P., and Parsons, S.F. (eds.), *Restoring Faith in Reason: A New Translation of the Encyclical Letter Faith and Reason of Pope John Paul II Together with a Commentary and Discussion* (London: SCM Press, 2002)

Lohfink, N. and N. Zenger, *The God of Israel and the Nations: Studies in Isaiah and the Psalms.* E.R. Kalin (tr.) (Collegeville, MN: Liturgical Press, 2000)

Martin, F., 'Male and Female He Created Them: A Summary of the teaching of Genesis Chapter One' *Communio* 20 (1993), 240-65.

_____, 'The New Feminism: A New Humanism?' *Josephinum Journal of Theology* 8:1 (2000), 5-26

Mays, J.L., 'The David of the Psalms' *Interpretation* 40 (1986), 143-55

McCann, J.C. (ed.), *The Shape and Shaping of the Psalter*, JSOTSupp 157 (Sheffield: Sheffield Academic Press, 1993)

Merriell, D.J., *To The Image of the Trinity: A Study in the Development of Aquinas' Teaching*, Studies and Texts 96 (Toronto: Pontifical Institute of Medieval Studies, 1990)

Robinson, H.W., *Corporate Personality in Ancient Israel*, J, Reumann (ed.), Facet Books, Biblical Series 11 (Philadelphia: Fortress Press, 1964)

Sokolowski, R., 'The Autonomy of Philosophy in *Fides et ratio*' in *Restoring Faith in Reason: A New Translation of the Encyclical Faith and Reason of Pope John*

Paul II together with a Commentary and Discussion, S.F. Parsons & L.P. Hemming (trs.) (London: SCM Press, 2002), 277-91

Soskice, J.M., *Metaphor and Religious Language* (Oxford: Clarendon Press, 1985)

Spaemann, R., *Personen: Versuche über den Unterschied zwischen 'etwas' und 'jemand'* (Stuttgart: Klett-Cotta Verlag, 1996)

Stoebe, J.H., 'hesed' in *Theological Lexicon of the Old Testament 2*, E. Jenni & C. Westermann (eds.) (Peabody, MA: Hendrickson, 1997)

Tate, M.E., *Psalms 51-100.* Word Biblical Commentary 20. (Dallas: Word Books, 1990)

Thiselton, A.C., *New Horizons in Hermeneutics: The Theory and Practice of Transforming Biblical Reading* (Grand Rapids: Zondervan/ Carlisle: Paternoster, 1992)

Wilson, G.H., *The Editing of the Hebrew Psalter*, SBL.DS. 76. (Chico: Scholars Press, 1985)

CHAPTER 4

A Chord of Three Strands:
Epistemology in Job, Proverbs and Ecclesiastes

Ryan P. O'Dowd

Introduction

Although no body of literature in the Old Testament has a more 'epistemological' texture than the wisdom literature, its epistemological insights have had very little influence on biblical and theological interpretation. The neglect of wisdom, and of its epistemology, is rooted in two aspects of the post-Enlightenment world.

First, the two-century hegemony of the historical-critical interpretation of Scripture produced imbalanced treatments of Old Testament texts. Scholars unable to situate wisdom within Israel's national history, or salvation history as whole, conveniently pushed it aside.[1] The discovery of other ancient Near Eastern wisdom writings in the middle of the twentieth century – particularly Amenemope in Egypt – sparked a new interest in the historical and social value of wisdom in ancient Israel.[2] However, wisdom study remains relatively young and in great need of development and integration within Old Testament biblical interpretation.

Secondly, the fragmented approach within philosophical studies that is characteristic of modern western philosophy, because of its tendency to divorce ontology and ethics (virtue) from epistemology and wisdom,[3] has perilously

---

[1] Cf. T.E. Fretheim, *God and World in the Old Testament: A Relational Theology of Creation* (Nashville: Abingdon, 2005), 200. Interestingly, W. Brueggemann, *Theology of the Old Testament: Testimony, Dispute, Advocacy* (Minneapolis: Fortress, 1997), 46-7, argues that this historical-critical era abandoned philosophy in exchange for history as its 'proper co-discipline'. Not only has this put philosophy at odds with the Bible (whatever their union looked like in other eras), but it demonstrates how the Enlightenment, with its scientific mode of reasoning, was resolved to neglect the theological and philosophical implications of wisdom in Old Testament interpretation.

[2] Cf. G. von Rad, *Wisdom in Israel* (London: SCM, 1970), 8-9.

[3] See W.J. Wood, *Epistemology: Becoming Intellectually Virtuous* (Leicester: Apollos, 1998), 15f, and K.J. Vanhoozer, 'Lost in Interpretation? Truth, Scripture, and Hermeneutics' in *Whatever Happened to Truth*, A. Köstenberger (ed.) (Wheaton: Crossway, 2005), 123. Quite significantly both Ricoeur and Levinas highlight the struggle to capture Judeo-Christian thinking, and particularly wisdom, in the Greek-dominated language and logic of the West. Both agree, however, that the effort is essential to philosophy, language and ethics. See R. Kearney, *Dialogues with Contemporary Continental Thinkers: Paul Ricoeur,*

overlooked the interconnectedness of wisdom, theology, and philosophy. Much like biblical and theological studies, the schools of thought in contemporary philosophy (analytical, Continental, postmodern, etc.) operate almost entirely independently of other philosophies and disciplines.[4]

The epistemological orientation of the wisdom literature provides fertile territory for a reassessment of the long-standing interdisciplinary silence between biblical, theological and philosophical studies. To this end, the rest of this study presents an epistemological analysis of the Old Testament wisdom literature, beginning with the most traditional wisdom book of Proverbs and progressing to an investigation of the more 'radical' or crisis-oriented books of Job and Ecclesiastes.[5] In the end, we will find it most natural to see these books intentionally crafted to present a diverse and yet unified description of what we know and how we know what we know. This description supplements the diversity found within the Old Testament narrative structure of creation and redemption and thus provides a new context for thinking about wisdom theologically and philosophically.

Epistemology in Proverbs

The book of Proverbs is commonly regarded as the most 'traditional' wisdom book in the Old Testament. I suggest that it also creates a framework within which the other books can and should be understood, for it sets the boundaries and structure of a wisdom worldview by painting a picture of the whole within which knowledge is to be sought.[6] We will examine the boundaries and structure along the lines of four epistemological categories – categories which are crucial to understanding wisdom

---

Emmanuel Levinas, Herbert Marcuse, Stanislas Breton, Jacques Derrida (Manchester: Manchester Univeristy Press, 1984), 41, 55.

[4] When I began working with epistemology in the Bible several years ago, I started with the Anglo-American tradition (justification, foundationalism, reliabilism, internalism, externalism, evidentialism, and coherentism) and slowly lost confidence that I could connect these ideas with what I found in the biblical text. Instead I found the most profitable ideas among Continental philosophers like Hamann, Jacobi, Hegel, Kirkegaard, Levinas, Ricoeur, and Gadamer whose attention to religion, ethics, and ontology in their epistemological discussions provided concepts and vocabulary suitable to biblical and theological description. To my knowledge these two traditions have very little interaction in the academy today, and consequently, most biblical scholars who attend to epistemology in the Bible do so through the Continental tradition. I hope that these facts, implicit in the material here, will provoke philosophers-by-trade to help biblical scholars understand why this is so.

[5] I regret my inability to address the contributions of Sirach and the Wisdom of Solomon in more than a tangential way in this study. Their contributions are, therefore, more significant than might appear here.

[6] Von Rad, *Wisdom*, 71 and A. Wolters, *The Song of the Valiant Woman: Studies in the Interpretation of Proverbs 31:10–31* (Carlisle: Paternoster, 2001), 26.

throughout the canon.[7] That is, knowledge in Proverbs is: (1) *reflexive*, (2) *of the whole*, (3) *from within* and therefore *hermeneutical*, and (4) endowed with theological and ontological *limits*.[8]

A Reflexive Knowledge

The editorial compilers of the proverbs begin their book with the warning that 'the fear of Yahweh is the beginning of knowledge' (Prov 1:7).[9] Proverbial knowledge, therefore, is not a rationalistic or empiricist project of assembling scientific facts. Rather it is a theological search for meaning which reacts responsively or *reflexively* to a religious encounter with Yahweh. Wisdom acts after, and because of, a divine encounter – not before it.

There is a richness and potency in wisdom's reflexivity which arises from the 'fear of Yahweh' phrase, embedded as it is the structure and theology of Proverbs. Not only does the phrase introduce the book of Proverbs in 1:7, but it appears thirteen more times, including 9:10 where it marks the seam between chapters 1-9 and 10-29, and in the book's conclusion where it is the most esteemed quality of the valiant woman (31:30). Its powerful and controlling presence in the book's structure can be diagrammed as follows (note especially the italicized text):

I. Proverbs 1-9
> *Introduction 1:7*
>> Father's first speech 1:29
>> As the knowledge of God 2:5
>> Lady Wisdom's call from creation 8:13
> *Lady Wisdom's last speech 9:10*

II. Proverbs 10-29
>> Individual proverbs 10:27; 14:27; 15:16, 33; 16:6; 19:23; 22:4; 23:17

III. Proverbs 30-31
> *Trait of the Valiant Woman, 31:30*[10]

---

[7] I argue this in my chapter 'Wisdom as Canonical Imagination: Pleasant Words for Tremper Longman' in C. Bartholomew, et al (eds.), *Canon and Interpretation* (Carlisle: Paternoster; Grand Rapids: Zondervan, 2006).

[8] I take the first three categories primarily from the material in Chapter 4 of O. O'Donovan's *Resurrection and Moral Order: An Outline for Evangelical Ethics* (Leicester: InterVarsity Press, 1986), 76–97.

[9] Or the beginning of 'wisdom' (9:10). In most of Proverbs 1-9 wisdom and knowledge are used synonymously.

[10] This threefold structure of the book of Proverbs (1-9; 10-29; 30-31) is central to its correct interpretation. See R.N. Whybray, *The Composition of the Book of Proverbs*, JSOTSup (Sheffield: JSOT Press, 1994), 153–6; Wolters, *Valiant Woman*, 134–54; and R.C. Van

Thus, as more than merely the beginning of wisdom, the fear of Yahweh stands as the book's motto and the 'culmination' of wisdom (2:5).[11] What, then, are we to make of this religious phrase in a book devoid of any historical allusions or reference to the Law, covenant or exodus?[12]

We must avoid the temptation to expect Proverbs to tell Israel's story of redemption. It is not a narrative; rather, it aims at general and universal concerns of order, ethics and knowledge. That said, the careful, repeated use of 'the fear of Yahweh' throughout Proverbs *reminds* the reader of Israel's redemptive history[13] and thus embeds wisdom in the worldview, or storied picture of the whole, which forms the foundation for Israel's religion. Wisdom and knowledge begin and are dependent on faithfulness to Israel's God and covenant. As Van Leeuwen states, 'The fear of the Lord is the key to Israel's epistemology ... for knowing the Creator puts one in the position appropriately to know the creation and humans within their divinely given possibilities and limits.'[14]

Historically, one can almost sense an anticipatory response to Kant's skeptical encounter with the knowledge of the noumenal realm (the divine and divine knowledge). Kant's skepticism leads him to a category-driven transcendental pursuit of knowledge from a premise of human autonomy, rather than knowledge flowing out of reflexive encounters with the divine. In his definition of *Aufklärung*, Kant says that enlightenment is

> leaving his self-caused immaturity. Immaturity is the incapacity to use one's intelligence without the guidance of another. Such immaturity is self-caused if it is not caused by lack of intelligence, but by lack of determination and courage to use one's

---

Leeuwen, *Proverbs*, vol. V, The New Interpreters Bible (Nashville: Abingdon Press, 1997), 24f.

[11] M.V. Fox, 'Ideas of Wisdom in Proverbs 1–9', *JBL* 116 (1997), 620.

[12] It is worth pointing to Ben Sira's familiar (loose) identification of wisdom with the torah (15:1; 17:11; 19:20; 24:23). Some see this as a transformation of wisdom and others as a nationalizing of wisdom. Neither of these is a necessary reading, for, as Schnabel has noted, both wisdom and torah have a 'cosmological and salvation-historical aspect', E.J. Schnabel, *Law and Wisdom from Ben Sira to Paul: A Tradition Historical Inquiry into the Relation of Law, Wisdom, and Ethics* (Tübingen: J.C.B. Mohr [Paul Siebeck], 1985), 90. Ben Sira maintains the universal and general availability of wisdom to all of creation. Cf. also Fox, 'Ideas', 632f.

[13] The phrase is used extensively and often with significant theological emphasis in Deuteronomy (4:10; 6:2; 10:16, etc.) and throughout the Deuteronomic History. Cf. M. Weinfeld, *Deuteronomy and the Deuteronomic School* (Oxford: Clarendon, 1972/ Winona Lake, IN: Eisenbrauns, 1992), 274–81.

[14] R.C. Van Leeuwen, 'Wisdom Literature', in K.J. Vanhoozer, C.G. Bartholomew, et al (eds.), *Dictionary for Theological Interpretation of the Bible* (Grand Rapids: Baker, 2005), 849.

intelligence without being guided by another. *Sapere Aude!* Have the courage to use your own intelligence! is therefore the motto of the enlightenment.[15]

Kant's autonomous appeal to universal law and normative categories do not yield the universally accepted standards for ethics or knowledge that he seeks. Instead they merely provide one more human perspective alongside many others at the same 'generic' level.[16] Proverbs assumes from the beginning that such human autonomy is neither transcendent nor universal and therefore not objective. Proverbial wisdom instead turns to Yahweh for the only relationship 'unqualified by any generic equivalences'[17] in pursuit of justice, knowledge, and order. Proverbs thus exchanges *Sapere Aude!* for 'the fear of Yahweh' as the motto of wisdom and knowledge. Autonomous self-confidence gives way trust in God (Prov 3:5).

In the next section we will explore this notion of reflexive knowledge under the category of ontology. However in making the transition to that point we must pause to examine briefly a paradoxical treatment of wisdom's epistemological premises in the research of Michael V. Fox. Perhaps the most respected Old Testament wisdom scholar today, Fox handles the epistemological assertions in Proverbs 1–9 with impressive lucidity and faithfulness to the whole of Proverbs. Thus, at many points, he affirms that: 'Wisdom both starts with the fear of God (1:7; 9:10) and leads to it;'[18] 'The book of Proverbs is not only about doing; it is about *knowing*;'[19] Wisdom is an 'ethical and religious message;'[20] the wisdom teacher imparts a 'power' or 'potential' which 'must be activated by God in order to become the faculty of wisdom;'[21] and 'The fear of God is the sphere within which wisdom is possible and can be realized, the *precondition* for both wisdom and ethical behavior.'[22] In other words, Fox recognizes (1) the unity of knowledge and ethics within the proverbs and (2) the fear of Yahweh as the epistemological condition for wisdom and knowledge.

In spite of this, however, in a recent contribution to the SBL Forum, Fox has caricatured the contemporary Christian and postmodern tendency to place biblical scholarship within contexts of religious presuppositions, calling it 'ideological

---

[15] I. Kant, 'What is Enlightenment?' in *The Philosophy of Kant*, C.J. Friedrich (trs.) (New York: The Modern Library, 1949), 132.

[16] I take the distinctions between generic and teleological sources of knowledge from O'Donovan, *Resurrection*, 33-52.

[17] Ibid., 33.

[18] M.V. Fox, 'The Pedagogy of Proverbs 2', JBL 113, no. 2 (1994): 238.

[19] Fox, 'Ideas', 613.

[20] Ibid., 632.

[21] Ibid., 619.

[22] M.V. Fox, *Proverbs 1–9: A New Translation with Introduction and Commentary*, AB (New York: Doubleday, 2000), 69, emphasis mine. In this context, Fox follows von Rad's description of the epistemological preconditions of knowledge in Wisdom in Israel, yet with qualifications that are not stated directly. In any case, I find much sympathy with von Rad, particularly his suggestion that for Israel there was 'one world of experience and that this was apperceived by means of a perceptive apparatus in which rational perceptions and religious perceptions were not differentiated' (Wisdom, 61).

scholarship and advocacy instruction'.[23] He argues, 'Faith-based study is a different realm of intellectual activity that can dip into Bible scholarship for its own purposes, but cannot contribute to it' and 'The best thing for Bible appreciation is [a] secular, academic, religiously-neutral hermeneutic', a '*Wissenschaft*.'[24]

Three important points come to mind in response to Fox's statements. For one, we can only wonder how Fox (and many other biblical scholars, for that matter) have missed the demolition of the naive presuppositions of *Wissenschaft* by the hands of literary, scientific, theological and philosophical scholars over the last two centuries.[25] Second, it is therefore highly conspicuous that his empiricism, objectivism, and rationalism escape the ideological label which he so freely applies to any kind of study other than his own. He merely assumes its transcendent value, seemingly without any awareness of the philosophical issues at stake. Most importantly, Fox's position begs the question of how he professes knowledge of wisdom in the wisdom literature which has so qualified itself within religious (ideological) and ethical preconditions.[26] We can only raise the questions here rather than pursue them with the scrutiny they deserve. At the very least, what must be emphasized is that biblical interpretation, epistemology, ethics and religion are not as easily divided as many scholars are inclined to believe, for the wisdom literature qualifies any understanding of its own message within the context of a religiously reflexive response to the God of creation and redemption.

Knowledge of the Whole

The reflexive origins of human knowledge in the wisdom literature opens learning into a picture of the whole. While this was mentioned above, it is necessary here to explore further the ontological nature of wisdom. That is, the unique rhetorical

---

[23] M.V. Fox, 'Bible Scholarship and Faith-Based Study: My View', SBL Forum (2006).

[24] Fox, 'Bible Scholarship'. This sentiment is not new for Fox, dominating his 'Review of C. Bartholomew, *Reading Ecclesiastes: Old Testament Exegesis and Hermeneutical Theory*', *Interpretation* 54 (2000): 195–96.

[25] Among the almost endless literature on this topic, I think specifically of F.C. Beiser, *The Fate of Reason: German Philosophy from Kant to Fichte* (Cambridge, MA; London: Harvard University Press, 1987); M. Bockmuehl, 'Reason, Wisdom and the Implied Disciple of Scripture', in D.F. Ford and G. Stanton (eds.), *Reading Texts, Seeking Wisdom* (London: SCM Press, 2003), 53-68; R.A. Clouser, *The Myth of Religious Neutrality: An Essay on the Hidden Role of Religious Belief in Theories* (Notre Dame: University of Notre Dame Press, 1991); S. Critchley, *Continental Philosophy: A Very Short Introduction* (Oxford: Oxford University Press, 2001); T.S. Kuhn, *The Structure of Scientific Revolutions* (Chicago: University of Chicago Press, 1996); and St. Toulmin, *Cosmopolis: The Hidden Agenda of Modernity* (Chicago: University of Chicago Press, 1990).

[26] I say this in jest of course, seeing the biblical material as anti-ideological by its very nature. See Chapter 5 of my 'The Wisdom of Torah: Epistemology in Deuteronomy and the Wisdom Literature.' PhD Thesis, The University of Liverpool, 2005.

invitation in Proverbs 1-9 for youths and sages to seek wisdom is embedded within several universal images that portray the reality into which this search is driven.

To see this it is necessary to recognize the role of two sets of voices in Proverbs 1–9 , which are often categorized as the 'ten admonitions' and 'five interludes'. In the admonitions[27] a mother and father appeal to their son to acquire wisdom, a wisdom which Fox helpfully locates in the 'words' and 'thoughts' of the speakers.[28] A more transcendent and sometimes mystical view of wisdom emerges in the highly poetic interludes[29] wherein two women, Lady Wisdom and Dame Folly, appeal to the young man erotically, sensually, emotionally, socially, economically, and in every other way, to walk in their respective paths. These two levels of speech, and their important seams and interrelations, correspond to two metaphors of the 'whole'.

The first is a creational metaphor of the whole, which is introduced in Proverbs 3:18-20 as the narrator equates Lady Wisdom with 'the tree of life' (3:18). The many scholars who reject a connection with the tree in Genesis 2:9 miss the abundance of intertextual clues that establish their theological relationship. For one, the phrase 'tree of life', though alluded to in texts like Psalm 1 and Jeremiah 17:8, is used explicitly only in Genesis 2-3, Proverbs 3:18; 11:30; 13:12; 15:4; and in Revelation 2:7; 22:2, 14, 19 – all passages with creational and re-creational contexts. Second, the immediate context in Proverbs 3 goes on to ascribe wisdom and knowledge to God for founding and establishing (*kûn*) the creation (3:19-20). The same language of wisdom and knowledge is also ascribed to Bezalel and Oholiab in Exodus 35:30ff who, with the Spirit of God upon them (cf. Gen 1:2), prepare the house for God's dwelling. This imagery appears again in Proverbs 24:3-4 where wisdom and knowledge are needed to 'build' and 'establish' (*kûn*) a house and 'fill' (*mālē'*) its rooms. The 'filling' echoes the divine command to be 'fruitful' and 'fill' (*mālē'*) the creation (Gen 1:22, 26; 6:11, 13, etc). Furthermore, the priests (Ex 28:5) and women who are 'wise of heart' and build God's 'house' (Ex 35:25) use the same rare materials (purple and scarlet cloth and fine linen) as the Valiant Woman of wisdom who cares for her own house in Proverbs (31:13, 19-25). In studying such clues, we find strong linguistic and thematic parallels between wisdom, the Spirit, God's work in creation, and humanity's corresponding responsibility to walk in his creation with wisdom.[30]

Perhaps an even stronger expression of the creational metaphor appears in the extended interlude by Lady Wisdom in Proverbs 8:1-36. In this speech, Wisdom

---

[27] 1:1; 1:8-19; 2:1-22; 3:1-12; 21-35; 4:1-9; 4:10-19; 4:20-27; 5:1-23; 6:20-35; 7:1-27.

[28] Fox, 'Ideas', 616–17.

[29] 1:20-33; 3:13-20, 6:1-19; 8:1-36; 9:1-18.

[30] These connections are noted by J.R. Middleton, *The Liberating Image: The Imago Dei in Genesis 1* (Grand Rapids, MI: Brazos, 2005), 85–87; R.C. Van Leeuwen, 'Building God's House: An Exploration in Wisdom', in J.I. Packer and S.K. Soderlund (eds.), *The Way of Wisdom: Essays in Honor of Bruce K. Waltke* (Grand Rapids: Zondervan, 2000), 204–11, and M.G. Kline, *The Structure of Biblical Authority* (Grand Rapids, MI: Eerdmans, 1972), 85.

attributes her origins to the beginning of God's creative work (8:22), pronouncing her expertise on the basis of having witnessed and even enjoyed the events of creation (8:23-31). The many allusions to order in this, her longest speech, express her appreciation for the order and fittingness to all God has made. Through a use of rhetoric, imagery and theology, wisdom is continually situated within this creational picture.

Her speech is complemented by a sexual/feminine metaphor which resides primarily in the interludes, though the rhetoric also runs over into the warnings about the adulterous woman in Proverbs 5. The metaphor consists of two women, Wisdom and Folly, who compete for the young man's attention as they represent two views of reality, or two perspectives on the whole. In other words, both women share an *interpretation of the world* which they seek to communicate to humanity. Wisdom alone is able to relate the particular to the universal, the individual to the whole. Fox again correctly connects the metaphorical world of these women with the ontological realities of the knower. Lady Wisdom's 'history is really ontology'. Imagining a Platonic analogy, he says: 'Lady Wisdom symbolizes the perfect and transcendent universal of which the particulars of human wisdom are imperfect images or realizations ... The wisdom of the mythos is an objective reality alongside God and man. It is the transcendent wisdom that is the universal of the infinity of wise things that humans can know and use.'[31] Because of her nearness to God and his creative acts, Wisdom is able to offer to humanity an unparalleled access to his view of reality and the knowledge that is true.

The ultimate consequence of the interplay of these metaphors is that Yahweh is the *Creator* and sole source of true knowledge. The creation and the creatures within in it, therefore, are understood 'as *creation*' and ordered within God's design and teleological purposes.[32] Humanity stands at a moral and epistemological crossroads between knowledge of God's world, of his order, and of his purposes for the whole, and distorted alternatives to that knowledge. Thus, contrary to Fox's inverted and rationalist and autonomous view of the whole in his own research, proverbial knowledge is rooted in the religious reality of Yahweh's ordering, crafting, and moving the cosmos according to his purposes. Furthermore, in a book which makes no mention of the covenants or of Israel's redemptive history, the frequent references to 'Yahweh', as opposed to 'Elohim', continually remind the reader of God's redemptive initiative and personal involvement with his creation. The fear of Yahweh continually resituates knowledge in the context of the fall from creation and the theological direction of redemption which apply to the structure of the whole.[33] Proverbial knowledge is acutely aware of the distorting powers of human autonomy

---

[31] Fox, 'Ideas', 629-31. Cf. Ricoeur's philosophical and hermeneutical description of this relationship in J.B. Thompson (ed. and trans.), *Hermeneutics and the Human Sciences* (Cambridge: CUP, 1981), 35–39.

[32] O'Donovan, *Resurrection*, 88. Cf. von Rad, *Wisdom*, 60–73.

[33] See A. Wolters, *Creation Regained: Biblical Basics for a Reformational Worldview* (Grand Rapids, MI: Eerdmans, 1985), for a description of the theological 'direction' and philosophical 'structure' of the created order.

and looks to a divine redeemer as the source and giver of truth and knowledge (Prov 2:6-7).

Knowledge from Within

A reflexive knowledge of the whole is also knowledge from within rather than from a distance. This point helps us to appreciate the distinction between proverbial epistemology and the disengaged and/or autonomous views of reason of the scientific and technological age. Such views, most commonly associated with Descartes, radicalize the 'subject-object relationship'; knowing is depicted in the scientific paradigm wherein the subject as scientist looks upon object of knowledge from the outside. This disengaged position seemingly gives the knower a purely objective view of the object.[34] Certainty is achieved through the knower's autonomous cognitive, empirical, or affective capacities and orientation.

The principal outcome of this strict subject-object distinction is a false or naive appeal to objectivity and a view of knowledge as *accumulation* – we know by adding discrete ideas together in our minds one by one. By contrast, Proverbs declares the learner's identity as a subject *of* and *within* the Creator's world. As a product of creation, the subject unavoidably shares historical and geographic space with the object and finds his or her knowledge shaped by that object. Thus, learning is not accumulated through rationalist or empiricist modes of knowing, as if through some Archimedian point of knowledge, but is more a process of discovery and recognition of one's surroundings. Through discovery, distorted and false interpretations of reality (of the whole), represented by Dame Folly, are exposed and exchanged for truer and closer interpretations of the whole as represented by Lady Wisdom. Wisdom is thus better described as hermeneutical rather than accumulative. Wisdom is a divinely initiated and guided interpretation of reality.

The most salient example of this hermeneutical mode of knowing is found in Proverbs 26:4-5. The overall context of this poem concerns situations of 'fittingness' for the fool (i.e. 'honor is not fitting for the fool' v. 1).[35] The climactic strophes in vv. 4-5 foist the reader into an irresolvable dilemma:

> Do not answer a fool according to his folly
>   Lest you become like him yourself.
> Answer a fool according to his folly
>   Lest he become wise in his own eyes.

This wonderful paradoxical scenario invites readers to imagine a safe place between answering and not answering the fool. This creates an illocutionary speech act which pushes readers through dilemmas to yield increased wisdom – i.e., knowledge which

---

[34] See Toulmin, *Cosmopolis*.

[35] Cf. R.C. Van Leeuwen, *Context and Meaning in Proverbs 25–27*, SBL.DS (Atlanta, Georgia: Scholars Press, 1988).

is truer of the whole than that which we had before. Wisdom in this situation does not come from adding facts to facts, but by comparing scenarios of behavior to what we know of the whole. Thus, in wrestling with the dilemma of answering a fool, we participate in the world from within and grow to understand that world with greater wisdom.[36]

In what we will see as central to understanding Job and Ecclesiastes, this kind of learning from within corresponds to the correct interpretation and ordering of reality. Dilemmas or quandaries, then, are the primary avenues for growth in wisdom and knowledge. The apparent crises in these books, rather than refuting Proverbs, extend its wisdom into new areas of interpretation.

The Limits of Knowledge

Finally, Proverbs establishes epistemological limits for wisdom. To understand this, we must appreciate how the wisdom books intertwine knowledge with ethics, justice and order. On this basis, the sayings in Proverbs are usually seen to project a naive, dogmatic deed-consequence or character-consequence scheme (*'Tun-Ergehen Zusammenhang'*) which corresponds to its naive view of knowledge and ontology (a naive idealism). It is then typically inferred that Job and Ecclesiastes respond to Proverbs for the failure of its naive consequentialism to match the experiences of life. Yet, this dogmatic reading of Proverbs fails for at least two reasons, and consequently, the belief that Proverbs embraces a naive epistemology resistant to Job and Ecclesiastes is also shortsighted.

For one, in the mode of highly analytical or positivist hermeneutics, the dogmatic reading has misconceived the limited nature of a proverb. Proverbs are pithy sayings and rarely, if ever, communicate universal exceptionless ideas (e.g., the righteous always prosper).[37] On the contrary, proverbs communicate general principles of order, the consistent outcomes of certain behaviors, and the general notion of cosmic (eternal) justice; they are not postulates for application at every particular level.

Second, Proverbs is composed in a way that opposes the common dogmatic/idealistic characterization. Studied more closely we find it communicating through a system of contradictions which show an honest awareness of the unpredictable realities of the lived life. That this is true should come as no surprise; proverbial collections of extra-biblical origin have long been known to embrace a sophisticated use of contradictions to communicate the realism of the worldview that encompasses the proverbs.[38] This use of systematic contradictions in Proverbs is increasingly well noted, and a few examples should suffice to demonstrate the point.

---

[36] Cf. O'Donovan's description of wisdom in the pluriformity of the moral order in *Resurrection*, 199–203.

[37] Cf. A. Taylor, *The Proverb* (Cambridge, MA: Harvard University Press, 1931); and Fox, *Proverbs 1-9*, 169-70.

[38] Taylor, *The Proverb*; and R.C. Van Leeuwen, 'Wealth and Poverty: System and Contradiction in Proverbs', *Hebrew Studies* 33 (1992), 25.

First, and most obviously, the individual proverbs are continually interrupted by contradictory voices. So, while the 'general' tendency in Proverbs is to be optimistic about righteousness and good behavior, and pessimistic about unrighteousness and laziness, many passages lament the reality of the opposite.[39] Proverbs frequently speaks of the wicked prospering or of the righteous having their wealth plundered (11:16; 13:23; 19:10; 21:6-7; 30:14). Second, Van Leeuwen has helpfully demonstrated another strong voice in Proverbs 30 which he categorizes as 'world upside down' (WUD) wisdom.[40] Here the sage communicates the anguish in seeing 'a servant who becomes king' or 'a godless fool who gets plenty to eat' (30:22). Third, the frequent use of the 'better than' sayings in Proverbs show an awareness of spectrums of behavior rather than a dogmatic cause-effect worldview (15:16-17; 16:1-16; 17:1; 28:6; cf. Sir 2:12; 1:28). Finally, in passages like Proverbs 3:9-10 and 11-12, contradictory voices are grouped together in one group of sayings where the ideal is accompanied by a warning which shows concern.[41] Fox concludes

> This lack of concern for a tight fit between deed and result is common in Proverbs ... It runs contrary to the theory of the 'deed-consequence connection' – the notion of tit-for-tat recompense – which is thought to be the essence of the Wisdom doctrine of retribution ... Intrinsic retribution does figure into many sayings, but it is part of a larger picture, in which wisdom as a whole brings about the total array of blessings.[42]

As such, Proverbs expresses an optimistic relationship between deed and consequence, yet does so in the larger context of its cautionary and contradictory voices. These voices discourage a simplistic reading of justice and reality, and, consequentially, a simplistic reading of epistemology in Proverbs; just as our knowledge of behavior and consequence is limited, so is our understanding of reality as a whole.

Epistemology in Job

Job is the Bible's book of justice, order and wisdom par excellence. Its narrative progresses on two levels which are enhanced and often complicated by various structural, thematic and aesthetic features. On the one hand, the book leads the reader through two perspectives of reality, the divine and the human, the latter of which is further divided between the perspectives of Job, Job's friends and the

---

[39] Cf. some 100 incidences of what J. Gladson calls 'retributive paradox' in Proverbs 10-29 alone: *Retributive Paradoxes in Proverbs 10–29* (Ann Arbor, MI: University Microfilms International, 1979).

[40] R.C. Van Leeuwen, 'Proverbs 30:21–23 and the Biblical World Upside Down', *JBL* 105 (1986): 599–610.

[41] See Van Leeuwen, 'Wealth and Poverty'.

[42] Fox, *Proverbs 1–9*, 170.

narrator.[43] Meanwhile, these two perspectives are narratively and rhetorically enhanced through the use of a frame narrative. The frame (1:1-3:1 and 42:7-16) is written in prose and presents the divine and orderly view of Job's scenario, emphasized by the thirty two uses of 'Yahweh' to refer to God. The intervening poetic body (3:2-42:6) recounts the human view of reality in Job's dialogues with his friends – dialogues which exclusively refer to God by the divine title *ʾĕlohîm*.[44] Furthermore, the prose frame emphasizes Job's upright, blessed, and quiet character which communicates a sense of Yahweh's cosmic order and justice, while the poetic body shows the cursed, despised, accused, and desperate Job who suffers the fate of local disorder and injustice. It follows that the implicit epistemology of this book has a bipolar character, resting on these two levels of reality, two levels of rhetoric, and two levels of justice and order.

Significantly, the narrator presents the story from within Israelite creation theology, as marked by echoes from Genesis. Job is an upright man, living on the land, where his name, his children, his flocks, and his families are blessed – a picture of Eden, Palestine and/or Paradise with harmony between humanity, creation and the divine. Similar to Genesis, Satan approaches Yahweh with the angels to introduce conflict into the story. Reminiscent of the cursed and prostrate serpent in Genesis 3, he comes from wandering about on the earth (1:7; 2:2; cf. Gen 3:14) and, like the serpent, seeks to disrupt the order within the Creator-creation relationship. Also, by agreeing to see Job afflicted, we hear an echo of the mysterious freedom of the serpent to tempt Eve with deception, followed by the foolish speech of a woman (2:9-10) and the loss of Eden's riches.[45] But in this case, the account of the fall is inverted: God willingly invites injustice into his ordered world, bringing suffering to the upright rather than punishing the disobedient as he does in Genesis.

With creation and justice thus tied together under a new sense of antithesis, the narrative turns to poetry (3:1) and begins to tease out the depths of the conflict – a conflict found especially in the intertextual play between this story and Genesis (and Proverbs). Thus, as with the creation narrative in Genesis 1:1–2:3, the narrative in Job 3:1–42:6 uses only the name *ʾĕlohîm* for God. Job's first speech in the poetic sections almost predictably turns from silence and worship (1:21; 2:10b) to a lengthy re-creational discourse of lament, suffering, cursing and despair (3:1-20). While we cannot reproduce the evidence here, Fishbane's impressive comparison of Genesis 1:1–2:4 and Job 3:13-20 demonstrates the astounding stylistic and verbal parallels

---

[43] See M.V. Fox, 'Job the Pious', *ZAW* 117 (2005), 351, who unfortunately fails to emphasize the perspective on reality represented by the friends. As we will see, this level is crucial to the narrator's purposes.

[44] Except for Job's nuanced reference to 'the fear of Adonai' in 28:28.

[45] I think it is significant that Eve was 'seeking' fruit that was pleasing to the eye and good for wisdom or prosperity (Gen 3:6) whereas Job's wife, whose ironic ends resemble the outcome of Eve's ambition, is labeled as one of the 'foolish women' for her counsel to Job to 'curse God and die'.

between them.[46] In sum, Job interprets his suffering in the context of his cosmological understanding of the whole, which – in this case, has proven insufficient. What he seeks is a new account of creation. This re-creation narrative – the poetic union of cosmological discourse with the onset of suffering or tragedy – is in fact common in the ANE, seen both in Akkadian literature and the *Egyptian Book of the Dead*,[47] thus reinforcing our confidence that Israel's wisdom literature associates local manifestations of justice and injustice with the cosmological understanding of the created order.

The remaining poetry of human speeches (chapters 4-37) accentuates the tension between the human and divine levels of knowledge and views of reality, grounded as they are in the context of cosmology and justice. Each of Job's four friends appeals to God's just character and the consequential outworking of the deed-consequence nexus in the created order: Eliphaz (4:7-9; 15:17-35), Bildad (8:3; 18:5-6), Zophar (11:13-20; 20:4-49), and Elihu (34:10-20). The most conspicuous epistemological aspect of these speeches is the diversity achieved in four distinct views of reality: (1) the friends' suspicion of Job's guilt and ignorance of his innocence, (2) Job's view of his innocence and yet the mystery of his suffering, (3) the narrator's knowledge of innocence and conditions of the suffering, yet his ignorance of the rationale, (4) and God's transcendent knowledge at all levels. The narrator is inviting new reflection upon creation towards a discovery of its previously undisclosed multifarious reality.

The tension between these views becomes palpably intense as readers, through the narrator's view of the friends, experience the consequences of misinterpreting the relationship between the particulars and the whole. All the while they remain ignorant of the divine rationale behind the conflict; God really has introduced injustice into his creation.[48] Thus, readers are simultaneously challenged to measure their perspectives on justice and knowledge against the narrator's picture of the whole, and yet also stop at the human limits of knowledge which even he cannot transcend. What gradually emerges is a judicial, cosmological and epistemological *struggle* or *dilemma* that gives way to wisdom by way of a reinterpretation of *the whole*, which, with its pre-established limits, is portrayed as an attunement to the structures of reality, rather than an exhaustive knowledge of particulars.[49] Like

---

[46] 'Jeremiah 4:23–26 and Job 3:3–13: A Recovered Use of the Creation Pattern', *VT* 21 (1971), 154.

[47] Fishbane, 'Jer 4:23-26 and Job 3:3-13', 155-57. This is noted also by R.S. Fyall, *Now My Eyes Have Seen You: Images of Creation and Evil in the Book of Job* (Leicester; Downers Grove: InterVarsity, 2002) and in Job 10 by W.P. Brown, 'Creatio Corporis and the Rhetoric of Defense in Job 10 and Psalm 139', in WP. Brown and S.D. McBride (eds.), *God Who Creates* (Grand Rapids, MI: Eerdmans, 2000), 107–24.

[48] G. Wilson, 'Preknowledge, Anticipation, and the Poetics of Job', *JSOT* 30 (2005): 243–56 argues that while the levels of ignorance provide anticipation of future dialogue and outcomes, the narratorial and divine levels of knowledge guide the reader to 'look elsewhere for the driving issue(s) behind the book's deliberations' (245).

[49] Von Rad, *Wisdom*, 210–12, 228.

Proverbs, this is wisdom from within – limited, and yet hermeneutically enabling greater fidelity between the universal and particular.

This message is perhaps most explicit in Job's lengthy speech in chapter 28 where he compares the relatively mundane task of finding the rarest of jewels and treasures in the depths of the earth with the near impossibility of finding wisdom. Twice he asks: 'But wisdom, where shall it be found and where is this place of understanding?' (v. 12; cf. v. 20). He concludes that 'God knows the way to it and he (alone) knows its place' (v. 23). Job's conflict with his knowledge of justice and order makes him skeptical about the possibility of human wisdom, yet he never abandons the superiority and even reliability of divine wisdom as evidenced by God's work in creation (28:23-27). Anticipating the end of the book, this pivotal chapter establishes the importance of recognizing human ignorance which gives way to piety and humility as established in God's order.[50]

The way in which any conflict resolution comes (or whether it comes) in these divine speeches (38–41) and in Job's restoration (42:7-20) is highly debated. Nevertheless, the distinctive epistemological texture of this episode provides invaluable insight into the larger theological message. To begin, there is a virtual consensus that God's 84 rhetorical questions in his speeches do not satisfy Job's request for vindication nor his desire to know God's rationale for his suffering. Rather, they appeal in various ways to the power, order and wisdom with which God created the world. In other words, as Job and his friends have appealed to cosmology in the midst of tragedy and epistemological dilemmas, God's rhetorical questions appropriately declare that as the Cosmological Author he alone holds the key to creation, its justice and its order: 'Where were you when I laid the foundations of the earth?' (38:4) and 'Would you discredit my justice?' (40:8).

Thus the primary epistemological point seems to be the limits of wisdom and the piety and humility required of humanity. Along with this, however, wisdom and knowledge are always grounded in creation theology, and God's 'non-answer' to Job's appeals points to a larger answer about the unseen order given to the universe. Job's and his friends' epistemological method were conditioned to view local injustice as incompatible with cosmic justice and order. Yet the divine speeches gather creation and justice together into an order which, just as it transcends human wisdom, also exceeds the original creation story in its goodness and vitality.[51] And so, bound up in this new picture of the cosmos is a strange new perspective about knowledge in the universe. Much like the stories of Isaac, Joseph and Jonah, Job's story reveals the possibility of a divine justice that transcends the apparent injustice toward the righteous [52] Reminiscent of the world upside down (WUD) wisdom of

---

[50] H. Fisch, *Poetry With a Purpose: Biblical Poetics and Interpretation* (Bloomington: Indiana University Press, 1988), 39; Fox, 'Job the Pious', 362.

[51] Fisch, *Poetry*, 39. Cf. Fox, 'Job the Pious', 364.

[52] Fisch, *Poetry*, 40–41; and E.A. Phillips, 'Speaking Truthfully: Job's Friends and Job', unpublished paper presented at the Evangelical Theological Society (2004).

Proverbs 16 and 30, this is a wisdom of a 'counter-order'.[53] Knowledge as created, ordered, and revealed by God often runs contrary to the natural instincts of human reason. Local instances of counter-order point to the good design in God's cosmic order.

Epistemology in Ecclesiastes

No Old Testament wisdom book offers a more conspicuous display of counter-order wisdom than Ecclesiastes, yet no Old Testament book has garnered more interpretative diversity and disagreement. I contend that much of this disagreement follows inattentive and inconsistent handling of the many rhetorical and epistemological cues within this book – cues I will address briefly here.

Ecclesiastes communicates its message in a unique fabric of structural and narrative artistry. Like Job, its frame narrator introduces (1:1-2) and concludes (12:9-14) the book, making one important interruption in 7:27. The speeches within the frame are that of Qohelet, an anonymous sage portrayed in a Solomonic guise.[54] Fox, who inspired new interest in frame-narrative analysis almost thirty years ago, represents the frame as a distancing voice in the book, telling the story of Qohelet's highly empirical search for wisdom. So, while his translation of the closing epilogue in 12:8-14 implies the narrator's strong reservations about Qohelet's wisdom, he still sees the narrator in a position of distanced neutrality which affords the reader the space to evaluate both sides of the book.[55] Similarly, Christianson notes what he calls 'redoubling' which results from the narrator's distanced position as a key strategy in leading readers into moral and epistemological self-examination.[56]

Representing a second major interpretative trend, Longman portrays the narrator as reproachfully and decidedly opposed to Qohelet's theology. In this case, Qohelet in the body emerges as a 'skeptic' whose theological message can be summarized as: 'Life is full of trouble and then you die.'[57] The frame-narrator in turn shuns these unproductive musings in favor of a more traditional admonition to fear God and keep his commandments in 12:13-14.[58]

---

[53] See B. Witherington III, *Jesus the Sage: The Pilgrimage of Wisdom* (Minneapolis: Fortress, 2000), 295, who rightly associates this counter-order with many of Jesus' sayings and Paul's 'foolish' wisdom in 1 Corinthians 1–4.

[54] See my 'Frame-narrative' in T. Longman and P. Enns (eds.), *Dictionary of the Old Testament: Wisdom Poetry and Writings* (Downers Grove: IVP, forthcoming). What follows here is adapted largely from that piece.

[55] 'Frame-Narrative and Composition in the Book of Qohelet', *HUCA* 48 (1977), 103–05.

[56] See *A Time to Tell: Narrative Strategies in Ecclesiastes* (Sheffield: Sheffield Academic Press, 1998) and 'Qohelet and The/His Self Among the Deconstructed', in A.A. Schoors (ed.), *Qohelet in the Context of Wisdom* (Leuven, Belgium: Leuven University Press, 1998), 425–33.

[57] *The Book of Ecclesiastes*, NICOT (Grand Rapids: Eerdmans, 1998), 34.

[58] *Ecclesiastes*, 274–84.

As much as these interpretations help accentuate the role of the frame-narrator, they underestimate the synthetic interaction that occurs between Qohelet's rhetoric and epistemology. Scholars like Bartholomew, Fisch and Seow (and Christianson at times), sensitive to the irony in Qohelet's rhetoric, detect signs which, rather than opposing the frame, allow Qohelet to stand more in line with the narrator. Seow even says, 'the perspective of the book is one and the same as the framework.'[59]

In brief summary, Ecclesiastes offers a dynamic interaction between frame, rhetoric and epistemology, leaving us with two key epistemological questions for the book: What does Qohelet want us to think about his search? And, what does the narrator want us to think about Qohelet's thought about himself searching? Of many, perhaps endless, subtle clues to these answers, I present four which demonstrate the way that irony yields a critique of certain modes of knowing.

1. In continuity with the rest of the wisdom literature, Qohelet expresses himself by engaging in creation theology. Most significant is his immediate appraisal of all things as 'obscure' (*hebel* [1:2]). While most English translations collapse *hebel* to 'vanity', an increasing number of commentators recognize the linguistic capacity of this word to point to a metaphorical 'ambiguity', 'vapor', or 'meaninglessness'.[60] Thus, while in Genesis 'God looked at all [*kol*] that he had made and *behold it was very good*' (*hinnēh tôb mĕōd* [1:31]), Qohelet 'looked on everything [*kol*] that is done under the sun and *behold it was all obscure*' (*hinnēh hakol hebel* [1:14; cf. 2:11]).[61] Genesis also depicts creation budding and developing out of nothing into bloom, whereas Qohelet's diagnosis of the motion of the sun, the wind, the streams, the sea, the toil of humanity, and time is that which is trapped in inescapable circularity (1:3-9; c.f. 3:1-15).[62]

Irony also results from Qohelet's juxtaposition of pre- and post-fall descriptions of creation which he does without explanation or clarification. For example, in contrast to humanity's hierarchical dominion over the 'beasts' (*bĕhēmâ* [Gen 1:26; 2:20]), Qohelet equates them: 'the children of man ... they are beasts' (*bĕhēmâ* [3:18]). Similarly, in contrast to humanity's unique formation out of 'dust' (*ʿāpār*) in Genesis 2:7, Qohelet adopts the language of Genesis 3 wherein all creatures are from 'dust' and helplessly return to 'dust' (*ʿāpār* [Eccl 3:20; Gen 3:19]). Verheij has identified Qohelet's distinctive use of vocabulary from Genesis 1-2 in Ecclesiastes 2:4-6, including: 'to plant', 'garden' (cf. *gānâ* with *gan* in Gen 2:8-9), 'tree', 'all', 'fruit', 'to drench', 'to sprout', and 'to work/make'.[63]

Qohelet also intermixes pre- and post-fall images of 'work' toward the same ironic ends. Thus, whereas in Genesis 1-2 work is humanity's privileged participation in God's creative work (1:27-30; 2:15), in the fall it becomes a cursed

---

[59] C.-L. Seow, *Ecclesiastes*, AB (New York: Doubleday, 1997), 38.

[60] See D.B. Miller, 'Qohelet's Symbolic Use of לבה', *JBL* 117 (1998), 437–54.

[61] A. Verheij, 'Paradise Retried: On Qohelet 2:4-6', *JSOT* 50 (1991), 114.

[62] Cf. Fisch, *Poetry*, 167; Seow, *Ecclesiastes*, 113-17; and O'Donovan, *Resurrection*, 79-80, 84.

[63] Verheij, 'Paradise', 114.

'pain' or 'toil' (Ecc 3:17). In this way it is especially striking that Qohelet repeatedly admonishes his audience to 'enjoy' their work (2:24; 3:18; 5:18-19), while his own work, which he identifies as seeking all things by wisdom (1:13; 7:23), is continuously lamented for its obscurity and fallenness (1:13-14, 17; 2:11, 17; 3:18-20; 7:23-24). Qohelet thus views creation as both ordered and disordered without any attempt to resolve the resulting tension. Qohelet's calculated reversals of the Genesis creation story are a part of his ironic rhetoric, which is ironic because it is the goodness of creation which he seeks to affirm, in spite of the obscurity he finds in human experience.[64]

2. Irony is also apparent in Qohelet's allusions to Proverbs and the ways of knowing prescribed there. Proverbs gives a stern warning of the ambitions of the 'heart' (*lēb*), representing a person's centre: 'Trust in Yahweh with all your *lēb* and do not lean on your own understanding' (3:5); 'Watch over your *lēb* with all diligence, for from it come the sources of life' (4:23). By contrast, Qohelet gives his heart to an unbounded search of all things. He speaks to his heart (1:16; 2:14, 15), 'sets' his heart (8:9; 9:1), 'explores' with his heart (2:3) and, in remarkable contrast to Proverbs, does not withhold his heart from pleasure (2:10).[65] Qohelet's search is flagrantly individualistic and unbounded.[66]

3. Qohelet's use of the heart also reflects a methodological and ethical irony in relation to Proverbs, for it stands in opposition to Proverbs' hermeneutical knowledge from within described above. Qohelet is not satisfied with deliberating the proverbial pictures of competing realities but pursues an unbounded accumulation of knowledge, seeking all things 'by wisdom' (*baḥokmâ* [cf. 1:13; 18; 7:23; 8:16]). Fox thus says, 'This faculty aims at increasing knowledge apart from its practical or prudential value ... [it is] an open-ended search for new knowledge and deeper understanding.'[67] This use of wisdom – and this epistemology – is found nowhere else in the Bible. The strangeness of it begs for resolution and, in this sense is ironic, deconstructing itself as its exhaustive search continuously ends in *hebel*.

4. Perhaps the strongest indication of Qohelet's irony emerges in his lengthy dialogue with Proverbs in 7:23–8:1a. The intertextual play with Proverbs, and with the rest of Qohelet's methodology, resides in the use of the verbs 'seek' (*bqš*) and 'find' (*mṣ'* [7:25, 28, 29; Prov 2:4; 11:27]). The context for Qohelet's use of these phrases is created by his stated purpose to 'seek[68] and search out all things by wisdom' (1:13). He restates his purpose in 2:1, 12; 4:1 and 7:23, leading the reader

---

[64] The affirmations of the goodness of creation appear sporadically, though perhaps not chaotically, throughout Qohelet's speech: Eccl 2:24-26; 3:12-13; 4:2-3; 5:18-20; 9:7-10; 12:13-14.

[65] M.V. Fox, *A Time to Tear Down and a Time to Build Up: A Rereading of Ecclesiastes* (Grand Rapids: Eerdmans, 1999), 77.

[66] On the emphatic individualism or hyper-subjectivity in Qohelet, see Christianson, *Time*, 34. The parallels with Kant's view of enlightenment, autonomy and maturity are remarkable; see Kant, 'Enlightenment'.

[67] *Time*, 74.

[68] *drš* (search) in 1:13 parallels *bqš* (search) in Chapter 7.

along with periodic echoes of the search introduced at length in the first two chapters: to look for things 'by wisdom' ([1:13; 7:23]). Yet, remarkably, the wisdom he seeks is 'far from him' (7:23), leading him to ask, 'who can find (*mṣ'*) it?' (v. 24; cf. Job 28:12, 20). The apparent obscurity of wisdom leads Qohelet to look for the 'scheme [*heśbôn*] of things' (7:25), a point he will come back to later. What he finds (*mṣ'*) initially is 'more bitter than death, the woman who is a snare ...' (7:26). This woman is remarkably like the adulterous woman in Proverbs 5 whose lips 'drip honey' (v. 3), but 'in the end ... is bitter as wormwood' (v. 4).[69] Yet, as I argued above, this adulterous woman in Proverbs is thematically and theologically interwoven with Dame Folly,[70] and the apparent implication is that Qohelet has 'found' the woman (path) whose way is not wisdom. His skepticism seems intentionally opposed to the hope of finding the wise woman of Proverbs 31:10-31 ('an excellent wife, who can find' [*mṣ'*]).[71]

When he continues in verse 27, the narrator interrupts with his only words between 1:2 and 12:9, '"Look", says Qohelet ...', signaling the importance of what follows in verses 27b-29:

> adding one thing to another
>> to *find* the *heśbôn* of things
>>> while I was still searching
>>>> but not *finding*
>>> One man among a thousand
>>>> I have *found*
>>> But a woman among all these
>>>> I have not *found*
>>>> See this alone I have *found*
>> That God made man upright
>>> But he has sought out many *hiśśĕbonôt*

Bracketed by the virtually synonymous and homonymous words *heśbôn* ('scheme', v. 27) and *hiśśĕbonôt* ('schemes', v. 29), the passage focuses on the character and results of Qohelet's search. By his 'adding' (7:27), 'wisdom [remains] far from him' (23); he has 'only' found one man – perhaps himself, or, more likely the prototypical Adamic humanity in search of the wrong tree (Gen 3:1-7). He has not found a woman,[72] who, in light of the context, is almost definitely Lady Wisdom, the embodiment of the ethical and religious pursuit of wisdom in Proverbs.[73] Rather,

---

[69] Seow, *Ecclesiastes*, 261-2.

[70] See W.P. Brown, *Ecclesiastes, Interpretation* (Louisville: John Knox Press, 2000), 84.

[71] M.V. Fox, *Ecclesiastes*, JPS (Philadelphia: Jewish Publication Society, 2004), 52; and Van Leeuwen, *Proverbs*, 260; both make this connection.

[72] That Qohelet has Genesis in mind is made more certain by his decision to follow Genesis 2 in pairing *'ādām* ('man'), rather than the more natural *'îš* ('man'), with *'iśśāh* (woman).

[73] It is particularly enlightening that Fox, 'Wisdom in Qohelet', in B.B. Scott et al (eds.), *In Search of Wisdom: Essays in Memory of John G. Gammie* (Louisville, KY:

Qohelet's wisdom is a *scheme* which resists God's created intentions for humanity – again echoing the ambitions of proto-humanity in Genesis 3.

In summary, Qohelet's is a wisdom that *adds* rather than one that *interprets*; a wisdom of parts rather than the whole; and a wisdom of self (an unbounded heart) rather than of tradition and modesty. Thus, when Qohelet 'sees' both order and disorder together in the world he is only able to juxtapose them and conclude that it is *hebel* (obscure). Yet, as the careful ironic interplay with Proverbs becomes increasingly pronounced, it becomes clear that Qohelet is aware of his method and is strategically deconstructing himself (his heart) as a knower and therefore his use of wisdom as a scheme (*ḥešbôn*). His hyper-subjectivist, empiricist and rationalistic wisdom, unable to account for what it sees, shows itself to be increasingly deficient. His argument works *with* the narrator, who, in concert with Qohelet's rhetoric throughout, concludes that 'when all has been heard, the end of the matter is to fear God and keep his commandments' (12:13). This ironically echoes the fear of Yahweh as the '*beginning* of wisdom' in Proverbs 1:7 and 9:10. By its absence at the beginning of the book we are able to infer that it is the solution to the obscurity and folly he has found.

Conclusion

Each book of Old Testament wisdom literature, and, to a certain extent, Sirach and the Wisdom of Solomon, contributes its own unique voice to the wisdom project: Proverbs with its concern for structure, foundations, scope, and limits, advertising the great treasure of the way of wisdom; Job's troubling story reinforcing the limits of wisdom, and presenting a picture of 'counter-order' which paradoxically corresponds with the exceeding goodness of God's creative mind; and finally, Ecclesiastes subjecting the search for wisdom to the tests of rational, empirical and subjective extremes, ironizing away the certainty-driven thirst for divine knowledge. Significantly, despite their unique differences, they all locate the knowledge of justice, righteousness, order, and meaning within the universal ontology of Yahweh's created order. They attest to the epistemological tension between wisdom and folly –

Westminster/John Knox Press, 1993), 128, is unable, or unwilling, to detect any moral or religious overtones in the passage, as much as he follows the logic of exegesis here. He says, 'The motive of this imperative is not a moral equation between wisdom and righteousness. In sharp contrast to Proverbs, but not to most of the Bible, Qoheleth does not regard wisdom as an ethical or religious virtue. A central principle of Proverbs that to be smart is to be righteous and being righteous makes you smart is not a truism. It is a new doctrine being expounded programmatically by the authors of Proverbs or, more likely, one layer of proverbial material ... He does pair righteousness and wisdom in 7:16 and 9:1, but he is bracketing the categories as positive values, not equating them.' It seems almost certain that Fox's epistemological presuppositions about wisdom and research as secular will not allow for a continuity between Proverbs' ethical qualifications on epistemology with the rest of the Old Testament or knowledge in general.

autonomy and faith in Yahweh. And together they usher wisdom seekers into an encounter with Yahweh, the source and guide of all knowledge.

It therefore seems most natural to see the books working together theologically, philosophically and existentially. How we hear them depends very much on our own reading intentions and methodology. Yet I believe that the kind of epistemological comparison presented here goes a long way toward demonstrating the artistry and genius integrated in and between them. Borrowing a musical metaphor, these books contain a polyphony of voices – sometimes atonal and conflicting – which, when heard together in the context of Israel's story, give way to a grand symphony. Thus, like Bach or Mozart's masterful and complex combination of keys and voices and tones, the wisdom literature achieves something which can only be heard together when all the instruments unite – one chord of three strands, played, tied or wound.

Bibliography

Beiser, F.C., *The Fate of Reason: German Philosophy from Kant to Fichte* (Cambridge, MA; London: Harvard University Press, 1987)

Bockmuehl, M., 'Reason, Wisdom and the Implied Disciple of Scripture' in D.F. Ford and G. Stanton (eds.), *Reading Texts, Seeking Wisdom* (London: SCM Press, 2003), 53–68

Brown, W.P., '*Creatio Corporis* and the Rhetoric of Defense in Job 10 and Psalm 139' in W.P. Brown and S.D. McBride (eds.), *God Who Creates* (Grand Rapids, MI: Eerdmans, 2000), 107–24

————, *Ecclesiastes*. Interpretation. (Louisville: John Knox Press, 2000)

Brueggemann, W., *Theology of the Old Testament: Testimony, Dispute, Advocacy* (Minneapolis: Fortress, 1997)

Christianson, E.S., 'Qohelet and The/His Self Among the Deconstructed' in A.A. Schoors (ed.), *Qohelet in the Context of Wisdom* (Leuven, Belgium: Leuven University Press, 1998), 425-33.

————, *A Time to Tell: Narrative Strategies in Ecclesiastes* (Sheffield: Sheffield Academic Press, 1998)

Clouser, R.A., *The Myth of Religious Neutrality: An Essay on the Hidden Role of Religious Belief in Theories* (Notre Dame, London: University of Notre Dame Press, 1991)

Critchley, S., *Continental Philosophy: A Very Short Introduction* (Oxford: Oxford University Press, 2001)

Fisch, H., *Poetry With a Purpose: Biblical Poetics and Interpretation* (Bloomington: Indiana University Press, 1988)

Fishbane, M., 'Jeremiah 4:23–26 and Job 3:3–13: A Recovered Use of the Creation Pattern' *Vetus Testamentum* 21 (1971), 151–67

Fox, M.V., 'Bible Scholarship and Faith-Based Study: My View' SBL Forum (2006)

————, *Ecclesiastes*. JPS. (Philadelphia: Jewish Publication Society, 2004)

————, 'Frame-Narrative and Composition in the Book of Qohelet', *Hebrew Union College Annual* 48 (1977), 83–106

_____, 'Ideas of Wisdom in Proverbs 1–9', *Journal of Biblical Literature* 116 (1997), 613-33

_____, 'Job the Pious', *Zeitschrift für die alttestamentliche Wissenschaft* 117 (2005), 351-66

_____, 'The Pedagogy of Proverbs 2', *Journal of Biblical Literature* 113:2 (1994), 233-43

_____, *Proverbs 1-9: A New Translation with Introduction and Commentary*. Anchor Bible. (New York: Doubleday, 2000)

_____, 'Review of C. Bartholomew, *Reading Ecclesiastes: Old Testament Exegesis and Hermeneutical Theory*', *Interpretation* 54 (2000), 195–96

_____, *A Time to Tear Down and a Time to Build Up: A Rereading of Ecclesiastes* (Grand Rapids: Eerdmans, 1999)

_____, 'Wisdom in Qohelet' in B.B. Scott, W.J. Wiseman and L.G. Perdue (eds.), *In Search of Wisdom: Essays in Memory of John G. Gammie* (Louisville, KY: Westminster/John Knox Press, 1993), 115–31

_____, 'Qohelet's Epistemology', *Hebrew Union College Annual* 58 (1987), 137-55

Fretheim, T.E., *God and World in the Old Testament: A Relational Theology of Creation* (Nashville: Abingdon Press, 2005)

Fyall, R.S., *Now My Eyes Have Seen You: Images of Creation and Evil in the Book of Job* (Leicester; Downers Grove: Inter-Varsity, 2002)

Gladson, J.A., *Retributive Paradoxes in Proverbs 10-29* (MI: University Microfilms International, 1979)

Kant, I., 'What is Enlightenment' in *The Philosophy of Kant*, C.J. Friedrich (tr.) (New York: The Modern Library, 1949),132-39

Kline, M.G., *The Structure of Biblical Authority* (Grand Rapids, MI: Eerdmans, 1972)

Kearney, R., *Dialogues with Contemporary Continental Thinkers: Paul Ricoeur, Emmanuel Levinas, Herbert Marcuse, Stanislas Breton, Jacques Derrida* (Manchester: Manchester Univeristy Press, 1984)

Kuhn, T.S., *The Structure of Scientific Revolutions* (Chicago: University of Chicago Press, 1996)

Leeuwen, R.C. van, 'Building God's House: An Exploration in Wisdom' in *The Way of Wisdom: Essays in Honor of Bruce K. Waltke*, J.I. Packer and S.K. Soderlund (eds.) (Grand Rapids: Zondervan, 2000), 204-11

_____, *Context and Meaning in Proverbs 25–27*. SBL.DS. (Atlanta, GA: Scholars Press, 1988)

_____, 'Proverbs 30:21–23 and the Biblical World Upside Down', *Journal of Biblical Literature* 105 (1986), 599-610

_____, 'Proverbs' in *The New Interpreters Bible* Vol. V (Nashville: Abingdon Press, 1997)

_____, 'Wealth and Poverty: System and Contradiction in Proverbs', *Hebrew Studies* 33 (1992), 25-36.

_____, 'Wisdom Literature' in *Dictionary for Theological Interpretation of the Bible*, K.J. Vanhoozer, C.G. Bartholomew, et al (eds.) (Grand Rapids: Baker, 2005), 847–50

Longman, T. III., *The Book of Ecclesiastes*. NICOT. (Grand Rapids: Eerdmans, 1998)

Middleton, J.R., *The Liberating Image: The Imago Dei in Genesis 1* (Grand Rapids, MI: Brazos, 2005)

Miller, D.B., 'Qohelet's Symbolic Use of □□□.' *Journal of Biblical Literature* 117 (1998), 437-54.

O'Donovan, O., *Resurrection and Moral Order: An Outline for Evangelical Ethics* (Leicester: Inter-Varsity Press, 1986)

O'Dowd, R.P., 'Frame-narrative' in *Dictionary of the Old Testament: Wisdom Poetry and Writings*, T. Longman and P. Enns (eds.) (Downers Grove: IVP, forthcoming).

_____, 'Wisdom as Canonical Imagination: Pleasant Words for Tremper Longman' in C.G. Bartholomew, et al (eds.), *Canon and Interpretation* (Milton Keynes: Paternoster/ Grand Rapids: Zondervan, 2006), 374-92

_____, 'The Wisdom of Torah: Epistemology in Deuteronomy and the Wisdom Literature' PhD Thesis, The University of Liverpool, 2005

Phillips, E.A., 'Speaking Truthfully: Job's Friends and Job', Unpublished paper presented at The Evangelical Theological Society, 2004

Rad, G. von., *Wisdom in Israel* (London: SCM, 1970)

Ricoeur, P., *Hermeneutics and the Human Sciences*, J.B. Thompson (ed. and trans.) (Cambridge: CUP, 1981)

Schnabel, E.J., *Law and Wisdom from Ben Sira to Paul: A Tradition Historical Inquiry into the Relation of Law, Wisdom, and Ethics* (Tübingen: J.C.B. Mohr [Paul Siebeck], 1985)

Seow, C.-L., *Ecclesiastes*. Anchor Bible. (New York: Doubleday, 1997)

Taylor, A., *The Proverb* (Cambridge, MA: Harvard University Press, 1931)

Toulmin, S., *Cosmopolis: The Hidden Agenda of Modernity*. Chicago: The University of Chicago Press, 1990

Vanhoozer, K.J., 'Lost in Interpretation? Truth, Scripture, and Hermeneutics' in A. Köstenberger (ed.), *Whatever Happened to Truth* (Wheaton: Crossway, 2005), 93-136

Verheij, A., 'Paradise Retried: On Qohelet 2:4–6' *Journal for the Study of the Old Testament* 50 (1991), 113-15

Weinfeld, M., *Deuteronomy and the Deuteronomic School* (Oxford: Clarendon, 1972/ Winona Lake, IN: Eisenbrauns, 1992)

Whybray, R.N., *The Composition of the Book of Proverbs*. JSOTSup. (Sheffield: Sheffield Academic Press, 1994)

Wilson, G., 'Preknowledge, Anticipation, and the Poetics of Job' *Journal for the Study of the Old Testament* 30 (2005), 243–56

Witherington, B. III, *Jesus the Sage: The Pilgrimage of Wisdom* (Minneapolis: Fortress Press, 2000)

Wolters, A., *Creation Regained; Biblical Basics for a Reformational Worldview* (Grand Rapids, MI: Eerdmans, 1985)

_____, *The Song of the Valiant Woman: Studies in the Interpretation of Proverbs 31:10–31* (Carlisle: Paternoster, 2001)

Wood, W.J., *Epistemology: Becoming Intellectually Virtuous* (Leicester: Apollos, 1998)

CHAPTER 5

'The Spirit of Wisdom and Understanding': Epistemology in Luke-Acts

Thomas D. Stegman, S.J.

There are many ways to approach the issue of 'epistemology in Luke-Acts'. One could use a concordance to track down Luke's use of terms such as *gnōsis* ('knowledge'), *alētheia* ('truth'), *epistamai* ('understand'), and *oida* ('know').[1] But this method tends to atomize the text, leaving one with a puzzle broken into hundreds of pieces. Another strategy might import certain philosophical questions to the text (e.g., 'How does Luke define 'knowledge'?'). The drawback here is that one might ask the wrong questions, or at least questions that Luke's text does not intend to address.

I propose, instead, to analyze key epistemological issues in Luke-Acts on terms set by the third evangelist himself. At the end of the prologue of his two-volume work, Luke explains his purpose in writing: that the reader might *know* 'certainty' or 'assurance' (*asphaleia* – Lk 1:4). In the first part of this essay I investigate Luke's expressed purpose and how he goes about fulfilling it. One of the critical issues throughout Luke-Acts is the correct understanding of Scripture. In the second section I analyze the importance of Scripture and its proper interpretation in Luke's plan to inculcate 'certainty'. Scripture tells a story in which God is the main protagonist. According to Luke, God is revealed preeminently in and through Jesus. In the third part I explore the role that Jesus plays in revealing proper knowledge about God in comparison with an approach from 'natural theology'. Knowledge of God, however, is not an end in itself for Luke; rather, it leads to the 'knowledge of salvation' (Lk 1:77) and to particular implications in the lives of its recipients. In the final section I touch briefly on some of the 'practical' aspects of knowledge that Luke's narrative suggests. I conclude each of the four parts by discussing the key epistemological issue(s) raised by the analysis.

---

[1] Although the Gospel of Luke and the Acts of the Apostles are separated in the canon of the New Testament by the Gospel of John, scholars are in agreement that Luke and Acts originally constituted a *single* two-volume work. Indeed, Acts 1:1 begins by referring to 'the first book', i.e. to the gospel. While neither document reveals its authorship internally, by the late second century tradition had named 'Luke' as the author of both writings. Following tradition, I refer to the author of both the gospel and Acts as 'Luke'.

I – Luke's Concern to Inculcate 'Certainty'

Luke begins his two-volume work by referring to the fact that 'many' have already undertaken to write a 'narrative' (*diēgēsis*) about 'the events that have been brought to fulfillment among us' (Lk 1:1).[2] The passive voice in the last clause is important, as Luke employs the divine passive to indicate that *God* is the ultimate protagonist of the various narratives that have been compiled. So why does Luke undertake to write yet another account? In 1:4 he offers the following reason: 'in order that you might know *asphaleian* concerning the words by which you have been instructed.' Although the RSV renders *asphaleia* as the equivalent of *alētheia* (i.e., 'truth'), Luke's wider usage of *asphal-* cognates suggests a different nuance, namely 'assurance', even 'certainty'.[3] Thus the third evangelist claims that his own narrative is written in order to inculcate 'certainty' in his readers.[4] That which sets Luke's account apart from others is his expressed commitment to tell the story 'in proper order' (*kathexēs* – 1:3), a point to which I will return shortly.

What drives Luke's concern to instill certainty among his readers? Most commentators interpret Luke-Acts as an apologetic work. For instance, some have regarded Luke as an apologist for Christianity vis-à-vis the Roman Empire (e.g., insisting that Christianity poses no threat to the Empire). Others have seen Luke as the champion of Paul (e.g., defending him from veering too far from the Judaism in which he was raised). The problem with such proposals is that they account only for certain parts of Luke-Acts while leaving much else unexplained. Luke Timothy Johnson has plausibly argued that Luke's real concern is *theodicy*.[5] To understand what Johnson means, one must place oneself in the position of a thoughtful Gentile Christian like Theophilus[6] (Lk 1:3; Acts 1:1). While such Gentile Christians would have rejoiced that God's message of salvation extends to 'all flesh' (Lk 3:6) and that God's people now include numbers taken from the Gentiles (cf. Acts 15:14), certain nagging questions emerge. The success of the Gentile mission seems to be – at least in large part – due to the rejection of the gospel by the Jews (e.g., Acts 13:44-47; 18:5-6; 28:23-28). But were not God's promises (e.g. to Abraham) made to the Jews? And have not the majority of them refused to accept Jesus as Messiah, thereby

---

[2] Unless otherwise noted, all translations of the biblical text are mine.

[3] See J.A. Fitzmyer, *The Gospel according to Luke*, 2 vols., AB 28–28A (New York: Doubleday, 1981–85), 1:300. Cf. Acts 21:34; 22:30; 25:26 (*to asphalēs*). More tellingly, see Acts 2:36 – 'let the whole house of Israel know *assuredly* (*asphalōs*).' In addition, cf. Acts 5:23; 16:23–24, where *asphal-* cognates indicate 'securing' one in prison.

[4] In the Greek text the phrase *tēn asphaleian* occupies the prominent end position for stronger emphasis.

[5] In what follows, I condense the argument found in L.T. Johnson, *The Gospel of Luke*, SP 3 (Collegeville, MN: The Liturgical Press, 1991), 9-10; and idem., *The Acts of the Apostles*, SP 5 (Collegeville, MN: The Liturgical Press, 1992), 7–9.

[6] Much ink has been spilled on the subject of identifying 'most excellent Theophilus.' Was he a real personage? If so, was he Luke's patron? A Roman official? A God-fearer or already a Christian? Or is Theophilus a symbolic name (meaning 'beloved of God') for all readers? For a helpful discussion, see Fitzmyer, *The Gospel according to Luke*, 1:299–300.

missing out on the fulfillment of God's promises? Has God truly been faithful to his people? And if not, why should Gentile Christians stake their lives in following such a God?

Luke addresses these questions and concerns by narrating the story of Jesus and the early church 'in order' (*kathexēs* – Lk 1:3). Luke's meaning here can be discerned at both the 'macro-' and 'micro-' levels of his story. At the macro-level, the function of Acts 1-7 is crucially important. While the gospel tells the story of the rejection of Jesus by his people (e.g., Lk 13:34-35; 19:41-44; 23:23-25), Luke makes clear that, after Jesus' resurrection and ascension, the message of salvation was *first* preached by the Spirit-empowered apostles in Jerusalem and its environs. And many Jews responded favorably to this proclamation. In fact, upon hearing Peter's Pentecost sermon (Acts 2:14-36), three thousand in the crowd – consisting solely of Jews (2:5) – responded by repenting and being baptized (2:41). In doing so, they received forgiveness of their sins and the gift of the Holy Spirit. The blessings poured out by the Spirit are, according to Luke, the fulfillment of the promises made to Abraham (Acts 2:33; 3:25). Moreover, the next four chapters of Acts are dotted with notices that more and more Jews believed in the gospel message and received the blessings of the Spirit (2:47; 4:4; 5:14; 6:7). In order to understand Luke's narrative properly, it is imperative not to pass over these notices too hastily. By means of them, the third evangelist describes, in effect, the restoration of Israel (and thereby the fidelity of God to his promises). The *subsequent* mission to the Gentiles – recounted through the remainder of Acts – can then be viewed as the continuation and growth of Israel, not her replacement.[7] Thus Luke offers 'the big picture' of God's workings among both Jews and Gentiles by telling the story 'in order'.[8]

Luke's aim to inculcate *asphaleia* by means of an 'orderly' narrative is also evident at the micro-level. The story of Peter and the Roman centurion Cornelius illustrates this well (Acts 10:1-11:18).[9] Acts 10 relates the encounter between the two, which resulted in Cornelius's baptism and in Peter's sharing table fellowship with Gentiles. The latter action led some fellow Jews to accuse him of violating God's law. Indeed, viewed solely from the vantage point of Jewish law, Peter was in the wrong.[10] His defense consisted in his narrating the events 'in order' (*kathexēs* – 11:4). That is, Peter carefully reported from his own experience the order of what had transpired: his strange vision through which he was directed to understand that

---

[7] See Johnson, *The Acts of the Apostles*, 8-9, 61, 80–81, 95, 107.

[8] With this 'big picture' in mind, Luke, especially in the latter half of Acts, can portray God as absorbing the predominant Jewish rejection of the gospel – which leads Paul to turn his missionary labors to the Gentiles – 'into a larger pattern which points toward God's victory.' See R.C. Tannehill, *The Narrative Unity of Luke-Acts: A Literary Interpretation*, 2 vols. (Philadelphia: Fortress, 1986–90), 1:12.

[9] Here I follow closely Tannehill, *The Narrative Unity of Luke-Acts*, 1:11–12. See also L.T. Johnson, *Scripture & Discernment: Decision Making in the Church* (Nashville: Abingdon, 1996), 91-98.

[10] As Johnson points out, 'The problem is a real one. For a Jew to eat without attending to ritual purity meant to lose his or her Jewish identity.' See *Scripture & Discernment*, 97.

God makes no distinction between Jews and Gentiles (11:5-10); the Spirit's prompting him to go to Cornelius's house (11:11-12); Cornelius's report that an angel had inspired him to seek out Peter (11:13-14); and Peter's preaching which led to the gift of the Spirit being bestowed upon Cornelius and his household (11:15-16). In the face of such experiences, Peter could not deny that God had given the same gift to the Gentiles as was bestowed on Jews 'who believed in the Lord Jesus Christ' (11:17). The end of this passage ought not to be overlooked. Peter's 'orderly' account convinced his fellow Jewish believers to understand that God was now working in new and surprising ways (11:18). In short, Acts 10:1-11:18 provides the key for understanding Luke's strategy as set forth in the prologue to the gospel: the third evangelist carefully orders the events he relates so as to make clear the divine plan of salvation behind those events.[11] This revelation of God's designs is what ultimately encourages 'certainty' among the readers of Luke-Acts.

Luke's expressed purpose in writing his two-volume work raises a critical question: what kind of certainty are we dealing with here? Philosophers regard certainty under two aspects: propositional (or logical) certainty and psychological certainty. The former refers to the manner in which statements or propositions are logically interrelated and set forth; the latter refers to a state of mind whereby one has subjectively attained assurance.[12] Undoubtedly, Luke seeks to instill a sense of psychological assurance in his readers (although such assurance must ultimately be bound up with faith). How does he accomplish this goal? Luke does not engage in syllogistic reasoning based on indisputable first principles. Nor does he set forth deductions from certain clear and distinct ideas. Rather, Luke writes a *narrative* – a special kind of history. Luke narrates a series of events that he interprets as *Heilsgeschichte*. The events he records find their ultimate meaning in the fact that they are saving events, events that are part of the unfolding of God's plan of salvation. It is this divine plan that Luke wants to make clear by offering an 'orderly' account, one that sets forth the 'logic' and unfolding of God's designs. Indeed, as Richard J. Dillon observes, 'the reader's "certainty" will be about *the significance of the reported events as God's action in history*, rather than about the mere factual truth of what is narrated.'[13]

Rudolf Bultmann famously accused Luke of watering down the challenge to faith that results from the gospel's fundamental proclamation. By 'historicizing' the story of Jesus and the early church, Bultmann thought that the third evangelist gave

---

[11] R.J. Dillon astutely observes that in Acts 11:5–17 Peter does not recount the events *precisely* as they were narrated in Acts 10. What Peter's reconstruction brings to the fore is a 'logical or idea-sequence' rather than a mere sequence of events in time. See 'Previewing Luke's Project from His Prologue (Luke 1:1-4)', *CBQ* 43 (1981), 205–27, here 220.

[12] See C.D. Rollins, 'Certainty', in P. Edwards (ed.), *The Encyclopedia of Philosophy*, 8 vols. (New York: Macmillan, 1967), 2:67–71, here 67.

[13] 'Previewing Luke's Project', 224 (italics added). To be sure, for the third evangelist the events themselves convey objective truth.

priority to evidence or objectivity over truth that is accessible only by faith.[14] Is this a fair criticism of Luke? François Bovon counters that Luke's project emits the optimism of one who believed that the search for truth – in this case, through historical means – would confirm the truth of the gospel message. This is the case because, for Luke, 'there is only one truth and one world.'[15] According to Bovon, what counted most heavily for evidence in Luke's time was '*rhetorical* argument', involving the strategy of persuasion – not, as is thought today, so-called 'objective evidence'. Luke's narrative history includes the presentation of the effective power of God's prophetic word (as found in Scripture) and of God's mediated activity within history. Because he construed the historical task thus (i.e., rhetorically), history and kerygma are inextricably intertwined for Luke.[16] Hence, the readers of Luke-Acts, while offered *asphaleia* by the third evangelist, must still respond with a decision of faith.[17]

Given what has been presented so far, it is easy to understand why one of Luke's key literary devices is prophecy and fulfillment, especially the fulfillment of God's promises.[18] The third evangelist instills certainty in large measure by demonstrating how Scripture has been fulfilled in Jesus and the early church. It is to the issue of Scripture and its correct interpretation that I now turn.

II – The Correct Understanding and Interpretation of Scripture

Luke regards Scripture (which, of course, in his day was what Christians now call the 'Old Testament') as the vehicle par excellence for conveying God's message and plan of salvation. This divine communication was for him not just a relic of the past, but a living word that continues to speak in the present. Like the other evangelists, Luke interprets Jesus' life, ministry, death, resurrection, and exaltation as the fulfillment of Scripture. Unique to the third evangelist, however, is his categorical

---

[14] 'The very fact that [Luke] writes an account of the origin and earliest history of the Christian Church – in which the eschatological Congregation, of course, would have no interest – shows how far removed he is from its own way of thinking. The fact that he wrote Acts as a sequel to his Gospel completes the confirmation that *he has surrendered the original kerygmatic sense of the Jesus-tradition and has historicized it.*' See *Theology of the New Testament*, K. Grobel (tr.), 2 vols. (New York: Scribner's, 1951–55), 2:117 (italics added).

[15] F. Bovon, *A Commentary on the Gospel of Luke 1:1–9:50*, Hermeneia, C.M. Thomas (tr.) (Minneapolis: Fortress, 2002), 24.

[16] Ibid (italics added). Bovon cites Aristotle's discussion on the search for the basis of conviction in *Rhet.*, 1.1.1355 b.7–12, 25–26.

[17] One omission in the above treatment is the role that 'signs and wonders' play – both in Jesus' ministry and in the Spirit-empowered missionary work of the early church – in the inculcation of *asphaleia*. Such 'signs and wonders' are ultimately evidence of the power of God (cf. Acts 14:3), and are included as such in Luke's 'orderly' narrative (as seen in Peter's recounting God's conferral of the Spirit upon the Gentiles in Acts 11:15).

[18] For Luke's use of prophecy, see Johnson, *The Gospel of Luke*, 15–21.

insistence that the story of the early church is the *continuation* of the unfolding of God's plans – plans that had been written down long before. In what follows, I trace four critical moments in Luke-Acts where the protagonists of the story offer specific – and *striking* – interpretations of Scripture.

Luke 4:16-30 offers the first detailed description of Jesus' public ministry. Entering the synagogue in his hometown of Nazareth (4:16), Jesus is handed a scroll of the prophet Isaiah (4:17). Finding the place he desired to read, Jesus proclaims a text that is, in fact, a conflation of LXX Isaiah 61:1-2 and 58:6.[19] This text speaks of the anointing of the prophet by 'the Spirit of the Lord', an anointing that empowers the prophet to preach good news to the poor, to proclaim release to prisoners and recovery of sight to the blind, to set free the oppressed, and to announce the Lord's year of favor (Lk 4:18–19). After reading the text and sitting down (4:20), Jesus offers an extraordinary interpretation of the text: it is being fulfilled *today* (*sēmeron* – 4:21). The Lukan Jesus boldly declares that the Isaian text – which originally served to announce the return of exiles from Babylon to Jerusalem – is a prediction that has been fulfilled, first of all, in the event of his baptism.[20] Moreover, Jesus intimates that the prophetic text will *continue* to be fulfilled in his ministry of teaching and healing. In fact, Luke 4:18–19 functions as a programmatic prophecy for Luke's first volume; the remaining narrative of the gospel sets forth what God has commissioned and empowered Jesus, as Son of God and Messiah, to do.[21] The Lukan Jesus asserts that the Isaian text concerning an anointed and empowered figure refers to himself.

The second critical 'moment' is the climax of Luke's gospel, namely the passion, death, and resurrection of Jesus. The risen Jesus explains to his disciples that 'all the things written in the Law of Moses and the Prophets and Psalms' about him – pertaining to his suffering and rising from the dead – had to 'be fulfilled' (Lk 24:44; cf. 24:27). Luke reports, without offering any specific examples, that Jesus interpreted all the passages concerning himself. This raises the question: where does the Old Testament speak about the suffering and vindication of Jesus? Luke offers several clues throughout both volumes of his text. For example, Jesus' final words at the last supper indicate that the manner of his upcoming death would fulfill the words of the prophet Isaiah – 'And he was reckoned among the lawless ones' (Lk

---

[19] Fitzmyer rightly argues that the wording of Luke 4:17 indicates that '[i]t sounds as if Jesus deliberately sought out the passage.' See *The Gospel according to Luke*, 1:532. For a description of the first century CE synagogue service, see idem., 1:531.

[20] That Luke intends to connect the anointing referred to in 4:18 with the descent of the Spirit upon Jesus at his baptism (3:22) is clear from the notices of Jesus' being led by the Spirit in 4:1 and 4:14. See C.H. Talbert, *Reading Luke: A Literary and Theological Commentary on the Third Gospel* (New York: Crossroad, 1982), 55.

[21] As Tannehill points out, both the Lukan Jesus' self-understanding of his call (4:43–44) and Luke's summaries of Jesus' preaching and healing evoke the language of the prophetic text cited in 4:18–19. So too does Jesus' description of his ministry (7:22) in response to the query from John the Baptist whether he is actually 'the one who is to come'. See *The Narrative Unity of Luke-Acts*, 1:77–82. C.f. Acts 10:38.

22:37; LXX Is 53:12). That Luke saw Jesus' suffering and death as the fulfillment of the fourth Isaian Servant Song is also evident from Philip's encounter with the Ethiopian eunuch (Acts 8:32-35; see LXX Is 53:7-8). Another example is Peter's Pentecost sermon where he interprets LXX Ps 15:8-11 – especially verse 10 ('You will not forsake my soul in Hades, nor will you allow your holy one to see decay') – as David's prophecy of the resurrection of Jesus (Acts 2:24-36, esp. vv. 30-31).[22] The implication from Luke 24 is that the risen Jesus now instructs his followers how to read and understand texts of Scripture. More precisely, Jesus teaches them to read Scripture 'messianically'.[23]

The third moment is the coming of the Holy Spirit upon the apostles at Pentecost (Acts 2:1-4). Filled with the Spirit, the apostles proclaim the 'the mighty works of God' to Jews who have gathered in Jerusalem from all over the Mediterranean world and from the east. Amazingly, each one hears the proclamation in his own language (2:5-12). Peter then interprets this event by citing LXX Joel 3:1-5. This text speaks of the coming day when God will pour out God's Spirit 'on all flesh' (Acts 2:17-21). Peter boldly claims that Joel's prophecy is now being fulfilled (2:16). Moreover, in setting forth Peter's Pentecost sermon, Luke makes a number of slight – but significant – alterations in the cited text. I call attention to two of them. First, Luke alters the beginning of the prophet's text from 'after these things' (*meta tauta*) to 'in the last days' (*en tais eschatais hēmerais*) in Acts 2:17. The third evangelist thus adds an *eschatological* orientation to Joel's words: God's gift of the Spirit to the church marks a new period in salvation history.[24] Second, Luke adds 'signs' (*sēmeia*) to 'wonders' (*terata*) in Acts 2:19. The phrase 'signs and wonders' functions as a leitmotif in Acts. Not only does Peter immediately describe Jesus as one attested to by God with signs and wonders (2:22); the Spirit-filled apostles are also depicted in this way.[25] Luke thus interprets the beginnings of the church as the fulfillment of prophecy. What is more, in doing so he takes the liberty of altering the biblical text.

The fourth critical moment takes place during the so-called Council of Jerusalem (Acts 15:1-21). At stake was whether or not Gentiles must be circumcised in order to become members of the people of God reconstituted around Messiah Jesus.[26] Following much debate among the apostles and elders (15:6-7a), Peter arises to

---

[22] An example from 'the law of Moses' is Peter's speech in Acts 3:12–26. In 3:22 Peter alludes to Deut 18:15-20, where Moses promised that God would 'raise up' a prophet like him. The latter is a reference to Jesus. Indeed, Stephen's speech in Acts 7 links the story of Moses – who suffered rejection from his people – with the story of Jesus (esp. 7:35–39). See Tannehill, *The Narrative Unity of Luke-Acts*, 2:91–97; c.f. Johnson, *The Gospel of Luke*, 18–19.

[23] See Johnson, *The Gospel of Luke*, 396.

[24] See J.A. Fitzmyer, *The Acts of the Apostles*, AB 31 (New York: Doubleday, 1998), 252.

[25] Cf. Acts 2:43; 4:30; 5:12; 6:8; 14:3; 15:12. See C.K. Barrett, *The Acts of the Apostles*, 2 vols., ICC (Edinburgh: T & T Clark, 1994–98), 1:137. For more on Luke's interpretation and adaptation of texts, see L.T. Johnson, *Septuagintal Midrash in the Speeches of Acts* (Milwaukee: Marquette University Press, 2002).

[26] Here I follow closely Johnson's presentation in *Scripture & Discernment*, 98–106.

speak. Alluding to his encounter with the Gentile Cornelius (10:24-48), Peter insists that God now makes no distinction between Jew and Gentile; both are saved 'through the grace of the Lord Jesus' (15:7b-11). Barnabas and Paul then recount the 'signs and wonders' that God worked through them during their first missionary journey, a ministry through which many Gentiles became disciples (15:12; cf. 13:1-14:28). Finally, James takes the floor. After affirming Peter's experience (15:14), James cites LXX Amos 9:11-12, a text that speaks both of the restoration of David's kingdom and of the invitation to Gentiles to join the people of God (Acts 15:16-18).[27] For James, this restoration and invitation have now come about through the life, death, and resurrection of Jesus and the outpouring of the Spirit. Hence he judges that Gentile Christians need not be circumcised (15:19). The remarkable feature of this passage is found in 15:15. James states there that 'the words of the prophets' – observe the plural – agree with what Peter has related, not vice versa. That is, as Johnson observes, 'it is the experience of God revealed through the narrative [first of Peter, then of Barnabas and Paul] which is given priority in this hermeneutical process.'[28]

What are the epistemological implications of the foregoing? One is the status of Scripture as a source of knowledge. Luke, in my opinion, would be in full accord with several observations that Thomas Aquinas made about Scripture in the opening question of the *Summa Theologiae* (the question concerning the nature and extent of Sacred Doctrine). First, Scripture is inspired by God and offers revealed knowledge that is necessary for salvation.[29] I noted above that the third evangelist makes several alterations in the text of LXX Joel 3:1-5 in Peter's Pentecost sermon in Acts 2:17-21. One of these changes is the addition of 'says God' (*legei ho theos*) in the opening line of the prophecy. Luke thereby makes explicit his conviction that *God* is, in the final analysis, the real author of Scripture. And as Zechariah intimates in the *Benedictus*, what God reveals is ultimately 'knowledge of salvation' (Lk 1:77). Second, Scripture 'has no science above itself'. That is the case because Scripture offers 'infallible truth' and 'incontrovertible proof'.[30] Luke's use of Scripture in Luke-Acts – especially at critical junctures in the narrative – reveals similar assumptions about Scripture as a certain and irrefutable source of knowledge.

Granted that Scripture provides sure, 'objective' knowledge, what guarantees that it is accurately understood and appropriated? Luke is unabashedly sanguine in his answer: the *Holy Spirit* empowers and assures the correct interpretation of Scripture. The four critical 'moments' set forth above make this abundantly clear. Jesus claims that he fulfills the Isaian prophecy in his own person and ministry only after the Spirit has descended upon him (Lk 3:22) and led him forth in power (4:1; 4:14). The

---

[27] The LXX version of Amos 9:11–12 differs from the Masoretic text in several important respects. See Barrett, *The Acts of the Apostles*, 2:727–28.

[28] Johnson, *Acts of the Apostles*, 271.

[29] *S.T.*, 1.1.1.

[30] *S.T.*, 1.1.8. The quotations are taken from *Summa Theologica*, 5 vols., English Province Dominicans (tr.) (Westminster, MD: Christian Classics, 1981), 1:5–6.

risen Jesus explains to his disciples all the passages from the Pentateuch, the Prophets, and the Writings that point to his suffering, death, and resurrection. Here it is significant to note that, for Luke, there is an intimate connection between the risen Jesus and the Spirit (see e.g., Acts 16:7).[31] Peter, after the descent of the Holy Spirit at Pentecost, is empowered not only to interpret that event by means of Scripture, but also to offer a christological reading of LXX Ps 15:8-11 (Acts 2:25-28). And in communicating the decision of the Jerusalem Council to Gentile Christians – a decision that involved an appeal to LXX Amos 9:11-12 – James refers to the inspiration of the Holy Spirit (cf. Acts 15:28).[32]

One of the extraordinary claims made in Luke-Acts is that God's plan of salvation (and thus the fulfillment of Scripture) *continues* to be enacted in the life of the church – at least up to the time of Luke's writing.[33] Such a claim raises several important questions. Does the nature of Luke's narrative imply that passages from Scripture, especially prophetic ones, are being fulfilled up to our own time today? The open-ended quality of the conclusion of Acts seems to suggest that this is a real possibility.[34] If so, how is the Holy Spirit's inspired interpretation and appropriation of biblical texts to be adjudicated? Or does the inclusion of Luke and Acts in the canon of the New Testament circumscribe the sacred history recounted in these two volumes and relegate it to the past (at least in terms of the fulfillment of Old Testament prophecy)? Moreover, the third and fourth critical moments discussed

---

[31] See Acts 2:32–33: 'This Jesus God raised up [from the dead]; we all are witnesses of that. Therefore, having been lifted up to the right hand of God, and also having received the promise of the Holy Spirit from the Father, [Jesus] has poured out this [i.e. the Spirit] which you see and hear.'

[32] As R.W. Wall observes, 'The content of James's reading of Scripture agrees with the intentions of its author, the Holy Spirit (see 1:16). Any interpretation of Scripture that is on target must enjoy a consensus that includes God's Spirit.' See 'The Acts of the Apostles: Introduction, Commentary, and Reflections', in L.E. Keck *et al.* (eds.), *The New Interpreter's Bible*, 12 vols. (Nashville: Abingdon, 1994–2002), 10:221.

For a study that sets forth, on the basis of Luke-Acts, the essential relationship between *prayer* and biblical hermeneutics, see C.G. Bartholomew and R. Holt, 'Prayer in/and the Drama of Redemption in Luke', in C.G. Bartholomew, et al (eds.), *Reading Luke: Interpretation, Reflection, Formation*, SHS 6 (Milton Keynes: Paternoster/ Grand Rapids, Mich.: Zondervan, 2005), 350-75. The first three of the four moments discussed above illustrate this relationship: Before reading the Isaian passages in the synagogue at Nazareth, Jesus experiences the Spirit's empowerment while at prayer (Lk 3:21-22); the risen Jesus interprets passages from Scripture immediately before the blessing and breaking of the bread (24:30-31); and Peter's Pentecost sermon follows the notice that he (and others) waited in prayer for Jesus' promised gift (Acts 1:14). I will return, with a narrower scope, to a 'prayer epistemology' in Part IV.

[33] This is the implication of the perfect tense of the participle *peplērophorēmenōn* in Luke 1:1.

[34] Observe how Luke's account ends with Paul's preaching the gospel 'unhindered, with all boldness' (Acts 28:31) – and not with the latter's martyrdom (about which surely Luke knew).

above raise the issue of the relationship between God's activity discerned in the present – activity that leads God's people in new directions – and the interpretation (or *re*interpretation) of Scripture, even to the extent of making alterations in the sacred texts. Is such a thing still possible today? If so, who determines whether and how God is acting, and how texts are to be (re)interpreted in light of God's action? Lastly, the interpretation of Scripture in Luke-Acts brings up the topic of the 'senses of Scripture'. For instance, when the Lukan Jesus declares that the Isaian texts are fulfilled in him and his ministry, does Luke imply that this is the literal sense of the passages in question? Or is the third evangelist drawing on a 'fuller sense' (*sensus plenior*) of those texts? Can one appeal to a fuller sense of biblical texts today?[35] Space constraints do not permit fuller treatment of these issues (which, admittedly, shade into the area of hermeneutics).

Scripture not only reveals God's plan of salvation, but *who God is*. While Scripture is an indispensable source of knowledge about God, it is not the only one. I turn now to two other ways in which Luke suggests that God can be known.

III – 'Natural Theology' and the Revelation of God through Jesus

Luke records two incidents in which Paul's preaching is marked by what we would call 'natural theology'.[36] The first occurs in Acts 14:15-17 during Paul and Barnabas's missionary work in Lystra. Paul has just healed a man crippled from birth (14:8-10). The crowds who witnessed the healing respond by hailing the two missionaries as Zeus and Hermes; moreover, they attempt to offer sacrifice to the two apostles (14:11-13). Horrified and appalled, Paul launches into a sermon. What is striking about this situation is that Paul faces a crowd of polytheists who are not familiar with the story of God as told in Scripture, but who are open to the divine power at work in their presence.[37] Paul begins by appealing to the living God whom he defines as *creator* (14:15). The apostle goes on to insist – through the use of three present tense participles – that this creator-God has left testimony to his existence and generosity: in 'doing good' (*agathourgōn*) by 'providing' (*didous*) rains and

---

[35] For a helpful discussion on the senses of Scripture, including the *sensus plenior*, see the Pontifical Biblical Commission's *The Interpretation of the Bible in the Church* (Boston: St. Paul Books and Media, 1993), 81–88.

[36] By 'natural theology', I refer to what can be known about God through nature. Several commentators have questioned whether Paul himself resorted to arguing from natural theology. For instance, Barrett remarks, '... it must be considered doubtful whether the Paul who is known to us from the epistles was accustomed to make, even to Gentiles, an approach that owed so much to natural theology.' See *The Acts of the Apostles*, 1.665. N.T. Wright counters that such an approach would have been compatible with Paul's theology of covenant and creation. See *Paul: In Fresh Perspective* (Minneapolis: Fortress, 2005), 38. Cf. Rom 1:19-21.

[37] As Tannehill indicates, Judaism's biblical story and belief in one God are the two major premises of most of the speeches in Acts. See *The Narrative Unity of Luke-Acts*, 2:179. The exceptions are this passage and Acts 17:22-31, to be discussed below.

fruitful harvests, thereby 'satisfying' (*empiplōn*) human hearts (14:17).[38] The Lukan Paul appeals to the observable provision of life and sustenance in order to assert the existence and goodness of the one Creator.

Paul's second appeal to natural theology occurs in his address to Epicurean and Stoic philosophers at the Areopagus in Athens (Acts 17:22-31). Here the apostle expands on the theme broached in 14:15-17. The 'logic' of his presentation depends on the relation of the creator and creation.[39] In 17:24-29 Paul makes three statements about who God is and then offers three implications for appropriate human response in worship of this God.[40] First, the apostle states that God, as 'Lord of heaven and earth,' is the creator of all that exists (17:24a). Thus God does not live in human-made shrines (17:24b). Second, he insists that God not only creates but also continues to *sustain* in existence all that is (17:25b). Thus people err if they think that God needs their service to fulfill some divine need (17:25a). Third, Paul argues that, although God is transcendent, God is also intimately involved in all aspects of the lives of human beings who are, indeed, his offspring; hence his transcendence does not preclude immanence (17:26-28). Nevertheless, humans – who are made to seek God (17:27a)[41] – are not to think that God can be represented by material means (17:29).[42] In short, the Lukan Paul attempts to help his Athenian interlocutors to reason to the truth about the one true God.

Prima facie Luke seems to sound an optimistic note about the possibility that natural theology can lead people to acknowledge and worship God. There are clues in both texts, however, that militate against such optimism. In Acts 14:16 Paul adverts to God's allowing the Gentiles of previous generations 'to go in their own ways'; they in fact did *not* succeed in finding their way to the one true God. The Lukan Paul refers to this as 'the times of ignorance' in 17:30, and adds that God has chosen to overlook such ignorance up to this point. But now things are different

---

[38] Barrett, citing the work of T.E. Page, observes that each participle is subordinate to the preceding one. See *The Acts of the Apostles*, 1:682. The use of *present* participles indicates that God's generous provision is ongoing.

[39] Tannehill rightly points out that this relation 'transcends every ethnic and racial difference. It is a relation rooted in creaturely existence as such, embracing, therefore, Jews and Gentiles equally.' See *The Narrative Unity of Luke-Acts*, 2:211.

[40] I follow here the analysis of C.H. Talbert, *Reading Acts: A Literary and Theological Commentary on the Acts of the Apostles* (New York: Crossroad, 1997), 162–64. Talbert offers parallels from ancient philosophic traditions to each of the statements about God as well as to each of the implications set forth for humanity.

[41] Fitzmyer captures this sense well: 'What Paul is speaking about here is not just the quest of God with the eyes of faith, but the instinctive searching of the human mind and heart for God in the traces that God has left in the creation and disposition of humanity in this world and on this earth. It is a form of natural theology.' See *The Acts of the Apostles*, 610.

[42] Barrett makes explicit the Lukan Paul's presupposition and logic: 'If human nature [marked by thinking and feeling] is what we know it to be, and if we who have human nature are God's children, the divine nature will be of no lower order. We deny our own proper being if we identify our progenitor with material objects.' See *The Act of the Apostles*, 2:849.

because God's self-revelation has taken on a radically new expression, namely through Jesus, the one whom God has raised from the dead (17:31).[43]

Jesus states explicitly in Luke 10:21-22 that he reveals God in an unsurpassable manner. Observe that this passage begins with the notice that Jesus speaks through the power of the Holy Spirit.[44] Luke thus signals the solemnity of what Jesus says here. Jesus asserts that God – whom he calls both 'Father' and 'Lord of heaven and earth' (10:21; c.f. Acts 17:24!) – desires to be revealed to the 'childlike'.[45] Then Jesus explains *why* he can reveal who God is: 'no one knows who the Father is except the Son' (Lk 10:22). That is, Jesus' unique relationship with God – expressed in terms of his unique Sonship – is what enables him to possess the knowledge of who God is and to reveal that knowledge.

What specifically does the Lukan Jesus reveal about God? Two examples will have to suffice here. The first is the underlying portrait of God given in Luke 12:22-34. After warning his disciples against the danger of greed by means of the parable of the rich fool (12:15-21), Jesus exhorts them not to be anxious about food and clothing. To make his point, Jesus offers the example of the ravens.[46] What can one learn from considering ravens? They do not sow or reap; nor do they have storehouses or granaries (contrast the rich fool). Nevertheless – and this is Jesus' key point – God takes care of them. The Lukan Jesus' teaching here acquires more sharpness when one realizes, as Robert C. Tannehill points out, that ravens were regarded as unclean (cf. Lev 11:15; Deut 14:14).[47] Jesus then argues from the lesser to the greater: if God provides generously for the 'unclean' ravens, how much more does God take care of those who respond to Jesus' call to follow him, those who are of much more value than birds (12:24)? Observe how Jesus teaches here as one who knows the Father's mind (12:30) and what God's pleasure is (12:32). Jesus appeals to God's generous, loving care in order to bolster his exhortation to his disciples to sell their possessions and give alms to others (12:33). Such is the way of God's kingdom – *imitatio Dei*. Indeed, Jesus teaches with more than words. His multiplying five loaves to feed five thousand demonstrates God's providential care and ability to feed; moreover, it affords the disciples the wherewithal to care for others (9:10-17).

---

[43] The (at best) lukewarm reception of Paul's message by the Athenians is, in my opinion, another clue that Luke is not overly confident in natural theology. The Lukan Paul's sermon here is *theo*logical almost to the exclusion of any christology (only the reference in Acts 17:31 to the 'man' appointed by God to judge, whom God raised from the dead). Was it this experience that convinced Paul, when he arrived in Corinth – his next stop on his missionary journey (18:1) – to preach only about 'Jesus Christ and him crucified' (1 Cor 2:2)?

[44] This is the first reference to the Holy Spirit since Jesus interpreted his anointing with the Spirit at his baptism (4:18–19).

[45] Fitzmyer points out that Luke uses *nēpioi* 'in the LXX sense' to denote those childlike persons who are open to and accept God's revelation in the Law. See *The Gospel According to Luke*, 2:873.

[46] Notice that, unlike Matthew who refers generically to 'birds' (*peteina* – Mt 6:24), Luke here offers a *specific* example – *korakes*.

[47] See R.C. Tannehill, *Luke*, ANTC (Nashville: Abingdon, 1996), 208.

A second and more dramatic example of Jesus' teaching about God is in Luke 15:3-32. In response to criticism over his consorting with 'sinners' (15:1-2), Jesus tells three parables in order to convey the compassionate and merciful character of God. God is like a shepherd who seeks the lost sheep and, upon finding it, places it with love and concern on his shoulders (15:3-7).[48] God is also like a woman who 'seeks diligently' for what she has lost (15:8-10). And most famously, God is like the father of the 'prodigal son'. First, the father endures his youngest son's ungrateful demand for his inheritance and his leaving home.[49] When the prodigal repents and seeks to be accepted back as a servant, the father's character emerges even more clearly.[50] The father catches sight of the son because he has been peering down the road, longing for the latter's return. Upon seeing the son, he feels compassion and, casting aside dignity and propriety, runs to embrace and kiss him, thereby signifying forgiveness. Furthermore, the father calls for a robe, ring, and sandals for his son, thereby indicating his restored status in the family. Lastly, the father calls for a lavish feast to celebrate the prodigal's return home. The Lukan Jesus thus presents God as marked by compassion. Jesus also embodies this compassion of God through his table fellowship with tax collectors and sinners (5:27-32) and his merciful regard for those who repent (7:36-50). And as was the case with the first example, Jesus reveals God's merciful character in order to exhort his followers to become merciful as God is (6:36) – even to the point of extending mercy to strangers (10:30-37).

The first epistemological implication to observe from the preceding paragraphs concerns the possibilities and limitations of natural theology. On the one hand, the Lukan Paul's sermons in Lystra and Athens suggest that, by observing the contingency of nature as well as its being continually sustained, people ought to be able to reason their way to 'the living God'. That is, Paul homes in on the possibility of reasoning based on the relationship of the creator to creation. On the other hand, Luke strongly suggests that such knowledge of God is insufficient. Generations of Gentiles wandered in error in 'times of ignorance' (Acts 14:16; 17:30). Luke would seemingly concur with the following assessment of Aquinas:

> Even as regards those truths about God which human reason could have discovered, it was necessary that man should be taught by a divine revelation; because the truth about God such as reason could discover, would only be known by a few, and that after a long time, and with the admixture of many errors.[51]

---

[48] Again, a comparison with Matthew is enlightening. Matthew 18:10–14 omits the detail of the shepherd lifting the sheep to his shoulders.

[49] As E. Schweizer comments, the father's 'powerlessness' here is actually a manifestation his of love, which does not coerce. See *The Good News according to Luke*, D.E. Green (tr.) (Atlanta: John Knox, 1984), 250.

[50] Here I follow the analysis of R.A. Culpepper, 'The Gospel of Luke: Introduction, Commentary, and Reflections', in L.E. Keck *et al.* (eds.), *The New Interpreter's Bible*, 12 vols. (Nashville: Abingdon, 1994–2002), 9:302–3.

[51] *S.T.*, 1.1.1. Quoted from *Summa Theologica*, 1.1.

Moreover, it was not just Gentiles who erred. In his speech to the Jews in Solomon's Portico (Acts 3:12-26), Peter acknowledges that they and their rulers acted in ignorance (3:17) when they put Jesus – 'the author of Life' (3:14) – to death. Thus not even those who had access to Scripture were initially able to understand God's self-revelation through Jesus and the unfolding of God's plan of salvation.[52] Indeed, the fulfillment of this plan through Jesus' suffering, death, and resurrection far exceeds the ability of reason alone to attain. This observation leads to a second implication.

Luke-Acts makes clear that God's self-revelation through Jesus can only be received and appropriated by *faith*. In the gospel Luke's use of *pist-* terminology pertains mostly to the attitude of those who approach Jesus for healing. Their faith involves not only recognizing the power of God at work in Jesus; it also entails trusting in Jesus to exercise that power for healing and life (cf. Lk 5:20; 7:9; 7:50; 8:48; 8:50; 17:19; 18:42). Indeed, it is for a lack of such trust that Jesus chides the disciples in 8:25. In Acts Luke employs *pist-* terminology to convey people's response to the apostles' preaching about God's offer of salvation through the life, death, and resurrection of Jesus (e.g. Acts 2:44; 4:4; 4:32; 8:12; 10:43) – the one whom God has made 'Lord' and 'Messiah' (2:36). This response of faith involves not only believing what God has done in and through Jesus; it also entails opening oneself to receive the Holy Spirit (cf. 10:44). In addition, Luke suggests in his second volume that the act of faith is inextricably bound up with *metanoia* (Acts 20:21). In fact, the turning point in Paul's speech in the Areopagus is his announcement of God's call to repent in 17:30. Prior to this point, the Lukan Paul's sermon can be categorized as natural theology (17:24-29). The call to repentance, however, leads to the proclamation of the gospel (17:31), and the only appropriate response to this kergyma is faith (17:34).[53]

IV – The Importance of Prayer for Knowing God's Will

The act of repentance within the response of faith illustrates that God's self-revelation has practical ramifications. So too does the point made above that Jesus reveals God's character in order to encourage his disciples to take on that character. In this final, and necessarily brief, section I turn to another practical implication: the role of prayer in determining God's will.

As the only Son of the Father (Lk 10:22), Jesus can uniquely reveal who God is. But Jesus is also 'son of Adam' (3:38), and as such serves as an exemplar of authentic human existence lived in faithful obedience to God. Throughout the gospel

---

[52] This, of course, jibes with what we saw in the second section above, namely that it is only through the Holy Spirit that Scripture is correctly interpreted and understood.

[53] I have purposely avoided the usual distinction made between reason and faith couched exclusively in cognitive terms. See e.g., the discussion in A.R. Jonsen, 'Faith: Patristic Tradition and Teaching of the Church', in *New Catholic Encyclopedia*, 15 vols. (Washington: The Catholic University of America, 2003²), 5:593–95, here 594–95. Faith for Luke involves more than an assent of the intellect.

Luke portrays Jesus as praying before pivotal moments of his ministry. In 3:21-22, immediately after his baptism and while at prayer, Jesus experiences the empowerment of the Spirit and hears God call him 'beloved Son'.[54] In 4:1-2 Jesus prays and fasts for forty days in the wilderness, and in doing so receives the wherewithal to withstand the devil's temptations and remain faithful to God.[54] In 6:12 Jesus prays all night before selecting his twelve apostles, an event that has great significance for Luke.[55] In 9:18 Jesus prays before solemnly declaring for the first time in the gospel that he must suffer and be put to death. A few verses later, in 9:28-29, while at prayer on a mountain, Jesus' appearance is transfigured in glory, and he discusses with Moses and Elijah his 'exodus' that will be accomplished in Jerusalem.[56] In 11:1, after spending time in prayer, Jesus teaches his followers to pray for the coming of God's kingdom which, as the Matthean version of the Lord's Prayer makes explicit, is tantamount to praying 'thy will be done' (Mt 6:10). In 22:41-42, on the night before he is put to death, Jesus prays that God's will be done. Finally, in 23:46 Jesus commits his life into God's hands. Luke's portrayal of Jesus at prayer emphasizes the latter's discerning God's will and receiving empowerment to faithfully obey.

The dynamic of prayer leading to people knowing and doing God's will continues in Luke's second volume. In Acts 1:13-14 the eleven apostles (sans Judas Iscariot), Jesus' mother, and certain other disciples are described as being devoted to prayer as they await the gift of the Spirit at Pentecost. In 1:24-25 they pray for guidance in choosing Judas's replacement in order to reconstitute 'the twelve'.[57] The monumental encounter between Cornelius and Peter is instigated by the inspiration and insight that both men receive in prayer: Cornelius in 10:1-6; Peter in 10:9-16 (cf. 11:5-17). This encounter, as we have seen, leads to the crucial decision made at the Council of Jerusalem. In 13:2-3, while at prayer, the prophets and teachers in the church in Antioch are led by the Spirit to send Barnabas and Paul on their first missionary journey. In fact, throughout his missionary labors, Paul is led to key decisions in moments of prayer. In 22:17-21 he testifies that his call to bring the

---

[54] Talbert astutely observes that '[f]rom the evangelist's perspective, Jesus is victorious in temptation because the empowering of the Holy Spirit enables him to hear Scripture's word addressed to his immediate needs.' See *Reading Luke*, 45. Such hearing is possible because implicit here is that Jesus is at prayer. Indeed, this passage evokes the stories of Moses (Ex 34:28) and Elijah (1 Kg 19:5-8), both of whom fasted for forty days in connection with a special encounter with God.

[55] The 'twelve apostles', as is often noted, play a crucial role in Luke's two-volume narrative. Not only do they symbolize the 'new Israel'; they are also the thread of continuity in the fulfillment of God's promises to Israel through the coming of Jesus, the gift of the Spirit, and the spread of the gospel to the Gentiles. Whereas the word 'apostle' rarely appears in the other three gospels, it occurs six times in Luke's gospel and twenty-eight times in Acts.

[56] This passage sets in motion Luke's lengthy treatment of Jesus' journey from Galilee to Jerusalem (9:51–10:44), a section that contains many of the latter's teachings that are found only in Luke's gospel (e.g. 10:25–37; 15:11-32; 16:11–19).

[57] See note 55 for the importance of 'the twelve' for Luke.

gospel to the Gentiles became clear to him at prayer. In 16:9-10 Paul receives a vision to take the gospel into Macedonia, while in 18:9-10 he is encouraged to persevere in his ministry at Corinth. Moreover, similar to Jesus, Paul is made aware that he must suffer (20:23). And in 23:11 he receives the risen Lord's encouragement and commission to proclaim the gospel in Rome (cf. 27:23-24).[58] In short, major characters in Acts receive practical guidance and empowerment while at prayer.

Luke's treatment of the efficacy of prayer has epistemological implications. First, the third evangelist suggests that God's revelation not only involves larger theological issues (such as those handled in the first three sections of this essay); revelation can also pertain to what is appropriately called '*practical* knowledge'. The revelation of God's will through prayer certainly occurs at pivotal moments in the narrative of Luke-Acts (e.g., important decisions made by Jesus and later by the apostles). Characters in Acts, moreover, come to prayerfully discern God's will in 'nitty-gritty' contexts: How do we distribute possessions (2:42-47; 4:32-37)? How do we take care of widows (6:1-6)? How do we promote table fellowship between Jews and Gentiles (15:19-21)? Second, observe that Luke connects the act of prayer with fasting and almsgiving. For example, in Acts 13:2-3 the Holy Spirit illuminates leaders of the church in Antioch as they both fast and pray. And in 10:1-2 Luke strongly intimates that Cornelius's almsgiving and constant prayer facilitate his openness to receiving a vision from an angel of God. Luke thereby suggests that, in addition to prayer, the pious practices of fasting and almsgiving help to make one more amenable to receiving insight into God's will. Third, Luke's portrayal of Jesus and the early church at prayer indicates that prayer involves more than just receiving knowledge of God's will. Jesus' teaching in Luke 12:47-48 – concerning those who know God's will but do not act accordingly – makes clear that knowledge alone does not suffice to produce proper behavior. In his own way, then, Luke weighs in on the age-old debate about the lack of congruence that exists at times between one's knowledge of what is good and the actions that one performs (or fails to perform).[59] According to the third evangelist, in addition to providing illumination, prayer supplies the wherewithal to *act* according to God's will. Thus Luke's 'prayer epistemology' touches not only the human intellect but also the human will.[60]

---

[58] Admittedly, Luke does not always explicitly state that Paul is at prayer at each of these moments. The third evangelist, however, has already shown that God grants 'visions' (*horamata*) to people at prayer (10:1–3; cf. 10:9–11). In connection with the former passage, Wall extrapolates the following Lukan principle: 'God responds to Cornelius's prayers with a vision. The missionary function of visions in Acts is to locate a person in the right place at the right time in order to receive God's benefaction.' See 'The Acts of the Apostles', 163.

[59] For both a brief sketch of the debate between Plato and Aristotle on the issue of 'weakness of will' and a concise treatment of Aquinas's explanation, see T.D. Stegman, 'Saint Thomas Aquinas and the Problem of *Akrasia*', *The Modern Schoolman* 66 (1989), 117–28.

[60] To be sure, much more can be said about 'prayer epistemology' in Luke. For instance, Bartholomew and Holt astutely observe that Luke suggests that it is only through Jesus' own prayer that his disciples are able to recognize his true identity. See 'Prayer in/and the Drama of Redemption in Luke', 356. Thus Jesus as intercessor – during both his earthly ministry

Conclusion

Luke's two-volume work does in fact raise many epistemological questions and issues: what constitutes 'certainty'; the use of narrative – particularly, an 'orderly' account of *salvation history* – in setting forth truth; the primacy of Scripture as a source of knowledge; the role played by the Holy Spirit in the correct interpretation and appropriation of Scripture; the possibilities and limitations of natural theology; the preeminence of Jesus in God's self-revelation; the necessity of faith for receiving God's self-revelation through Jesus; and the importance of prayer for both coming to know and then acting on God's will. If one were to seek a unifying thread in a 'Lukan epistemology', one such thread is the Holy Spirit. The Spirit directs the course of events 'in order' (*kathexēs*), making possible Luke's inculcation of *asphaleia* (e.g. Acts 10-15). The Spirit is both the source of inspiration of Scripture (Acts 1:16) and the means of properly understanding it (e.g. Acts 2:1-4, 16-21). It is by the Holy Spirit that Jesus, who is God's unsurpassable self-revelation to humanity, is conceived (Lk 1:35) and led throughout his life and ministry (e.g., Lk 4:1, 14). The Spirit enables people to receive the gospel message in faith (Acts 10:44; 11:15-17). And it is the Spirit who communicates to people in prayer, offering illumination and power (e.g., Acts 4:31; 20:23). Indeed, the Spirit in Luke-Acts resembles the description of 'the Spirit of God' found in Isaiah 11:2:

> the Spirit of wisdom (*sophia*) and understanding (*synesis*),
> the Spirit of counsel (*boulē*) and strength (*ischys*),
> the Spirit of knowledge (*gnōsis*) and piety (*eusebeia*).

The prominence of the Spirit for a Lukan epistemology has implications for philosophers in terms of both the knowing subject and what is potentially knowable. Concerning the human person as 'knower', it is insufficient to refer solely to traditional epistemic powers or 'faculties' such as sensation, cognition, and intuition. An adequate philosophical anthropology also has to account for the 'faculty' of the knower that is capable of enlightenment by God's Spirit. In this vein, Paul's description of human beings as comprised of 'spirit (*pneuma*) and soul (*psychē*) and body (*sōma*)' in 1 Thessalonians 5:23 has relevance insofar as the 'spirit' is understood here as that aspect of humanity which is open to the illuminating and empowering actions of the Holy Spirit. Concerning that which is potentially knowable (i.e., objective knowledge), a Lukan epistemology suggests that the fullness of this knowledge entails not only persons, things, events, etc., but also the significance of such persons, things, and events in light of the divine plan for salvation. That is, full knowledge of this type requires discerning the Spirit's presence and revelatory impetus. Moreover, because the Spirit always moves ahead

---

(see Lk 9:18-20) and now in his existence as risen Lord – mediates correct perception of who he is and his significance for our salvation. Of course, the appropriation of this knowledge requires receptivity on the part of Jesus' followers (then and today), a receptivity that includes prayerful listening to and reflection on Scripture.

of the church – leading it forward according to God's will and redemptive mission – constant discernment is required to follow the Spirit's lead.

Granted the need for such ongoing discernment, a second unifying thread of a Lukan epistemology is prayer. By prayer I refer (at least in part) to a quiet, reverent posture of openness before God in order to listen to the divine Word and to observe the movements of the Spirit. Prayer opens the human spirit to the presence and activity of the divine Spirit. Through prayer individuals and communities come to greater knowledge of God's self-revelation, of God's saving actions in and through Jesus, and of God's will for them to participate in the ongoing work of redemption. Such knowledge is *transformative* of individuals and communities as they become protagonists and agents in the unfolding story of salvation. Thus, if the Lukan epistemology as set forth above has any merit, then I submit that philosophers need to seriously consider that, while the private study and classroom are necessary places wherein to conduct philosophical inquiry, the oratory and sanctuary are even more indispensable.

Bibliography

Aquinas, T., *Summa Theologica*, English Province Dominicans (tr.), 5 vols. (Westminster, MD: Christian Classics, 1981)

Barrett, C.K., *The Acts of the Apostles*, 2 vols., International Critical Commentary (Edinburgh: T & T Clark, 1994–98)

Bartholomew, C.G. and R. Holt, 'Prayer in/and the Drama of Redemption in Luke', in C.G. Bartholomew, J.B. Green, and A.C. Thiselton (eds.), *Reading Luke: Interpretation, Reflection, Formation*, Scripture and Hermeneutic Series 6 (Milton Keynes: Paternoster/ Grand Rapids, MI: Zondervan, 2005), 350-75

Bovon, F., *A Commentary on the Gospel of Luke 1:1–9:50*, Hermeneia, C.M. Thomas (tr.) (Minneapolis: Fortress, 2002)

Bultmann, R., *Theology of the New Testament*, K. Grobel (tr.), 2 vols. (New York: Scribner's, 1951–55)

Culpepper, R.A., 'The Gospel of Luke: Introduction, Commentary, and Reflections,' in L.E. Keck *et al.* (eds.), *The New Interpreter's Bible*, 12 vols. (Nashville: Abingdon, 1994–2002), 9:1-490

Dillon, R.J., 'Previewing Luke's Project from His Prologue (Luke 1:1-4)', *Catholic Biblical Quarterly* 43 (1981), 205–27

Fitzmyer, J.A., *The Acts of the Apostles*, Anchor Bible 31 (New York: Doubleday, 1998)

_____, *The Gospel according to Luke*, 2 vols., Anchor Bible 28–28A (New York: Doubleday, 1981–85)

Jonsen, A.R., 'Faith: Patristic Tradition and Teaching of the Church', in *New Catholic Encyclopedia*, 15 vols. (Washington: The Catholic University of America, 2003[2]), 5:593–95

Johnson, L.T., *The Acts of the Apostles*, Sacra Pagina 5 (Collegeville, MN: The Liturgical Press, 1992)

_____, *The Gospel of Luke*, Sacra Pagina 3 (Collegeville, MN: The Liturgical Press, 1991)

_____, *Scripture & Discernment: Decision Making in the Church* (Nashville: Abingdon, 1996)

_____, *Septuagintal Midrash in the Speeches of Acts* (Milwaukee: Marquette University Press, 2002)

Pontifical Biblical Commission, *The Interpretation of the Bible in the Church* (Boston: St. Paul Books and Media, 1993)

Rollins, C.D., 'Certainty,' in P. Edwards (ed.), *The Encyclopedia of Philosophy*, 8 vols. (New York: Macmillan, 1967), 2:67-71

Schweizer, E., *The Good News According to Luke*, D.E. Green (tr.) (Atlanta: John Knox, 1984)

Stegman, T.D., 'Saint Thomas Aquinas and the Problem of *Akrasia*', *The Modern Schoolman* 66 (1989), 117–28

Talbert, C.H., *Reading Acts: A Literary and Theological Commentary on the Acts of the Apostles* (New York: Crossroad, 1997)

_____, *Reading Luke: A Literary and Theological Commentary on the Third Gospel* (New York: Crossroad, 1982)

Tannehill, R.C., *Luke*, Abingdon New Testament Commentaries (Nashville: Abingdon, 1996)

_____, *The Narrative Unity of Luke-Acts: A Literary Interpretation*, 2 vols., Foundations and Facets (Philadelphia: Fortress, 1986–90)

Wall, R.W., 'The Acts of the Apostles: Introduction, Commentary, and Reflections' in L.E. Keck *et al.* (eds.), *The New Interpreter's Bible*, 12 vols. (Nashville: Abingdon, 1994–2002), 10:1-368

Wright, N.T., *Paul: In Fresh Perspective* (London: SPCK/ Minneapolis: Fortress, 2005)

CHAPTER 6

Christ, the Spirit and the Knowledge of God: A Study in Johannine Epistemology

Cornelis Bennema

Introduction

Contemporary Christian philosophers and theologians have devoted considerable time to the study of epistemology, but biblical scholars have largely neglected the subject. As a consequence, Christian philosophical and theological examinations of human knowledge often draw only superficially upon Scripture. In fact, I am aware of only a few contributions to the subject of Johannine epistemology – the focus of this study – but these are inadequate in that they deal only with certain aspects of John's epistemology, and especially the crucial role of the Spirit has been neglected.[1] This chapter seeks to address this problem in a wider perspective and against the background of contemporary questions in epistemology.

The aim of this study is to elucidate the epistemology of the Johannine literature in relation to its theology and in particular its soteriology, since the purpose of both the gospel and the epistles is soteriological (Jn 20:30-31; 1 Jn 5:13). Our task is simply to *infer* an epistemology from the Johannine literature that is based on Johannine words, themes and concepts, which we might then call a 'Johannine' epistemology. The key questions we will address are as follows: Can people know God? What hides knowledge of God from people? How does God make himself known? How does one acquire knowledge of God? What are the roles of Jesus and

---

[1] M.R. Ely, *Knowledge of God in Johannine Thought* (New York: Macmillan, 1925); I. de la Potterie, '*Oida* et *ginōskō*: Les deux modes de la connaissance dans le quatrième évangile', *Biblica* 40 (1959), 709-25; J. Gaffney, 'Believing and Knowing in the Fourth Gospel', *TS* 26 (1965), 215-41; J. Painter, 'Johannine Symbols: A Case Study in Epistemology', *JTSA* 27 (1979), 26-41; J.H. Neyrey, 'John III: A Debate over Johannine Epistemology and Christology', *NovT* 23 (1981), 115-27; *idem*, 'The Sociology of Secrecy and the Fourth Gospel' in F.F. Segovia (ed.), *What is John? Vol. II: Literary and Social Readings of the Fourth Gospel* (Atlanta: Scholars Press, 1998), 79-109; M.M. Thompson, *The God of the Gospel of John* (Grand Rapids: Eerdmans, 2001), Ch. 3; H.C. Kee, 'Knowing the Truth: Epistemology and Community in the Fourth Gospel' in D.E. Aune, T. Seland and J.H. Ulrichsen (eds.), *Neotestamentica et Philonica: Studies in Honor of Peder Borgen*, NovTSup 106 (Leiden: Brill, 2002), 254-80.

the Spirit in one's knowledge of God? What is the dialectic between knowledge and belief? What is the purpose of knowledge?[2]

Regarding the scope of this study, we shall investigate primarily the Gospel of John but also consider the Johannine Epistles.[3] Further, although epistemology *per se* is concerned with both how we know what we do and what justifies us in believing what we do, this study will only consider the former, i.e., we will examine the Johannine concept of knowledge rather than the justification of that knowledge. Moreover, we will not explore John's concept of general knowledge but, more specifically, the knowledge *of God* (i.e., about God). Finally, besides divine revelation as the main source of knowledge of God for John, we will also consider human perception as a source of knowledge, especially since visual, aural and cognitive perception are common in the Johannine literature.[4]

We will first delineate the Johannine epistemic language and the method we shall follow in section I. The epistemic themes that are defined in section I will be arranged under three major headings, forming sections II-IV respectively. In section II it is argued that the human condition of epistemic darkness is matched by a divine response of illuminating revelation. However, as section III explains, an escape from this darkness by a proper human response of belief to this divine initiative can only be achieved with further divine help in the form of the Spirit as a cognitive agent. In section IV we will demonstrate that being in a saving relationship with the Father and Son, the believer has ongoing access to further knowledge, and the Spirit continues to provide cognitive assistance. After having presented these main aspects of John's epistemology, section V will attempt to explain the dialectic between knowledge and belief, and section VI will then formulate a coherent Johannine epistemology. Finally, we shall summarize our findings and draw some conclusions.

Since certain terminology shall be used in this study in slightly specialized ways to make appropriate distinctions, we employ the following definitions:[5] 'sensory perception' describes the activity of becoming aware of something through the senses; 'cognitive perception' is the conscious mental activity or process of

---

[2] Since John writes from within a theistic worldview, we are not concerned with questions regarding God's existence.

[3] Although we remain agnostic whether the gospel and the epistles of John have common authorship (an author we call 'John'), the similarities in language, style and theology suggest that they at least belong to the same school of thought. The limitations of our study prevent us from indulging in the possible environments of John's epistemology, but for a plausible Jewish wisdom background, see C. Bennema, *The Power of Saving Wisdom: An Investigation of Spirit and Wisdom in Relation to the Soteriology of the Fourth Gospel*, WUNT II/148 (Tübingen: Mohr Siebeck, 2002), Ch. 2.

[4] Other sources of knowledge are testimony, memory, consciousness and reason. See R. Audi, *Epistemology: A Contemporary Introduction to the Theory of Knowledge* (London/New York: Routledge, 1998), Chs. 2-5. We refer to testimony and memory in fn. 42 and fn. 49 respectively, and consciousness and reason come partly under our concept of cognitive perception.

[5] Section I shows that these definitions are based on Johannine words.

acquiring and evaluating information and understanding through thought/reason, experience and sensory perception in order to determine the meaning and significance of what is perceived; 'truth' is conformity with reality, and, particularly for John, 'truth' is the divine reality – the reality of God and divine things. This study upholds a distinction in the definition of belief by contemporary epistemologists and by John. Epistemology in general defines 'belief' as 'accepting a particular proposition as true', whereas Johannine 'belief' (which Christians generally call 'faith') *also* connotes (as we will see) personal allegiance to Jesus and following him as a disciple.[6] Hence, we shall use 'to believe' and 'belief' in our chapter in this Johannine sense. The word 'adequate' is used to qualify knowledge and belief as both authentic (true, valid, genuine) *and* sufficiently salvific. Finally, we use the term 'agent' to refer to someone who produces or causes an effect.

I – John's Epistemic Language

One approach to defining the semantic domain of Johannine epistemology would simply be to identify all the individual Johannine words with epistemological under- and overtones. A possible danger of this approach, however, is that we may read meaning into these words that is foreign to John or overlook their interrelationship in John's thought. Nor do we want to engage in diachronic word studies, since the etymology of a word is not necessarily the hermeneutical key to its meaning.[7] We thus propose another, more comprehensive method, namely, a thematic and conceptual synchronic approach to the Johannine epistemic language. That is, we shall identify within the Johannine literature epistemic themes and concepts (which are naturally made up of individual words) as the main building blocks. This approach has two advantages. First, as just indicated, a primarily synchronic approach is a safer road to John's thought world. Second, context rather than individual words produces meaning, and hence we choose themes and concepts as the context for words to understand John's epistemology.

We have identified the following main epistemic themes and their associated Greek terms:[8]

1. epistemic darkness (*skotia, skotos, tuphlos, tuphloun, ou ginōskein/eidenai, ou katalambanein, ou blepein/horan/theōrein/theasthai, ouk akouein, ou noein*)
2. illumination/enlightenment (*phōs, phainein, phōtizein*)
3. Jesus' revelation/teaching (*exēgeisthai, emphanizein, phaneroun, gnōrizein, anaggellein, didaskein, didaskalos, didachē*)

---

[6] Without intending a difference in meaning, we prefer the categories 'to believe' and 'belief' rather than 'to have faith' and 'faith', partly because John exclusively uses the verb *pisteuein* and never the noun *pistis* (except for 1 Jn 5:4).

[7] This point has been made clear by J. Barr, *The Semantics of Biblical Language* (Oxford: OUP, 1961).

[8] We do not claim to be exhaustive in our themes or that these words do not have other denotations and connotations, but merely elucidate their *epistemic* dimension.

4. saving truth (*alētheia*)
5. sensory perception (*blepein, horan, theōrein, theasthai, akouein*)
6. cognitive perception and understanding (*ginōskein, eidenai, mimnēskesthai, mnēmoneuein, eraunan, noein*)
7. the Spirit as a cognitive agent
8. people's response (*pisteuein, pistos, [para]lambanein*)
9. the relationship between the Father and Son
10. the relationship of the believer with the Father and Son (*koinōnia, philos, hen einai, menei en*).

These epistemic themes can subsequently be grouped in the following thematic clusters or concepts: (i) people's epistemic darkness and Jesus' illuminating revelation (themes 1-4); (ii) people's perception of, and responses to, Jesus' revelation, and the assistance of the Spirit (themes 5-8); (iii) people's epistemic relationship with the Father and Son (themes 9-10). After having done the groundwork, we are now in a position to flesh out these concepts in the following three sections.

II – Epistemic Darkness and Illuminating Revelation

This section examines John's understanding of the human epistemic condition and the divine response to it. Regarding the human condition, the Prologue already introduces this theme, which is not surprising since the Prologue sets the agenda for the rest of the gospel (as most scholars agree). The darkness in 1:5 can be understood, *inter alia*, as an *epistemic* darkness since the verb *katalambanein* can either mean 'to overcome, overpower' or 'to comprehend, understand'. We do not need to choose between these potential meanings; this word is an example of John's literary technique of *double entendre*.[9] That the epistemic denotation of *katalambanein* is also in view is clear from the context, which speaks about witnessing, (not) knowing, accepting and believing (1:6-13). This cognitive darkness is a characterization of the general epistemic human condition. The life-giving Logos-Light came into the world (1:4, 9) but the world did not know him (1:10); the Light shines in the darkness (of the world) but the darkness did not understand or grasp it (1:5).[10] Thus, John's evaluation of the epistemic condition of humanity is a

---

[9] Cf. R. Bultmann, *The Gospel of John*, G.R. Beasley-Murray (tr.) (Philadelphia: Westminster Press, 1971), 48 fn. 1; C.K. Barrett, *The Gospel According to St John* (London: SPCK, 1978[2]), 158; D.A. Carson, *The Gospel According to John* (Leicester: IVP, 1991), 120, 138.

[10] Contra Lesslie Newbigin, *The Open Secret: Sketches for a Missionary Theology* (Grand Rapids: Eerdmans, 1978), 197-99, we take 1:9 as a reference to the incarnation since the context refers respectively to the Baptist's testimony to Jesus (1:6-8) and to people's reaction to Jesus (1:10-13). Cf. C.H. Dodd, *The Interpretation of the Fourth Gospel* (Cambridge: CUP, 1953), 281-84; Barrett, *Gospel*, 160-61; G.R. Beasley-Murray, *John*, WBC 36 (Dallas: Word, 1991), 12. Carson, *Gospel*, 119-22, and Bultmann, *Gospel*, 45-46, even think that 1:5 already refers to the incarnation. Besides, if the Prologue hints at natural revelation in 1:4-5, 9, does John perhaps indicate that all religions contain partial revelation/knowledge of God?

pessimistic one: the world is enveloped in an epistemic darkness, and hence its people reject the Logos-Light (1:11; cf. 3:19-20). Nevertheless, although the world as 'world' may not improve in its condition (3:19; 16:8-11; 1 Jn 2:15-17; 4:1-6),[11] those people who are given to Jesus *from the world* by the Father (17:6)[12] are able (with divine help) to accept and believe in him (e.g., those in 1:12-13, the Twelve, the Samaritan woman). Therefore, John is able to write to the believers in his church(es) that this darkness is passing away (1 Jn 2:8).

The theme of epistemic darkness is also expressed by the concept of 'blindness'. Despite their claim to knowledge (9:24, 29) and 'sight' (9:40-41), the Pharisees are ironically diagnosed with epistemic blindness (9:41). Darkness and blindness are implicitly related in 12:35, in that the person who walks in the darkness does not know where she goes (i.e., she experiences epistemic blindness). In 1 John 2:11, darkness and blindness are explicitly related: (being in) darkness causes spiritual blindness. In fact, the phrase 'to blind the eyes' in 1 John 2:11 and John 12:40 (where it is paralleled by 'to close the heart/mind'), is an idiomatic expression for 'to cause not to understand' and hence denotes epistemic blindness. Those who are in darkness are epistemically blind and need epistemic illumination or enlightenment.

Another way of expressing epistemic deficiency is by a lack of sensory and cognitive perception – people do not 'see', 'hear' (i.e., understand) or know the meaning and significance of Jesus' words. As mentioned above, Jesus' assessment of the Pharisees in 9:39-41 was that they were not able to 'see'. People whose eyes are blinded are not able to 'see'/understand (12:40). In a fierce debate with 'the Jews', Jesus asked them why they were not able to 'hear'/understand his word (8:43; cf. 8:47). As already noted, the world does not have knowledge of Jesus (1:10, 26; 8:14; 9:29; 16:3), or of God (7:28; 8:55; 15:21; 16:3; 17:25; 1 Jn 3:1) or of the Spirit (14:17), nor is it able cognitively to penetrate Jesus' words (8:27, 43; 10:6).

In fact, epistemic darkness or dullness, referring to a lack of *adequate* understanding or knowledge of God and Jesus, is the general condition of the world and its people.[13] Nicodemus, for example, is portrayed as someone who is interested in and sympathetic towards Jesus, yet also as one who is and remains in the darkness (at least on the basis of John 3).[14] Or consider the Jewish religious authorities, who

---

Also, what would this imply for religious pluralism or relativism that says that all religions are equally valid?

[11] 'World' is in some sense personified as the great opponent of Jesus. Cf. H. Sasse, '*Kosmeō, ktl.*' in *TDNT*, 3:894.

[12] Rather than reading a doctrine of predestination or election into John, I suggest that these texts show the priority of divine initiative over human response. Cf. D.A. Carson, *Divine Sovereignty and Human Responsibility: Biblical Perspectives in Tension* (London: Marshall, Morgan & Scott, 1981), Chs. 11-12.

[13] Cf. J.G. van der Watt, 'Salvation in the Gospel According to John' in *idem* (ed.), *Salvation in the New Testament: Perspectives on Soteriology*, NovTSup 121 (Leiden: Brill, 2005), 107.

[14] Note the symbolism of 'by night' in 3:2. For a detailed interpretation of Nicodemus, including the possibility that he made cognitive progression and eventually came to adequate belief, see Bennema, *Power*, 168-81.

become increasingly alienated from Jesus because they are not able to take in his words (6:41, 52; 8:12-59; 10:1-39). Even many of Jesus' own disciples turn their backs on him because they find his teaching too difficult to understand (6:60, 66). Ironically, these people who are entrenched in epistemic darkness nevertheless make claims to knowledge (Nicodemus in 3:2; 'the Jews' in 5:38-40; 6:42; 7:27; 8:54-55; the Pharisees in 9:24, 29). Yet, though the epistemic darkness has been lifted for those who have come to an adequate belief, they do not have perfect knowledge. They still know in part, and misunderstanding or lack of understanding remains. The disciples, for example, continue to struggle in their understanding of Jesus' words (14:9; 16:18; 20:9). Hence, an epistemic 'cloudiness' remains, but they have been sufficiently enlightened to come to a saving knowledge of God.[15]

Why is knowledge of God hidden from people? Why are people not able to 'see', 'hear' and know God/Jesus? John suggests a few reasons. One reason is that, according to John's dualistic worldview, all people belong naturally to the realm below (3:6; 8:23). The person who is 'from below' cannot 'see' God (1:18; 6:46) and does not have the necessary epistemic 'sight' that is needed to enter into the realm above (3:3). People are not able to 'see' and 'hear', i.e., to understand, because they are not from God, they are not 'from above' (3:3; 8:23, 47). There is no natural contact between the two realms (cf. 1:10; 3:6, 31; 14:17; 1 Jn 4:4-6),[16] and therefore Jesus functions as the mediator between them (1:51; 3:13, 31-36). To 'see' the kingdom of God (i.e., to enter into the divine realm of salvation) requires a birth 'from above', a birth of water and Spirit (3:3, 5), and, as we shall see in section III, this epistemic 'sight' is provided by the Spirit. Elsewhere John restates people's inability to 'see' and know God as epistemic blindness and closed hearts (i.e., the minds of some people are closed to cognitive perception and understanding) (12:39-40).[17] Another reason is sin. Part of the work of the Spirit-Paraclete is to convince the world of sin, which is in its very essence disbelief in Jesus (16:8-9).[18] In 8:31-36, Jesus explains that knowledge of the truth will set people free from sin, which implies that sin keeps people from attaining saving knowledge. Moreover, in the

---

[15] Neyrey argues that, even for insiders, there is a hierarchy of knowledge (i.e., various degrees of being 'in the know') ('Sociology', 98-105).

[16] The realm above is characterized by, or as, 'heaven', 'Father', 'Son', 'Spirit', 'revelation', 'knowledge', 'free', 'light', 'love', 'truth', 'life' (1:32; 3:13, 31; 6:38; 12:28). The characteristics of the realm below are 'earth', 'world', 'devil', 'hate', 'sin', 'death', 'evil', 'lies', 'darkness', 'flesh', 'slave' (3:19, 31; 8:23, 44; 12:35; 17:16, 25; 1 Jn 3:1).

[17] John 12:39-40 is probably not a description of the *general* epistemic condition of humankind (although lack of perception and knowledge of the divine is a general condition of people), but, more specifically, the condition of those who *oppose* Jesus. This passage, then, may simply refer to the resulting condition and inevitable consequence of rejecting Jesus rather than the result of divine predestination: by rejecting Jesus one *remains* blind (cf. 9:39-41).

[18] We take *hoti* as explicative rather than causal. Cf. M. Turner, *The Holy Spirit and Spiritual Gifts: Then and Now* (Carlisle: Paternoster, 1999 [rev. ed.]), 86-87.

light of 8:34-35 and 15:15, a slave of sin has no knowledge of God. Hence, sin has affected the intellect in that it has caused epistemic darkness.[19]

The divine response to the epistemic darkness of people is light or epistemic illumination. The Logos-Light came into the darkness to enlighten people by revealing the Father (1:4-5, 9, 18).[20] This theme is later developed as Jesus is portrayed as the life-giving light of the dark world (8:12; 9:5; 12:35-36, 46). But how, and in what way, is Jesus the light of the world? We suggest that Jesus is the light of the world precisely in his capacity of revealer. The world's problem is that it does not have (adequate) knowledge of God and hence remains in darkness, but Jesus' illuminating revelation expels darkness and gives life. Jesus can be the perfect revealer of divine reality because: (i) he has an intimate relationship with the Father (1:18), including a sharing of knowledge (10:15); (ii) he has open access to heaven/revelation (1:51; 3:12-13); (iii) he only reveals what he sees the Father doing and hears the Father speaking (3:32; 5:19; 8:26, 28; 15:15); (iv) he is endowed with the Spirit, which is primarily an empowerment of revelatory wisdom to reveal God (1:32; 3:34).[21] In his revelatory teaching, Jesus reveals the Father and himself in terms of their identity, character, mission and the nature of their relationship.[22] Jesus often uses mundane objects (bread, water, light, etc.) as symbols in his teaching to point to a deeper reality. John thus employs a *symbolic epistemology* as a response to the problem of human epistemic darkness, in that the Johannine symbols are the key to knowing Jesus and hence God.[23]

In presenting Jesus and his revelation as the key to knowing God, John introduces a significant epistemological paradigm shift. For Judaism at large, the source of knowledge of God was the law, and the Gospel of John reflects this understanding (5:39; 7:49; 9:28-29). With the coming of Jesus, however, the epistemic foundation for knowing God has now become Jesus himself and the revelation he brought.[24] For John, then, the main source of knowledge of the divine is *Jesus' revelation*, in that knowledge of God is revealed to people in and by Jesus. Hence, Jesus supersedes the law as the epistemic basis for knowledge of the divine (1:17-18; 5:39, 46). Ironically, Jesus points out to 'the Jews' that if their epistemology based on the law

---

[19] In turn, epistemic darkness causes sin to remain (9:41; 15:22). Others also mention some causes/conditions of not believing/knowing (e.g., Gaffney 'Believing', 233-35; Neyrey, 'Sociology', 97).

[20] In 1:9, *phōtizein* means 'to illuminate', 'to give understanding'. The verb *exēgeisthai* ('to make fully known') in 1:18 has the connotation of 'to reveal'.

[21] Concerning the last point, see fn. 35 below.

[22] Since Jesus' revelation and teaching are inextricably linked we do not make a significant distinction between them. Bultmann and others have argued that there is little or no definable content to Jesus' revelation/teaching (Jesus merely reveals that he is the Revealer) but this contention is mistaken (Bennema, *Power*, 117-20). Jesus' signs also have a revelatory character. They reveal, for example, Jesus' identity (6:14; 7:31), aspects of his character (2:11), and the nature of his relationship with the Father (10:38; 14:11).

[23] See especially Painter, 'Symbols', for the epistemic potential of Johannine symbols.

[24] Cf. Painter, 'Symbols', 34.

had been correct, they would have been able to make this new epistemological shift, since the law points to Jesus (5:39-40, 46-47; 7:19). However, as it is, this shift was too scandalous for many, as the growing opposition to Jesus and his claims demonstrates (e.g., 6:41, 52, 60, 66; 7:1, 32; 8:31-59).

Although it is evident *that* Jesus' revelation/teaching illuminates and gives life (e.g., 4:1-42; 5:24; 6:63, 68), it is less clear *why* this is so. We suggest that Jesus' revelation is life-giving because it contains saving truth which may result in saving knowledge. In 8:31-36, Jesus states that his teaching contains truth that will set people free from sin. Moreover, Jesus speaks God's words, which are truth that purifies (3:34; 17:17; Cf. 15:3). Thus, Jesus communicates divine truth through his teaching, and knowledge of this truth will liberate (8:26, 31-32, 40). Besides, 17:3 explains that eternal life is (the result of) knowledge of the divine, which comes from accepting Jesus' teaching (17:8). In other words, truth is the reality of God and divine things, which is revealed to the world in and by Jesus; truth is the saving content or aspect of Jesus' revelatory teaching.[25] Knowledge of the truth is salvific because it is knowledge of the identity, character, work and relationship of the Father and Son, and this knowledge *of God* will prepare a person to become *from God* (see section III). It must be noted that this knowledge is *revealed* knowledge (i.e., it cannot be achieved by human experience or reason alone, cf. 1:18; 15:15; 17:6-8).

Conclusion

The world is enclosed in epistemic darkness; people do not have (saving) knowledge of God. The reason for this epistemic darkness is that people do not belong to the realm of God and cannot access this divine realm. The solution, then, must come from the realm above, and the divine response to this crisis is illuminating revelation. The Logos-Light enlightens the epistemic darkness through his revelation of God (in terms of the identity, character, mission and relationship of the Father and Son). Thus, for John, the primary source of knowledge of God is divine revelation, presented as Jesus' person and his teaching. This revelatory teaching contains saving truth or knowledge of the divine, and for those who accept this revelation, the darkness is passing away.[26] Nevertheless, the acceptance of Jesus and his revelation requires cognitive effort, and the question is whether people are up to this task. To this issue we now turn.

---

[25] If Jesus as the Word is full of truth (1:14) then probably his words are also. Cf. I. de la Potterie, 'The Truth in Saint John' in J. Ashton (ed.), *The Interpretation of John* (London: SPCK, 1986), 54-57. For the concept of knowing the truth as a mode of behaviour within the community of faith, see Kee's article 'Truth'.

[26] Interestingly, the Old Testament prophets also attribute Israel's exile and spiritual bankruptcy to her lack and rejection of knowledge (of Yahweh) (Is 1:3; 5:13; 56:10-11; Jer 8:7; 9:3, 6; 14:18; Hos 4:1, 6; 5:4). However, they could also describe Israel's restoration in terms of, or in relation to, knowledge (Is 11:9; 33:6; 43:10; 60:16; Jer 3:15; 24:7; 31:34). Not surprisingly, then, the envisaged Messiah is expected to be endowed with revelatory knowledge (Is 11:2; 53:11).

III – Human Response and Further Divine Help

This section elucidates the Johannine view of human sensory perception, cognitive perception and belief, and the concept of the Spirit as an epistemic agent. John's categories of 'seeing' and 'hearing' operate on two levels: at one level, people literally hear Jesus' words and see his signs; at another level, people are invited to perceive and understand the spiritual reality or significance of what is seen and heard (e.g., 3:3; 5:24-25; 8:47; 14:9).[27] Similarly, the verbs *ginōskein* and *eidenai* can simply mean 'to know, to have knowledge of', but in John, they frequently denote 'to understand', 'to perceive' (e.g., 1:48; 2:25; 5:42; 6:15; 8:43; 13:12; 17:3; 20:9; 21:17).[28] Thus, the cognitive penetration of the deeper, spiritual significance of what has been heard and seen should result in an adequate understanding or knowledge of the Father and Son.

In reality, however, people struggle to understand, misunderstand or fail to understand.[29] Nicodemus, for example, misunderstands *anōthen* as 'again' instead of 'from above' (3:3-4), and he fails to understand the meaning of the birth of water-and-Spirit (3:5-10). It is clear that Nicodemus has a cognitive problem – he does not understand Jesus' revelation.[30] In John 4, the Samaritan woman also struggles for understanding but she makes, with Jesus' help, such cognitive progression that she acquires saving knowledge of Jesus and even brings her own people to him.[31] After a long struggle to understand Jesus' words, 'the Jews' essentially fail to understand and reject Jesus (6:41-59; 8:31-59; 10:1-39). Even many of Jesus' 'disciples' find his teaching too demanding, and probably also too difficult to penetrate, and they defect (6:60-66). Because of this lack of understanding and cognitive inability, people are

---

[27] Cf. Thompson, *God*, 105-17, 142, for the concept of 'seeing' God in Jesus, although she may have over-emphasized 'seeing' at the expense of 'hearing'. Besides, Thompson does not explain that the Spirit provides true epistemic 'seeing'. C.R. Koester, however, over-emphasizes the concept of 'hearing' at the cost of 'seeing' ('Hearing, Seeing, and Believing in the Gospel of John', *Biblica* 70 [1989], 327-48).

[28] Cf. the semantic domains of *ginōskein* and *eidenai* in the Louw-Nida lexicon. John does not differentiate between these two verbs (contra de la Potterie, '*Oida*', 709-25).

[29] In John, misunderstanding functions as a hermeneutical device: the misunderstanding of the character in the story and Jesus' subsequent explanation benefits the reader. See esp. D.A. Carson, 'Understanding Misunderstandings in the Fourth Gospel', *TB* 33 (1982), 59-91; R.A. Culpepper, *Anatomy of the Fourth Gospel: A Study in Literary Design* (Philadelphia: Fortress Press, 1987), 152-65.

[30] Neyrey observes that Jesus' statement in 3:3 is an attack on Nicodemus' knowledge professed in 3:2, and the fact that Nicodemus must *ask a question* in 3:4 demonstrates a lack of certain knowledge ('John III', 119).

[31] For a full elaboration of the story, see Bennema, *Power*, 181-96. We disagree with F.J. Moloney, *The Gospel of John* (Collegeville: Liturgical Press, 1998), 131, who concludes that the Samaritan woman, like Nicodemus, only arrives at a partial faith.

not able to make an adequate belief-response to Jesus; they remain stuck at the level of sensory perception and hence in darkness.[32]

As we saw in the previous section, the problem of this epistemic darkness is that people are 'from below', not from God, and do not know God (8:23, 47, 55; 1 Jn 3:1). People often move merely at an earthly or physical level and are not able to go beyond that. Nicodemus' problem, for instance, is that he is not born 'from above' and therefore does not understand the things 'from above'. Hence, sensory perception (a literal or physical seeing and hearing) needs to be followed or complemented by cognitive perception (a spiritual seeing and hearing that understands the significance of what is literally seen and heard).[33] People are, in fact, challenged to think 'from above'.[34] However, by nature they are not able to do so, and further divine help is needed. What is needed is a cognitive agent 'from above' who can assist people in thinking 'from above' and consequently in accessing the realities 'from above'.

This cognitive or epistemic divine agent is *the Spirit*. The Spirit, according to the Gospel of John, is instrumental in the process of bringing people to knowledge, belief and hence salvation. First, the Spirit provides Jesus with revelatory wisdom and knowledge that probably forms the basis for his teaching/revelation (1:32-34; 3:34-36).[35] Subsequently, the Spirit also actively reaches out to people *through* Jesus' teaching, mediating this saving wisdom or knowledge to people so that they might come to an adequate understanding and belief-response. We must elaborate this latter concept.[36]

---

[32] Neyrey looks at this issue from a different (perhaps complementary) angle. In a sociological analysis of knowledge and secrecy in the Gospel of John, Neyrey argues that information about Jesus is controlled, i.e., only certain people are given selected information about Jesus. According to Neyrey, this secrecy or information control was John's conscious strategy to distinguish between insiders (those 'in the know') and outsiders (those '*not* in the know') in order to provide security for and to classify roles and social standings within the Johannine group ('Sociology', *passim*).

[33] In fact, this concept of a two-level seeing and hearing is confirmed by the semantic domain of *blepein, horan, theōrein, theasthai* and *akouein*, which allows for a connotative meaning of 'to come to understand' (cf. the Louw-Nida lexicon).

[34] This phrase dovetails nicely with the concept of setting one's mind on divine things and of the renewal of the mind in other parts of the New Testament (Mt 16:23; Mk 8:33; Rom 8:5; 12:2; Eph 4:23; Phil 2:5; Col 3:2, 10).

[35] The coming and remaining of the Spirit on Jesus in 1:32 probably alludes to Isaiah 11:2 which describes the Messiah as being empowered with the Spirit of wisdom, understanding, knowledge and liberating power. Subsequently, 3:35 explains that God has given the entire revelation to Jesus, and 3:34 clarifies that Jesus can bring this revelation because he is empowered with the Spirit. The picture that emerges is that Jesus can carry out his salvific ministry of revealing God precisely because the Spirit empowers him with wisdom and knowledge. Thus, Jesus' revelation or teaching is Spirit-provided and Spirit-empowered. See further Bennema, *Power*, 161-67. Cf. Turner, *Spirit*, 57, 60.

[36] For an extensive treatment of the Spirit's cognitive functions, see Bennema, *Power*, Chs. 4-5.

Those people who accept (i.e., believe in) Jesus are born from God and become part of God's family (1:12-13). John 3:3, 5 subsequently elucidates this birth from God as a birth from the Spirit, which alludes to the eschatological cleansing and transformation of Israel that God will bring about by means of his Spirit (Ezek 36:25-27; 37:1-14). When Nicodemus enquires how this new birth into the realm of salvation might be accomplished (3:9), Jesus replies that this will happen through looking in belief at the one lifted up on the cross (3:14-15). However, Jesus also points out in 3:10-13 that Nicodemus has a cognitive problem – he is not able to grasp Jesus' revelation and to respond in belief, which is symbolized by his fading out of the conversation after 3:9. The text seems to imply then that a birth of the Spirit is accomplished through some sort of understanding of Jesus' revelation, especially an understanding of the significance of the cross.[37]

When we recognize the allusions to the Wisdom of Solomon, we can probe further *how* this understanding of the cross and the consequent spiritual birth will come about. First, as Wisdom shows Jacob the kingdom of God (Wis 10:10), so Jesus shows Nicodemus the way to the kingdom of God in 3:3, 5. Second, 3:12 finds a parallel in Wisdom of Solomon 9:16: if 'earthly things' are already difficult to understand, how much more 'heavenly things'? Wisdom of Solomon 9:17-18 goes on to explain that Solomon will only be able to understand the 'heavenly things', and hence experience salvation, if God sends Wisdom and the accompanying Spirit. Coming back to John, if the Spirit is the agent of the birth 'from above' and if this birth requires a true understanding of the cross, then it follows that the Spirit may also provide such saving knowledge. Thus, I suggest that the Spirit facilitates a true understanding of the cross and subsequently a birth into the realm above.

We now turn to Jesus' encounter with the Samaritan woman in John 4, where Jesus is depicted as the source of 'living water' (4:10, 14). Judaism knows of four possible referents for 'living water': (i) life or salvation (Is 12:3; 35:6-7; 55:1-3; Jer 17:13; Zech 14:8); (ii) cleansing or purification (Lev 14:5-6; Num 19:17-19); (iii) the Spirit (Is 44:3); (iv) divine wisdom or teaching (Prov 13:14; 18:4; Is 11:9). It is likely that all these possible referents are in view, so we need not choose between them.[38] Combining these four referents, I suggest that 'living water' is a metaphor for Jesus' Spirit-imbued wisdom teaching that cleanses and gives eternal life to those who accept it.[39]

In 6:63, we find the cognitive role of the Spirit in a nutshell: 'The Spirit is the one that gives life, the flesh does not benefit anyone; the words that I speak to you are Spirit and life.' That the Spirit gives life (6:63a) has already been observed in John

---

[37] Cf. Turner, *Spirit*, 68-69; Bennema, *Power*, 168-81.

[38] These possible referents of 'living water' in Judaism are also present in John: (i) based on 1:32; 3:34, we had inferred that Jesus was endowed with the Spirit in order to speak God's words (i.e., to provide divine teaching); (ii) in 6:63, Jesus asserts that his teaching is Spirit-empowered and produces eternal life; (iii) in 7:38-39, 'living water' is explicitly identified as the Spirit; (iv) in 15:3, Jesus confirms the cleansing abilities of his teaching (cf. 17:17).

[39] Cf. R.E. Brown, *The Gospel According to John*, AB 29, 2 vols. (London: Chapman, 1971), 1:178-79; Turner, *Spirit*, 61-63; Bennema, *Power*, 183-85.

3–4, where we learned that the Spirit facilitates entry into eternal life through a spiritual birth and empowers Jesus' life-giving teaching. The phrase, 'the flesh does not benefit anyone' (6:63b), is more puzzling because the referent of 'flesh' is uncertain. It could refer to the human, unbelieving mind. Like the contrast in 3:6 between 'flesh' and Spirit, 6:63b may refer to the unbeliever who is locked in her 'fleshly' or human thinking, and then to the life-giving activity of the Spirit which illuminates the human mind. Plausible as it may sound, there are two reasons why I suggest that 'flesh' refers to Jesus' life instead, in particular to the giving of his life in death on the cross. First, in 6:51-58, 'flesh' also refers to Jesus' death. Second, 6:62 refers to Jesus' ascent and return to glory, starting at the cross, and 6:63 then sheds further light on this event. However, if 'flesh' in 6:63b refers to Jesus' death on the cross, how do we explain that this is of no benefit to people? I suggest that one needs to understand the significance of the cross before Jesus' death can be life-giving. Only when Jesus' death on the cross is understood as the supreme expression of God's love for this world, as God's way to deal with sin and provide eternal life – only then is Jesus' death of benefit. Consequently, 6:63c then also becomes clear: Jesus' words are Spirit and life in that the Spirit reveals the meaning and significance of Jesus' life-giving teaching. Jesus' revelation (which culminates at the cross) can only be life-giving if its meaning and significance is properly perceived and understood, and it is the Spirit who will facilitate this cognitive perception and retrieval of saving knowledge. Thus, the Spirit gives life particularly in his role of a cognitive agent – facilitating people's understanding of Jesus and his teaching and hence assisting them to produce an adequate belief-response that will result in a life-giving relationship with Jesus.[40]

This concept of the Spirit moving people from sensory to cognitive perception and knowledge coheres with the notion of the Spirit of truth in John 13–17. After Jesus' departure, the Spirit-Paraclete will mediate or reveal to believers the life-giving truth present in Jesus' teaching (16:13) in order to inform their testimony to the world (15:26-27).[41] Since the disciples have already encountered and experienced the Spirit in and through Jesus' words, Jesus' assertion that the disciples already 'know' this Spirit is then not surprising (14:17). Moreover, as we have argued elsewhere, the combined ministry of the Spirit-Paraclete and the disciples is in strong continuity with Jesus' earthly ministry, and, consequently, the Spirit-Paraclete is expected to be similarly active in and through the disciples' testimony, leading to similar results (cf. 17:20). In other words, the disciples' Spirit-imbued testimony will evoke belief because it is based on Jesus' historical teaching and because the same Spirit who actively reached out to people through Jesus' teaching will also reach out to the world through the disciples' testimony. When people are confronted with the combined testimony of the Spirit-Paraclete and the disciples, they are essentially confronted with the life-giving teaching of Jesus himself. Thus,

---

[40] Turner, *Spirit*, 66-67; Bennema, *Power*, 202-04; *idem, Excavating John's Gospel: A Commentary for Today* (Delhi: ISPCK, 2005), 83-84.

[41] Cf. de la Potterie, 'Truth', 62-63.

the disciples' Spirit-informed testimony is expected to have the same cleansing and liberating effect as Jesus' Spirit-imbued teaching. To draw on 6:63, *the disciples' words are 'Paraclete' and 'life'*, in that their testimony is prepared and empowered by the Paraclete, which provides eternal life if it is accepted.[42]

But how will the disciples' Spirit-empowered testimony evoke belief? I suggest that the *aim* of the Spirit-Paraclete's prosecution of the world in 16:8-11 is ultimately soteriological. First, as Jesus' aim was to save and not to condemn (3:17), and as Jesus was the first paraclete (14:16), it is natural to assume that the mission of the Spirit-Paraclete, as a continuation of Jesus' mission, is salvific. Second, the Spirit-Paraclete cannot directly convict the world (14:17) but channels this conviction *through* the disciples' testimony (15:26-27) – a testimony which is aimed at evoking belief (17:20). Therefore, the Spirit-Paraclete brings a case against the world, with the intention that people will repent and come to believe in Jesus.[43] In this process, the Spirit-Paraclete acts as an epistemic agent, assisting unbelievers in cognitively perceiving the disciples' testimony so that they may come to adequate belief on the basis of their new understanding. 'Spirit of truth', then, denotes an epistemic function of the Spirit-Paraclete, namely, the Spirit who communicates truth and facilitates saving knowledge.

Conclusion

According to John, people in general do not know God and are not 'from God'. People need to *know God* through an understanding and acceptance of Jesus' revelatory teaching that contains saving truth, and consequently to become *'from God'* through a new birth. To put it differently, sensory perception of Jesus and his teaching should be followed by cognitive perception of the spiritual significance of what has been observed at a sensory level, and result in an adequate belief-response in order to give life.[44] This implies that belief in the Johannine sense has both a

---

[42] Bennema, *Power*, 241-47. Thus, besides revelation, the Gospel of John also regards testimony as an important source of knowledge. First, the disciples' Paraclete-imbued testimony, which is rooted in Jesus' historical revelation/teaching, is a source of saving knowledge (cf. 17:20). Second, the text of the Gospel of John and the Letters are, in their testimony to Jesus, also a source of knowledge (19:35; 20:30-31; 21:24-25; 1 Jn 1:1-4; 5:13). The Spirit-Paraclete functions as a facilitator of cognitive perception and knowledge to those who encounter Jesus' revelation through the oral and written testimony. Third, the testimonies of the Baptist and the Samaritan woman are sources of belief (1:7; 4:39), and the implication of 5:39, 46-47 is that Moses' written testimony is also supposed to be a source of knowledge and belief.

[43] Cf. Bennema, *John's Gospel*, 176.

[44] If John's epistemology is compared with that of Greek philosophy, it is more Aristotelian than Platonic, since for Aristotle knowledge depends on sense experience (cf. also Epicurean epistemology) whereas for Plato knowledge is innate and essentially a recollection of a priori ideas. Cf. E. Ferguson, *Backgrounds of Early Christianity* (Grand Rapids: Eerdmans, 1993²), 314-15, 321, 352.

cognitive aspect (one needs to perceive/understand Jesus' teaching) and a *volitional* aspect (one needs to accept Jesus' teaching and commit oneself to him). The Spirit is an epistemic agent in that the Spirit facilitates cognitive perception and knowledge, so that people can think 'from above' about Jesus and his teaching, and produce an adequate belief-response. The Spirit thus creates and provides the basis for a new, Christ-centered epistemology. In other words, in John's view the knowledge of God is *Spirit-informed* and *christocentric*.

IV – An Epistemic Relationship with the Father and Son

The intimate relationship between the Father and Son is primarily characterized by life (5:21, 26), love (3:35; 5:20; 14:31; 15:9), knowledge/truth (8:55; 10:15; 14:6; 17:17) and glory (17:1-5). This relationship of life, love, knowledge/truth and glory between the Father and Son is not exclusive; believers are drawn and participate in this saving relationship through a birth 'from above'. Recognizing and understanding the identity, mission and relationship of the Father and Son enables a person to make an adequate belief-response and to partake in this divine relationship (1 John 1:3 calls this participation '*koinōnia* with the Father and Son'). This intimate relationship between the Father, Son and believer is also expressed in other ways, such as the oneness-language (*hen einai* [10:30; 17:11, 21-23]), the indwelling-language (*menei en* [6:56; 10:38; 14:10-11, 20; 15:4-7; 17:21, 23; 1 Jn 2:6, 24, 27-28; 3:6, 24; 4:12-13, 15-16]), and Jesus' calling his disciples 'friends' (15:13-15). Both concepts of 'oneness' and 'indwelling' between the Father, Son and believer are metaphors for an intimate relationship between them.[45] Besides, the believing community consists of those who 'hear' and know Jesus' voice (10:3-4, 16).[46] There is, in fact, a *perpetual* flow of life, love, knowledge/truth and glory between the Father, the Son and the believer (cf. 5:21, 26; 10:14-15; 14:6, 13, 21; 15:9-10; 16:13; 17:5, 22; 1 Jn 1:2; 2:24-25; 3:1; 4:7-19; 5:11-12; 2 Jn 2). The implication, then, is that a believer who continues in her fellowship with the Father and Son continues to have access to the truth or divine reality, and hence to knowledge of the divine.[47]

---

[45] Cf. the concept of the believer remaining in Jesus' word and love, and vice versa (8:31; 15:7, 9-10).

[46] Cf. Thompson, *God*, 142-43, who concludes that seeing, and hence knowing, God must be interpreted as *communion* with and *experience* of God, since seeing demands the presence of the one who is seen.

[47] Note the tremendous claims regarding the knowledge of the Johannine believers, expressed, for example, by the phrase '(by this) we/you know that ...' (1 Jn 2:5, 18, 21; 3:5, 14-16, 19, 24; 4:2, 6, 13; 5:2, 15, 18-20). Moreover, people's participation in the divine reality or truth is expressed by phrases such as 'doing the truth' (3:21), 'to worship in truth' (4:23-24), 'being of the truth' (18:37; 1 Jn 3:19), 'witnessing to the truth' (18:37; 19:35; 21:24; 3 Jn 12), 'knowing the truth' (8:32; 1 Jn 2:21; 2 Jn 1), 'walking in the truth' (2 Jn 4; 3 Jn 3–4).

In fact, in order to remain in a life-giving relationship the believer needs a *continuous* knowing and understanding of the Father and Son. The knowledge generated, received or made accessible in one's relationship with the Father and Son is probably also precisely the knowledge needed to *sustain* the believer's relationship with the Father and Son. We can explain this concept of the need for continuous knowledge as follows.

The knowledge available to the believer in her relationship with the Father and Son forms the basis on which she can know the will of the Father and Son, be obedient to Jesus' commandments, and thus demonstrate discipleship (cf. 7:17; 8:31-32; 10:4; 13:17; 15:15; 15:27–16:4; cf. Jesus' obedience because he knows the Father [8:55; cf. 2:24-25; 13:1; 18:4]). This discipleship based on knowledge guarantees and sustains the believer's participation in the relationship with the Father and Son, and subsequently guarantees the believer's access to further knowledge, which is necessary to remain in this saving relationship (cf. 1 Jn 2:3-6; 4:7). In other words, continuous belief (as expressed primarily in discipleship) guarantees the continuation of the relationship and hence the access to further knowledge. Moreover, belief and knowledge stimulate and inform one another. Continual belief warrants continual access to further knowledge, and further knowledge of God, his will and commandments will probably motivate continual belief.

In this entire dynamic process, the Spirit continues to be the facilitator of cognitive perception and knowledge. First, as the Spirit of truth, the Paraclete will continue to mediate to believers the truth present in Jesus' teaching – to enhance their own spiritual growth *and* to inform and prepare their life-giving testimony to the world (cf. section III). Second, as Teacher, the Paraclete will enable believers to recall Jesus' revelatory teaching and cognitively to perceive and understand it more fully (14:26; 16:12-15).[48] The Paraclete's anamnesis (14:26) is closely related to (if not an aspect of) the Paraclete's teaching; consequently the explicit examples of the disciples' anamnesis (2:17, 22; 12:16) can be most likely ascribed to the work of the Paraclete (esp. since 2:22 and 12:16 mention that the recalling happened *after* Jesus' glorification). The Paraclete's recalling or bringing to memory of Jesus' words leads to, or is expected to result in, knowledge (and belief) (2:17, 22; 12:16; 14:26; 15:20; 16:4, 21).[49] Third, in the light of the activities ascribed to the 'anointing' in 1 John 2:20, 27, this 'anointing' most probably refers to the Spirit-Paraclete. Hence, Jesus' promise of the Paraclete's teaching concerning all truth, and the resulting knowledge, have become a present reality in the Johannine church(es) (1 Jn 2:20).

Conclusion

A believer has made the transition (through a new birth) from the realm below to the realm above, and hence participates in a relationship of life, love, knowledge/truth and glory with the Father and Son. The Spirit continues to function as an epistemic

---

[48] See also Bennema, *Power*, 228-34.

[49] Thus, John also regards memory as an important source of knowledge.

agent, in that the Spirit-Paraclete continues to facilitate cognitive perception and knowledge of Jesus' teaching in order to sustain the believer's salvation.[50] John, then, seems to portray a *relational* epistemology, in that knowledge of the divine can only be attained in a relationship with the Father and Son by the Spirit.

V – The Johannine Dialectic between Knowledge and Belief

In sections III-IV, we argued that a certain degree of knowing is required for an adequate Johannine belief-response. That is, one needs cognitively to perceive and understand something of the identity, character, mission and relationship of the Father and Son in order to commit oneself to a personal relationship with Jesus. Hence, we are not asserting a general philosophical principle that we must know a proposition *p* before we can believe *p*. For John, *pisteuein* is not simply to accept a proposition as true, but *also* involves personal allegiance to Jesus in discipleship, based on a certain degree of knowledge of God.[51] Thus, for John, believing involves some knowing; indeed, it is *a knowing belief*.[52]

Regarding the juxtaposition between knowledge and belief, two passages in the Johannine literature seem to assert that *ginōskein/eidenai* follows *pisteuein* (i.e., belief constitutes knowledge) (10:38; 1 Jn 5:13); two passages put *ginōskein* and *pisteuein* on an equal footing (6:69; 1 Jn 4:16);[53] and two passages seem to indicate that *pisteuein* involves *ginōskein/eidenai* (16:30; 17:8). Hence, a clear-cut case for the priority of one or the other cannot be made.[54] There are, however, reasons to think that some knowing or understanding is required for adequate Johannine belief. We have argued that Jesus' revelation is not empty (see fn. 22) but is informative in that it contains saving truth of the Father and Son, and it is precisely on the basis of the cognitive penetration or understanding of this truth that an adequate belief-response can be made.

A few instances serve to illustrate this concept. We noted that Nicodemus's lack of cognition and knowledge prevented adequate belief (cf. 3:11-12), and the

---

[50] In fact, there seems to be no limit to the believer's Spirit-aided access to truth and knowledge of the divine: the Spirit will guide into *all* truth (16:13); the 'anointing' will teach about *all* things (1 Jn 2:27).

[51] Cf. Dodd, *Interpretation*, 178, 182, 184.

[52] Cf. Bultmann's concept of 'knowing faith', which denotes that *ginōskein* is a constitutive element or structural aspect in *pisteuein* ('*Ginōskō, ktl.*' in *TDNT*, 1:713; *Theology of the New Testament*, 2 vols. [London: SCM Press, 1952, 1955], 2:73-74; *Gospel*, 435 fn. 4).

[53] In the case of 6:69 and 1 Jn 4:16, we probably deal with a hendiadys (i.e., 'to know' and 'to believe' express essentially one idea). See H. Ridderbos, *The Gospel of John: A Theological Commentary* (Grand Rapids: Eerdmans, 1997), 249 fn. 177; C.G. Kruse, *The Letters of John* (Leicester: Apollos, 2000), 165-66.

[54] Cf. Bultmann, *Gospel*, 435 fn. 4; R. Schnackenburg, *The Gospel According to St John*, 3 vols. (London: Burns & Oates, 1968-82), 1:565-66; *idem*, *The Johannine Epistles* (Tunbridge Wells: Burns & Oates, 1992), 221; Brown, *Gospel*, 2:513; *idem*, *The Epistles of John*, AB 30 (New York: Doubleday, 1982), 524-25; Barrett, *Gospel*, 307.

implication is that an adequate belief-response requires adequate understanding or knowledge. In 4:41-42, the Samaritans' knowledge (that Jesus is the saviour) is the *basis* for their belief; to argue *vice versa* disregards the causal use of *gar* ('for', 'because'). In 4:50, the royal official 'believed' Jesus' word (i.e., he accepted it as true) but when that 'belief' had been confirmed (i.e., had become knowledge) the royal official (and his household) believed in the Johannine sense of being saved (4:51-53). Besides, if one of the reasons for unbelief is a lack of cognitive perception and knowledge (see previous sections), then the opposite must also be true: cognitive perception and knowledge is a potential basis for Johannine belief. In 17:8, for instance, the disciples' belief is based on knowing certain truths (as present in Jesus' words). Finally, in 1 John 4:1, believers are encouraged to believe only after discernment (*dokimazein*), i.e., after acquiring the necessary knowledge on which to judge. Thus, the Johannine literature seems to indicate that belief in the Johannine sense includes at least an element of knowing.[55]

I am not arguing for *perfect* or *complete* knowing or understanding prior to belief in the Johannine sense (because who then would qualify?), but at least for *some* intellectual grasp of Jesus and God before one can make an adequate belief-response. I merely assert that *some* true and sufficient insight into Jesus' identity, mission and relationship with God is needed in order to believe adequately. I remain deliberately reticent, however, to spell out what, according to John, is sufficient or adequate knowledge for saving belief. In popular language, John would not advocate faith in a god whom we do not know; rather, he promotes faith in a God whom we understand to be a God who embodies love, is faithful and able to save. Johannine belief is *not* a leap into the epistemic dark or unknown. Instead, Johannine belief has an epistemic basis; it is an intellectual decision to accept the truth claims of Jesus and his teaching (the cognitive element) and to commit oneself to him in discipleship (the volitional element).[56]

Although many people believed in Jesus, not every 'believing' is a saving or adequate belief for John. In 2:23-25, for example, Jesus' decision not to entrust himself (*ouk episteuen*) to those who 'believed' in him reveals that their 'belief' was inadequate or defective. Indeed, this is spelled out further in John 3, where Nicodemus, who is one of these people, displays a deficient knowledge of the divine

---

[55] Contra I. de la Potterie, *La Vérité dans Saint Jean*, 2 vols. (Rome: Biblical Institute Press, 1977), 2:553-58. An interesting observation is that knowing is frequently attributed to Jesus but believing is not. Does this imply that Jesus did not need to believe because he has (perfect) knowledge, and hence that knowledge is superior to belief (so Gaffney, 'Believing', 224)? We do not need to speculate about this; we simply argue that Johannine belief *includes* some knowledge. Moreover, for John, belief also involves personal commitment to Jesus, following Jesus as a disciple, etc., which is not applicable to Jesus. Interestingly, Jesus' decision not to entrust (*ouk episteuen!*) himself to people was based on his knowledge of them (2:24).

[56] Cf. the disciples' volitional decision to stay with Jesus in 1:38-39; 6:67-69.

and hence is not able to come to an adequate belief-response.[57] The 'belief' of 'the Jews' in 8:30-31 is certainly inadequate, as Jesus' dialogue with them points out in 8:31-59. Finally, 6:60-66 indicates that many of the 'disciples' left Jesus because they found his teaching too difficult to understand or too demanding to accept in order to continue their belief in him. Hence, there cannot be an adequate belief-response without prior understanding; a certain degree of knowing is a prerequisite of even an initial adequate belief-response. Nevertheless, once in a saving relationship with the Father and Son, further knowledge may confirm or warrant previous, and stimulate further, belief-responses.[58]

Conclusion

Although John's epistemology asserts that an initial belief-response is based on some knowing, once a person is brought into a saving relationship with the Father and Son, knowledge and belief stimulate and inform one another. To be more precise – and that is where perhaps some tension remains – for John, an adequate degree of understanding or knowing is necessary for saving belief, and hence it can be called a 'knowing belief', which in turn leads to deeper knowledge of the divine. Thus, for John, knowledge and belief have a *cyclical* or *spiral* relationship: knowledge of the divine is available to the believer through the aid of the Spirit, and this knowledge stimulates and informs further belief, which guarantees access to further knowledge. The Johannine concept of 'knowing belief' is essentially *one* epistemic concept in which the two ingredients – knowledge and belief – are inextricably interwoven with one another.[59] In addition to the cognitive aspect, Johannine belief also involves a volitional element, namely a commitment to a trusting relationship with Jesus.

VI – Towards a Johannine Epistemology

Having outlined the main aspects of John's epistemology, we are now in a position to present a more coherent Johannine epistemology. John's epistemic starting point is his negative assessment of humanity as being characterized by epistemic darkness: people lack a saving knowledge of God. The divine response to this condition is the coming of Jesus to the world and the illuminating revelation that he brings. This life-giving revelation contains truth (i.e., saving information about God and divine reality), especially knowledge about the identity, character, mission and relationship of the Father and Son (e.g., 1:17-18, 51; 3:12, 31-36). In general, people are unable

---

[57] Nicodemus is one of those who believed in Jesus in 2:23, because 2:23-25 is narratologically linked to 3:1ff: (i) the word 'man' is repeated in 2:25 and 3:1; (ii) the antecedent of 'him' in 3:2 is Jesus in 2:24-25; (iii) the phrase 'the signs that he was doing' in 2:23 is repeated by Nicodemus in 3:2.

[58] Cf. Bennema, *Power*, 124-34, 152-54.

[59] Although 'believing' and 'knowing' may be correlated concepts for John, they are nevertheless distinct (contra Bultmann, *Theology*, 2:73-74). However, the contrast Gaffney suggests between the two is probably overstated ('Believing', 239-40).

to understand Jesus' revelation unless the Spirit mediates to them the saving truth present in Jesus' revelation and assists them in understanding its meaning and significance. The human belief-response consists (i) of an acceptance of this mediated divine truth, in which this information of the divine *becomes* one's *personal* knowledge of the divine, and (ii) of a personal allegiance to Jesus in discipleship. In other words, with the aid of the Spirit the truth in Jesus' revelation is appropriated by the believer so that it becomes her own knowledge of the divine (the cognitive aspect) *and* she commits herself to a trusting relationship with the Father and Son (the volitional aspect). In fact, the witness of the Spirit provides the warrant that makes true belief knowledge; that is, the Spirit enables belief in such a way that the belief appears as knowledge (cf. 16:13-15; 1 Jn 2:20-21). Thus, belief in the Johannine sense becomes, or virtually is, knowledge because it is a warranted true belief from the moment we have it.[60]

The Spirit-facilitated acceptance of Jesus and his saving revelation by the believer results in a birth of the Spirit into the family of God. In this intimate relationship with the Father and Son, the believer has access to further divine truth, and the Spirit continues to be involved as an epistemic agent, assisting the believer to appropriate these truths. Hence, further human belief-response, expressed in continuing discipleship, then, indicates at the same time the further appropriation of personal knowledge of the divine (e.g., a greater knowledge of God, his will, commandments, etc.). This reveals that there is an important *interaction* between the divine Spirit and the human mind: (i) the Spirit mediates divine truth and facilitates human cognition and understanding; (ii) the human mind, enhanced by the Spirit, accepts and appropriates this saving truth so that it becomes personal saving knowledge of the divine. Thus, *knowledge of God is attained through the Spirit-enabled understanding and believing of the divine revelation of saving truth in Jesus.* This understanding of John's epistemology can be best visualized in the following diagram:[61]

---

[60] I am grateful to Robin Parry for this insight. Cf. Dodd, *Interpretation*, 186, who calls faith a form of knowledge, and Bultmann's concept of knowing faith (see fn. 52 above).

[61] See also the more comprehensive diagram in Bennema, *Power*, 152.

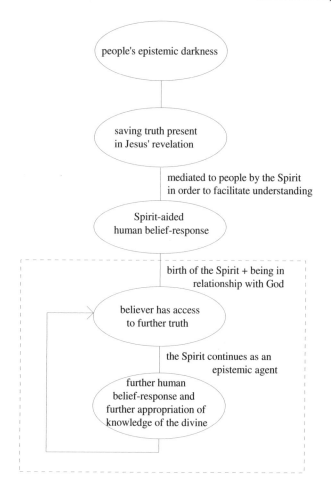

Excursus: A Comparison between Johannine Epistemology and Contemporary Epistemology

We need to reflect further on our model of Johannine epistemology in relation to contemporary epistemology. At first sight, there seems to be a tension. Some contemporary epistemology advocates an epistemic hierarchy with regard to perception as a source of knowledge: perception leads to beliefs, and beliefs may constitute knowledge.[62] Even the definition of knowledge as 'true belief plus something else', a definition which goes back to Plato[63] and is held by virtually every epistemologist,[64] regards belief as a necessary but not a

---

[62] See, e.g., Audi, *Epistemology*, Ch. 1.

[63] In his *Theaetetus*, 201c-d, Plato identifies knowledge (*epistēmē*) as true belief (*alēthēs doxa*) plus an 'account' (*logos*), although it is debatable whether Plato's *logos* is what contemporary philosophers mean by justification. See L. Zagzebski, 'What is Knowledge?' in J. Greco and E. Sosa (eds.), *The Blackwell Guide to Epistemology* (Oxford: Blackwell, 1999), 114 fn. 18. Moreover, a definition of knowledge as 'justified true belief' has been more

sufficient condition for knowledge. According to John, however, belief involves a certain degree of knowing since Johannine belief is not simply the acceptance of a proposition as true but also involves a commitment to Jesus based on a certain degree of knowledge of God. In other words, for John, belief requires cognitive perception and understanding of the truth present in Jesus' revelation. In that case, is John's epistemology opposed to a modern understanding of knowledge, or can the two views be reconciled?

We suggest the latter option is correct for several reasons. First, perhaps we should recognize that there are various contemporary epistemolog*ies* rather than one uniform theory of knowledge, and some of these are comparable to John's epistemology. For example, Alvin Plantinga, one of the leading Reformed epistemologists, develops an epistemology based on theories of Thomas Aquinas and John Calvin, which advocates that faith involves an explicitly cognitive element.[65] Plantinga distinguishes between 'belief' (accepting a proposition as true) and 'faith' (a cognitive activity that includes personal commitment).[66] What Plantinga and other Reformed epistemologists call 'faith' we have labeled 'belief' (since John does not use the noun 'faith').

Second, following from the first point, John and modern epistemologists work with different definitions of 'belief'. Epistemology in general defines belief as accepting a specific proposition as true, whereas John seems to understand belief as a broader concept, which also includes connotations of discipleship (abiding, following, obeying, etc.), participation in and personal allegiance to Jesus. This concept of Johannine 'belief' is generally called Christian 'faith'. Hence, although both contemporary epistemology and John admit that belief contains a cognitive component, in that it is at least an intellectual assent to a proposition, for John belief also includes a volitional and affective aspect (i.e., relating to will, attitude and motivation).

Third, as we argued in sections IV-V, Johannine belief and knowledge stimulate and inform one another; they form two entwined hermeneutical spirals. Knowledge of the divine is available to the believer through the aid of the Spirit, and this knowledge stimulates and informs further belief, which guarantees access to further knowledge. Hence, for John, knowledge and belief have a cyclical or spiral relationship. For John, knowledge-belief is one salvific package, in that a saving belief requires or contains a certain adequate degree of knowledge of the divine.

---

difficult to retain after Edmund Gettier's classic article 'Is Justified True Belief Knowledge?', *Analysis* 23 (1963), 121-23.

[64] E.g. (with various nuances), Audi, *Epistemology*, Ch. 8; Zagzebski, 'Knowledge', 92-116; W. Alston, 'Perceptual Knowledge' in J. Greco and E. Sosa (eds.), *The Blackwell Guide to Epistemology* (Oxford: Blackwell, 1999), 223-42.

[65] A. Plantinga, *Warranted Christian Belief* (Oxford: OUP, 2000), esp. Ch. 8. Other eminent Reformed epistemologists are, for instance, William Alston, Nicholas Wolterstorff and C. Stephen Evans, and some of them have crossed the disciplinary boundary of philosophy into theology: e.g., N. Wolterstorff, *Divine Discourse: Philosophical Reflections on the Claim that God Speaks* (Cambridge: CUP, 1995); C.S. Evans, *The Historical Christ and the Jesus of Faith: The Incarnational Narrative as History* (Oxford: OUP, 1996).

[66] Plantinga, *Belief*, 244ff.

Fourth, some systematic theologians and Christian philosophers adhere to the theory that personal knowledge involves belief and propositional knowledge ('knowing that').[67] Likewise, many biblical scholars distinguish between John's usage of *pisteuein hoti* and *pisteuein eis*.[68] However, a difference in syntax does not necessitate a difference in meaning; both 'beliefs' can be adequate/salvific and it may simply reflect a variation in Johannine style.[69] Moreover, instead of distinguishing between propositional and personal knowledge, or between 'belief that' and 'belief in', we argue that for John knowledge and belief is always personal since it is acquired or expressed within a relationship with Jesus and is based on trust, openness, commitment, obedience, etc. In 6:69, for example, Peter's propositional knowledge and belief occurred while he was already in a relationship with Jesus. Similarly, in 14:10-11 Jesus encourages Philip and the other disciples, who are already in a relationship with him, to assent to a certain propositional belief. Finally, the Johannine community, in its fellowship (*koinōnia* [1 Jn 1:3]) with the Father and Son, possessed much propositional knowledge (see fn. 47 above).

Conclusion

For John, accepting or believing Jesus' revelation requires cognitive perception; people need to understand in order to believe. To believe, in the Johannine sense, means to understand and accept the truth in Jesus' revelation so that one obtains personal saving knowledge of the divine. Once in relationship with Jesus, belief and knowledge seem to form a hermeneutical spiral. Hence, John advocates a *knowing belief*. At the same time, however, to believe involves a volitional act, i.e., an act of the will that involves choice or decision – to commit oneself to a personal allegiance to Jesus in discipleship.[70] In short, Johannine belief consists of a *cognitive* and a *volitional* element – to believe is both an act of the intellect and of the will.[71] John's epistemology seems to show much convergence with that of the so-called Reformed epistemologists, and in particular with the epistemological model of Alvin Plantinga.[72]

---

[67] Cf. M. Polanyi, *Personal Knowledge: Towards a Post-Critical Philosophy* (Chicago: University Press, 1962), *passim*; L. Newbigin, *Proper Confidence: Faith, Doubt and Certainty in Christian Discipleship* (London: SPCK, 1995), esp. Chs. 1, 4, 7.

[68] E.g., Dodd, *Interpretation*, 182-86; Gaffney, 'Believing', 228-32; Brown, *Gospel*, 1:512-13; Schnackenburg, *Gospel*, 1:559-63; R. Kysar, *John the Maverick Gospel* (Louisville: WJKP, 1993 [rev. ed.]), 93-94.

[69] John is quite capable of doing so. There is, for instance, no difference in meaning between John's usage either of *ginōskein* and *eidenai* (see fn. 28 above), or of *filein* and *agapan*.

[70] Amongst the specific volitional acts that John mentions are: following Jesus, abiding in Jesus, obeying Jesus' commandments, accepting Jesus.

[71] See also Scott MacDonald's stimulating article in which he discusses the cognitive and volitional components of faith, although he gives more weight to the volitional aspect ('Christian Faith' in E. Stump [ed.], *Reasoned Faith: Essays in Philosophical Theology in Honor of Norman Kretzmann* [Ithaca: Cornell University Press, 1993], 42-69).

[72] Cf. Plantinga, *Belief*, esp. Chs. 6-8.

Conclusions

Epistemologically, John's analysis of humanity (apart from Christ) is negative: people do not have (adequate/saving) knowledge of God and are enveloped in an epistemic darkness. The divine response is twofold. First, as the Light, Jesus brings illuminating revelation that gives life. Second, since people's epistemic condition of darkness prevents them from cognitively penetrating Jesus' revelation, the Spirit opens up Jesus' revelation and mediates its saving truth to people. That is, the Spirit aids people in their understanding of Jesus' revelation and in the appropriation of divine truth as personal saving knowledge of the divine. Hence, John's epistemology is primarily a *pneumatological* and *christocentric* epistemology. It is christocentric in that knowledge of God is revealed and anchored in Jesus. It is pneumatological in that the Spirit functions as an epistemic agent who facilitates cognitive perception and unlocks the truth that is present in Jesus' teaching so that it can be accepted as saving knowledge of the divine. This saving truth is the epistemic constituent of Johannine belief, and the implication of this interrelationship between knowledge and belief is that we cannot have a non-intellectual or anti-intellectual attitude towards the Christian faith.

One question we posed in the introduction – What is the purpose of knowledge? – has not yet been answered. For epistemology in general, the pursuit of knowledge often seems to be an end in itself.[73] Contemporary epistemology seems to have indulged itself in eating from the tree of knowledge and to have forgotten the real source and aim of knowledge. For John, however, there are three related purposes of knowledge. The first purpose of knowledge, the knowledge of God at any rate, is *salvific*. Cognitive perception or understanding of the truth in Jesus' revelation makes possible an adequate belief-response and saving knowledge of God that brings a person into a saving relationship with the Father and Son. Within this relationship the believer has access to further knowledge of the divine that may stimulate proper discipleship as a means of sustaining one's saving relationship with the Father and Son. Thus, John's epistemology is directly related to and serves his soteriology, since knowledge of God is salvific. Looking at the *Sitz im Leben* of the Johannine church(es), we may learn *why* John puts so much emphasis on knowledge. Both the gospel and the letters testify to the existence of defective or inadequate christologies (e.g., 1:10-11; 6:42; 8:19, 31-59; 9:24; 1 Jn 2:22; 4:2-3). In facilitating knowledge about the true identity of Jesus, the Spirit assists in the confession of a correct christology (cf. 16:13-15; 1 Jn 4:2), which has direct bearing on the believer's soteriological status.

The second purpose of knowledge is *ethical* and related to the first one. The knowledge that is available to the believer in her relationship with the Father and Son is transformative in that it provides knowledge of God's character, will, commandments, work, etc., and this knowledge is naturally expected to affect a person's will, attitudes, motivations and actions. This ethical aspect of knowledge is

---

[73] The more recent subdiscipline of virtue epistemology is an exception to this.

the focus of the more recent discipline of virtue epistemology.[74] An important implication can be drawn in the area of Spirit and ethics. If the Spirit facilitates cognitive perception and transformative knowledge, and if orthodoxy (right thinking) is inextricably linked to orthopraxis (right acting), then the Spirit is also significantly related to right morality; a Spirit-informed epistemology must affect people's praxis. Further study must work out how and to what extent the Spirit is involved in Johannine ethics.

The third purpose of knowledge is *evaluative*. If we extrapolate John's admonition in 1 John 4:1-6, the believer is urged to use her Spirit-provided knowledge to examine and evaluate (*dokimazein*) teachings that she hears or reads in the light of authentic Christian doctrine, i.e., in the light of Jesus' revelation of the truth. Moreover, the conclusion that we cannot have a non-intellectual or anti-intellectual attitude towards the Christian faith also extends, for example, to the area of Christian experience. In some sectors of the church there is the tendency to over-emphasize the experiential or emotional side of salvation or the Christian faith to the extent that the cognitive dimension is almost neglected or denied, but this will not do since our cognitive, volitional and affective facilities are all involved. The Spirit, who facilitates knowledge, is presumably also related to orthopathos (right feeling/experience), in that the Spirit helps believers to interpret and evaluate correctly their religious experiences on the basis of their newly perceived knowledge. John's concept of knowledge, then, is not so much that of 'theoretical' knowledge but one that is personal and practical. The knowledge that is acquired in a personal relationship with Jesus through the aid of the Spirit should be used to evaluate ('judge') doctrine, praxis and experience, and the Spirit, then, is also expected to assist the believer in this evaluative process.[75]

In conclusion, John's epistemology is pneumatological and christocentric in nature, is soteriological, ethical and evaluative in its aim, and has cognitive, relational, volitional and affective aspects. We argued that the Johannine notions of knowledge and belief are so closely correlated – stimulating and informing one another – that they essentially constitute one epistemic concept of 'knowing belief'. The extent to which our model of John's epistemology informs, confirms or subverts contemporary epistemologies is an issue that needs to be examined further.

---

[74] Virtue epistemology has its roots in ancient Greek philosophy (cf. Ferguson, *Backgrounds*, 309, 321, 337-38), but has only received attention in recent years. See, e.g., E. Sosa, *Knowledge in Perspective* (Cambridge/New York: CUP, 1991); J. Greco, 'Virtues and Vices of Virtue Epistemology', *CJP* 23 (1993), 413-32; L. Zagzebski, *Virtues of the Mind* (Cambridge/New York: CUP, 1996); W.J. Wood, *Epistemology: Becoming Intellectually Virtuous* (Leicester: Apollos, 1998); A. Fairweather and L. Zagzebski (eds.), *Virtue Epistemology: Essays on Epistemic Virtue and Responsibility* (Oxford: OUP, 2001).

[75] Cf. the Pauline concept of *dokimazein* in, e.g., Rom 12:2; 1 Cor 11:28; 2 Cor 13:5; Gal 6:4; Eph 5:10; Phil 1:10; 1 Thes 2:4; 5:21. See also A. Munzinger, *Discerning the Spirits: Paul's Hermeneutic of Theological and Ethical Verification* (Cambridge: CUP, 2007).

Bibliography

Alston, W., 'Perceptual Knowledge' in J. Greco and E. Sosa (eds.), *The Blackwell Guide to Epistemology* (Oxford: Blackwell, 1999), 223-42

Audi, R., *Epistemology: A Contemporary Introduction to the Theory of Knowledge* (London/New York: Routledge, 1998)

Barr, J., *The Semantics of Biblical Language* (Oxford: OUP, 1961)

Barrett, C.K., *The Gospel According to St John* (London: SPCK, 1978[2])

Beasley-Murray, G.R., *John*. Word Biblical Commentary 36 (Dallas: Word, 1991)

Bennema, C., *The Power of Saving Wisdom: An Investigation of Spirit and Wisdom in Relation to the Soteriology of the Fourth Gospel*. WUNT II/148 (Tübingen: Mohr Siebeck, 2002)

————, *Excavating John's Gospel: A Commentary for Today* (Delhi: ISPCK, 2005)

Brown, R.E., *The Gospel According to John*. Anchor Bible 29; 2 vols. (London: Chapman, 1971)

————, *The Epistles of John*. Anchor Bible 30. (New York: Doubleday, 1982)

Bultmann, R., *Theology of the New Testament*. 2 vols. (London: SCM Press, 1952, 1955)

————, '*Ginōskō, ktl.*', in *Theological Dictionary of the New Testament*, 1:689-719

————, *The Gospel of John*. G.R. Beasley-Murray (tr.) (Philadelphia: Westminster Press, 1971)

Carson, D.A., *Divine Sovereignty and Human Responsibility: Biblical Perspectives in Tension* (London: Marshall, Morgan & Scott, 1981)

————, 'Understanding Misunderstandings in the Fourth Gospel', *Tyndale Bulletin* 33 (1982), 59-91

————, *The Gospel According to John* (Leicester: IVP, 1991)

Culpepper, R.A., *Anatomy of the Fourth Gospel: A Study in Literary Design* (Philadelphia: Fortress Press, 1987)

Dodd, C.H., *The Interpretation of the Fourth Gospel* (Cambridge: CUP, 1953)

Ely, M.R., *Knowledge of God in Johannine Thought* (New York: Macmillan, 1925)

Evans, C.S., *The Historical Christ and the Jesus of Faith: The Incarnational Narrative as History* (Oxford: OUP, 1996)

Fairweather, A. and L. Zagzebski (eds.), *Virtue Epistemology: Essays on Epistemic Virtue and Responsibility* (Oxford: OUP, 2001)

Ferguson, E., *Backgrounds of Early Christianity* (Grand Rapids: Eerdmans, 1993[2])

Gaffney, J., 'Believing and Knowing in the Fourth Gospel', *Theological Studies* 26 (1965), 215-41

Gettier, E., 'Is Justified True Belief Knowledge?', *Analysis* 23 (1963), 121-23

Greco, J., 'Virtues and Vices of Virtue Epistemology', *Canadian Journal of Philosophy* 23 (1993), 413-32

Kee, H.C., 'Knowing the Truth: Epistemology and Community in the Fourth Gospel' in D.E. Aune, T. Seland and J.H. Ulrichsen (eds.), *Neotestamentica et Philonica: Studies in Honor of Peder Borgen*. NovTSup 106 (Leiden: Brill, 2002), 254-80

Koester, C.R., 'Hearing, Seeing, and Believing in the Gospel of John', *Biblica* 70 (1989), 327-48

Kruse, C.G., *The Letters of John* (Leicester: Apollos, 2000)

Kysar, R., *John the Maverick Gospel* (Louisville: WJKP, 1993 [rev. ed.])

MacDonald, S., 'Christian Faith' in E. Stump (ed.), *Reasoned Faith: Essays in Philosophical Theology in Honor of Norman Kretzmann* (Ithaca: Cornell University Press, 1993), 42-69

Moloney, F.J., *The Gospel of John* (Collegeville: Liturgical Press, 1998)

Munzinger, A., *Discerning the Spirits: Paul's Hermeneutic of Theological and Ethical Verification* (Cambridge: CUP, 2007)

Newbigin, L., *The Open Secret: Sketches for a Missionary Theology* (Grand Rapids: Eerdmans, 1978)

————, *Proper Confidence: Faith, Doubt and Certainty in Christian Discipleship* (London: SPCK, 1995)

Neyrey, J.H., 'John III: A Debate over Johannine Epistemology and Christology', *Novum Testamentum* 23 (1981), 115-27

————, 'The Sociology of Secrecy and the Fourth Gospel' in F.F. Segovia (ed.), *What is John? Vol. II: Literary and Social Readings of the Fourth Gospel* (Atlanta: Scholars Press, 1998), 79-109

Painter, J., 'Johannine Symbols: A Case Study in Epistemology', *Journal of Theology for Southern Africa* 27 (1979), 26-41

Plantinga, A., *Warranted Christian Belief* (Oxford: OUP, 2000)

Polanyi, M., *Personal Knowledge: Towards a Post-Critical Philosophy* (Chicago: University Press, 1962)

Potterie, I. de la, '*Oida* et *ginōskō*: Les deux modes de la connaissance dans le quatrième évangile', *Biblica* 40 (1959), 709-25

————, *La Vérité dans Saint Jean*, 2 vols. (Rome: Biblical Institute Press, 1977)

————, 'The Truth in Saint John' in J. Ashton (ed.), *The Interpretation of John* (London: SPCK, 1986), 53-66

Ridderbos, H., *The Gospel of John: A Theological Commentary* (Grand Rapids: Eerdmans, 1997)

Sasse, H., '*Kosmeō, ktl.*' in *Theological Dictionary of the New Testament*, 3:867-98

Schnackenburg, R., *The Gospel According to St John*. 3 vols. (London: Burns & Oates, 1968-82)

————, *The Johannine Epistles* (Tunbridge Wells: Burns & Oates, 1992)

Sosa, E., *Knowledge in Perspective* (Cambridge/New York: CUP, 1991)

Thompson, M.M., *The God of the Gospel of John* (Grand Rapids: Eerdmans, 2001)

Turner, M., *The Holy Spirit and Spiritual Gifts: Then and Now* (Carlisle: Paternoster, 1999 [rev. ed.])

Watt, J.G. van der, 'Salvation in the Gospel According to John' in *idem* (ed.), *Salvation in the New Testament: Perspectives on Soteriology*, NovTSup 121 (Leiden: Brill, 2005), 101-31

Wolterstorff, N., *Divine Discourse: Philosophical Reflections on the Claim that God Speaks* (Cambridge: CUP, 1995)

Wood, W.J., *Epistemology: Becoming Intellectually Virtuous* (Leicester: Apollos, 1998)

Zagzebski, L., *Virtues of the Mind* (Cambridge/New York: CUP, 1996)

_____, 'What is Knowledge?' in J. Greco and E. Sosa (eds.), *The Blackwell Guide to Epistemology* (Oxford: Blackwell, 1999), 92-116

CHAPTER 7

Knowledge of the Mystery:
A Study of Pauline Epistemology

Mary Healy

The theme of knowledge has not generally been considered a prominent subject of Paul's attention. Indeed, one is hard pressed to find a thorough and systematic treatment of the topic in contemporary biblical studies.[1] Observing that the word *gnōsis* itself (like *sophia* and other related terms) is relatively infrequent outside the Corinthian correspondence, where it occurs in polemical contexts,[2] exegetes have usually concluded that the term reflects the slogans of his opponents, which Paul takes up as the occasion demands but then drops as having little significance in its own right.[3] However, this dismissal of *gnōsis* as a distinctively Pauline concept neglects its place within a whole network of themes treating of the cognitive dimension of salvation in Christ. One indication that knowledge is not a peripheral matter for the Apostle but rather an object of intense theological reflection and pastoral concern is the fact that the Pauline correspondence contains well over half of the New Testament occurrences of an array of cognition-related terms, including knowledge (*gnōsis* and *epignōsis*), wisdom (*sophia*), mind (*nous*), conscience (*syneidēsis*), revelation (*apokalypsis*), thought (*noēma*), understanding (*synesis*),

---

[1] I.W. Scott's excellent monograph, *Implicit Epistemology in the Letters of Paul: Story, Experience and the Spirit*, WUNT 2, 205 (Tübingen: Mohr Siebeck, 2006), is a welcome exception, being the first book-length study of knowledge in Paul since Jacques Dupont's *Gnōsis. La connaissance religieuse dans les épitres de Saint Paul*, published a half century ago (Louvain: Gabalda, 1949). J.D.G. Dunn's monumental *Theology of Paul the Apostle* (Grand Rapids: Eerdmans, 1998), illustrates the lacuna in contemporary scholarship in that it provides no section or chapter explicitly treating Paul's notions of knowledge or revelation.

[2] *Gnōsis* appears 16 times in 1–2 Corinthians; 7 elsewhere in Paul; *sophia* (wisdom) 18 times in 1–2 Corinthians; 10 elsewhere in Paul; *sophos* (wise) 11 times in 1 Corinthians; 5 elsewhere in Paul.

[3] See, for instance, J.D.G. Dunn, *Jesus and the Spirit. A Study of the Religious and Charismatic Experience of Jesus and the First Christians as Reflected in the New Testament* (Philadelphia: Westminster, 1975), 217; G. Fee, *The First Epistle to the Corinthians*, NICNT (Grand Rapids: Eerdmans, 1987), 11, 100; H. Conzelmann, *1 Corinthians*, Hermeneia, J.W. Leitch (tr.) (Philadelphia: Fortress, 1975), 57-59. To contest this explanation is not to deny that Paul, on occasion, noticed and took advantage of his interlocutors' favorite catchwords and adages, as is apparently the case, for instance, in 1 Corinthians 6:12f; 8:1, 4; 10:23.

mindset (*phronēma*), disclosure (*phanerōsis*), thinking (*phrēn*), to think (*phroneō*), to make known (*gnōrizō*), and to be ignorant (*agnoeō*).[4] Knowledge of God and of Christ plays an important role not only in the Corinthian correspondence but also in Romans and Philippians, and receives an even more developed treatment in the later letters. In fact, the basic vocabulary of knowledge, *gnōsis*, *ginōskō* and *oida*, appears more often in Paul than that of faith, *pistis* and *pisteuō*.[5] While numbers never tell the whole story, this fact at least challenges the assumption that knowledge is a relatively insignificant concern for the Apostle.

In light of this evidence, it is not only valid but vital to bring epistemological questions to the study of the Pauline correspondence. What does Paul have to say about the knowledge of God and how it is attained? In what way, if at all, does he see knowledge of God as different from ordinary knowing? How does knowledge relate to faith, one of his principal themes? Paul himself, of course, never addressed these questions in a systematic philosophical manner. Nevertheless, by carefully probing his writings, we can obtain some insight into the underlying assumptions and conceptual framework that shape his thought.[6] For instance, even if Paul never consciously thought about the question of whether there are different 'modes' of knowing, his statements may logically presuppose a particular answer to that question. The contention of this essay is that Paul's writings, *ad hoc* and contingent as they are in addressing diverse pastoral situations, are theologically and philosophically robust: that is, subjecting them to penetrating questions does not cause them to dissolve into a morass of inconsistencies or ambiguities. Of course, this presupposes that due attention is paid to the context, the setting in life, and the particular purposes of a given letter. But once this is done, then the most significant and provocative interpretive questions can be raised.

One of the key texts where Paul directly addresses the human epistemic situation is 1 Corinthians 2:6-16. Much of his cognitive terminology converges in this passage, which describes a hidden wisdom imparted to believers by the Spirit, and

---

[4] There are also several cognitive verbs with strong but somewhat less disproportionate representation in Paul, including know (*oida*, *ginōskō* and *epiginōskō*), understand (*noeō*), reveal (*apocalyptō*), and manifest (*phaneroō*).

[5] This is the case if one excludes the Pastoral Letters, which characteristically speak of faith in the sense of the content of Christian doctrine rather than the act of believing or trusting God.

[6] Such an inquiry rests on the assumption that in the most important sense of the term, Paul's thought is consistent. That is, although he may have used words or images in very different senses in various contexts, and although in many respects his thought is inchoate relative to later systematic theology, his work is not fraught with logical or ontological contradictions. Recent scholarship has emphasized the contingency of Pauline thought; see Dunn, *Theology of Paul*, 6–12; J.A. Fitzmyer, 'Pauline Theology', *NJBC*, 1382-416, §§24-30. However, the fact that Paul was writing letters to particular churches, occasioned by particular pastoral situations, does not in itself imply that his overall theological vision is incoherent. Apparent contradictions in Paul can often be resolved by appreciating the analogous use of terms or by distinguishing different contexts in which given statements apply.

goes on to draw a contrast between those who do and do not understand the Spirit's revelation.[7] Appreciation of this passage has been compromised by the early twentieth-century tendency to suspect 'Gnostic' influence,[8] and the more recent view of the unit as polemical irony rather than a straightforward statement of Paul's own thought.[9] Recovered from these interpretive dead ends, the passage has much to contribute to our understanding of Pauline epistemology. This study will probe the epistemological claims of 1 Corinthians 2:6-16, using it as a springboard to explore the views of knowledge underlying the entire Pauline corpus.[10]

---

[7] Knowledge and revelation are treated in a dynamic rather than a conceptual manner in 1 Corinthians 2:6-16; the nouns *gnōsis* and *apocalupsis* do not occur. However, in their verbal form these terms are central to the passage. *Gnōsis* does appear later as keyword in Paul's dialogue with the Corinthians: 1 Cor 8:1-11; 12:8; 13:2, 8; 14:6; 2 Cor 2:14; 4:6; 6:6; 8:7; 10:5; 11:6. *Apocalupsis* occurs in the discussion of spiritual gifts in 1 Corinthians 14:6, 26.

[8] The Gnostic hypothesis first gained prominence through R. Reitzenstein, *Hellenistic Mystery Religions: Their Basic Ideas and Significance*, PTM 15, J.E. Steely (tr.) (Pittsburgh: Pickwick, 1978), 432; and R. Bultmann, '*ginōskō*', *TDNT*, I, 689–719; *ibid.*, *Faith and Understanding*, L. Smith (tr.) (Philadelphia: Fortress, 1987), 70–72; and was further developed by W. Schmithals, *Gnosticism in Corinth: An Investigation of the Letter to the Corinthians*, J. Steely (tr.) (Nashville: Abingdon, 1971), 141-55; and U. Wilckens, *Weisheit und Torheit: Eine exegetisch-religionsgeschichtliche Untersuchung zu 1 Kor 1 und 2*, BHT 26 (Tübingen: Mohr/Siebeck, 1959). But as several studies have shown, the alleged evidence for a developed form of pre-Pauline Gnosticism is scant and anachronistic. See W.D. Davies, *Paul and Rabbinic Judaism: Some Rabbinic Elements in Pauline Theology* (London: SPCK, 1948), esp. 191–200; Dupont, *Gnosis*; Pearson, *Pneumatikos-Psychikos Terminology*; R.McL. Wilson, 'Gnosis at Corinth', in M.D. Hooker and S.G. Wilson (eds.), *Paul and Paulinism. Fs. C.K. Barrett* (London: SPCK, 1982), 102–14.

[9] For this widespread view, see R.W. Funk, *Language, Hermeneutic, and the Word of God: The Problem of Language in the New Testament and Contemporary Theology* (New York: Harper, 1966), 303; B.A. Pearson, *The Pneumatikos-Psychikos Terminology in 1 Corinthians*, SBL.DS 12 (Missoula, MT: Society of Biblical Literature, 1973), 32; R.A. Horsley, 'Wisdom of Word and Words of Wisdom in Corinth', *CBQ* 39 (1977), 224-39; J. Davis, *Wisdom and Spirit: An Investigation of 1 Corinthians 1.18–3.20 against the Background of Jewish Sapiential Traditions in the Greco-Roman Period* (Lanham, MD: University Press of America, 1984), 125; and Fee, *First Corinthians*, 98–99. J. Murphy-O'Connor characterizes the entire passage as 'mental gymnastics intended to bemuse the Corinthians' ('The First Letter to the Corinthians', *NJBC*, 802). See the critique, however, by R. Scroggs, 'Paul: ΣΟΦΟΣ and ΠΝΕΥΜΑΤΙΚΟΣ', *NTS* 14 (1967), 33–55; and P. Stuhlmacher, 'The Hermeneutical Significance of 1 Cor 2:6–16', C. Brown (tr.), in G. Hawthorne and O. Betz (eds.), *Tradition and Interpretation in the New Testament: Fs. E. Earl Ellis* (Grand Rapids: Eerdmans, 1987), 328–47, esp. 334.

[10] Because of space limitations, this study will focus primarily on the seven 'undisputed' letters. However, passages in Colossians and Ephesians (whether written by Paul himself, by a scribe assisting him, or by a later disciple) confirm and develop the epistemological insights of the earlier letters. Cf. esp. Col 1:25–2:3; Eph 1:17f; 3:16–19.

Revelation in Paul

A close examination of 1 Corinthians 2:6-16 shows a two-way dynamic, where *knowing* is the human act that follows, and corresponds to, God's act of *revealing*. Paul's affirmation that God 'has revealed [these things] to us through the Spirit' (v. 10) is parallel to 'We have received the Spirit from God, that we might know the things bestowed on us by God' (v. 12). For Paul (as for the New Testament in general, deriving from the Old Testament), in human knowledge of God, it is always God who takes the initiative by revealing himself. Thus to investigate Paul's epistemology we will begin with his view of the 'downward' divine act of revelation, then proceed to the 'upward' human act of knowing.

Revelation as God's Self-disclosure

In 1 Corinthians 2:7-10a, Paul identifies the content of God's revelation as his eternal plan, 'decreed before the ages for our glory' and accomplished through the crucifixion of 'the Lord of glory'. Paul thereby indicates that divine revelation is fundamentally rooted in an historical event – the incarnation and redemptive death of Christ.[11] In v. 10b he further identifies that content with the 'depths of God', implying that revelation is the disclosure within the world not only of particular truths but of the inmost divine mystery. For Paul, revelation in its most fundamental sense is thus God's definitive communication of *himself* through the person and life of Jesus Christ.

This conclusion accords with other Pauline texts. As the Apostle emphasizes particularly in Galatians, the self-revelatory intervention of God in history has given rise to a distinct 'before' and 'after' which can be demarcated by various phrases: 'before faith came', 'until faith should be revealed', 'until Christ came' (Gal 3:23f), 'at the right time God sent forth his Son' (Gal 4:4), 'now that you have come to know God, or rather to be known by God' (Gal 4:9). These statements, taken together, suggest that God's revelation is simultaneously both a self-*disclosure* and a self-*gift* through his Son.[12] It is historically particular, yet universal in scope: through Christ, God's love and covenant righteousness have been irrevocably manifested in the world, inaugurating a new dispensation (cf. Rom 3:21; 2 Cor 3:7-9). The Christ-event has manifested in history the ineffable divine attributes: God's love (Rom 5:8);

---

[11] Scott argues persuasively that 'there is a narrative structure to the Apostle's knowledge' (*Implicit Epistemology*, 5, 95-118). That is, 'Paul's theological knowledge is structured as a grand unified story, an epic narrative of the relationship between human and its creator which stretches from creation to the final eschatological fulfillment' (108), with the Christ event as its pivotal moment.

[12] Cf. Rom 8:32; Gal 2:20; Eph 5:2, 25.

righteousness (Rom 1:17; cf. 3:21f, 25); glory (Rom 9:23); and faithfulness to his promises (Rom 15:8).[13]

Paul's preferred term for expressing the content of divine revelation is *mystērion* (1 Cor 2:1, 7), a term that acquires increasing prominence throughout his writing career.[14] Besides accenting the veiled and hidden character of what is revealed, this word has the advantage of uniting all the various dimensions of God's salvific design in a comprehensive unity. By designating the object of revelation as mystery, Paul indicates that it remains permanently subject to God's free initiative and beyond the controlling grasp of the human intellect. As mystery, it cannot be confined to determinate doctrinal formulations, though it can require them for its correct preservation (cf. 2 Thes 2:15; 1 Cor 11:2; 15:1-8).

Revelation as Personal Encounter

A further characteristic of revelation emerges from the fact that Paul associates it with the event of the Corinthians' own conversion in 1 Corinthians 2:10-12: God 'revealed' the mystery when they 'received' the Spirit (both verbs are in the aorist). Thus divine 'revelation' took place for the Corinthians at the moment when the good news of Christ was preached to them. This notion too finds expression throughout the epistles. In Romans 16:25, the cosmic 'revelation of the mystery' is parallel to 'the preaching of Jesus Christ'. Paul describes his own work of evangelization with a wealth of revelatory vocabulary, using terms like 'manifest' (*phaneroō*), 'make known' (*gnōrizō*), 'enlighten' (*phōtizō*), 'reveal' (*apocalyptō*), and 'fulfill the word of God' (*plēroō ton logon tou theou*).[15] The apostles are 'stewards of the mysteries of God' (1 Cor 4:1), through whom God 'spreads the fragrance of the knowledge of him everywhere' (2 Cor 2:14). Not only the words of the Christian missionaries but their lives, marked by sacrificial love and willingness to suffer for the gospel, contribute to the revelation of the mystery, as they 'carry in the body the death of Jesus, so that the life of Jesus may also be manifested in our bodies' (2 Cor 4:10f). For the Apostle, God's self-revelation in Christ is essentially linked with, and carried forward in, the apostolic proclamation of the gospel.

The premise throughout, however, is that the apostles are not initiators but mediators in an undertaking in which Christ himself remains the primary agent: 'we are ambassadors for Christ, God making his appeal through us' (2 Cor 5:20). This assumption has two significant implications. First, each act of preaching and hearing the gospel in faith involves an encounter between Christ himself and the hearer (cf. 1 Thes 2:13; 2 Cor 5:20; 13:3). Second, God's revealing activity is not confined to the

---

[13] Similar affirmations can also be made of God's power and his wrath against sin: 'God, desiring to show (*endeiknymi*) his wrath and make known (*gnōrizō*) his power ...' (Rom 9:22; cf. 1:18).

[14] Cf. Rom 16:25f; Col 1:25f; 2:2; 4:3; Eph 1:9; 3:5, 9f; 6:19.

[15] Cf. Rom 1:16f; 3:21; 15:19; 1 Cor 2:1f; 2 Cor 2:14; 4:4–6; Col 1:25–28; 4:4; Eph 3:7–10; 6:19.

irretrievable past of the Christ-event but continues in the Church as the good news is proclaimed and human hearts open to it in faith.[16] 'For Paul the act of revelation takes place wherever Christ manifests and makes himself known.'[17] In other words, an interior divine work takes place in the listeners coincident with the exterior preaching of the gospel. Paul describes his own paradigmatic experience on the Damascus road as 'a revelation of Jesus Christ' (Gal 1:12); that is, his conversion involved Christ making himself known to Paul and being recognized in his living presence and divine sonship.[18] In another phrase laden with meaning, the Apostle declares that God 'was pleased to reveal his Son in me (*en emoi*)' (Gal 1:16), suggesting that God illuminated Paul's mind from within, bringing about a compelling recognition of the lordship of Jesus. Although Paul's own experience was unique in that it took place without a human intermediary, his consistent use of revelation language indicates that he regards the conversion of others in essentially the same terms.[19] Those who receive the gospel encounter not only a cogent preacher but Christ himself, making himself known through the human intermediary.

Paul assumes that his Corinthian readers will well remember the initial opening of their minds to revelation and recognize it as a foundation for the increasing knowledge of God to which he is urging them (1 Cor 2:10; cf. 1 Thes 1:5; 2:13; Gal 3:2). This in turn presupposes that the Spirit's work of revelation within them continues and grows to the degree they are open to it. Revelation thus involves an ongoing activity of the Spirit within each believer, beyond the initial proclamation and acceptance of the gospel. Whenever the gospel is announced, the Spirit is present, imparting understanding and bringing the truth to life. Following the initial act of conversion, the Spirit brings about a progressively more profound interior enlightenment, within both the individual and the community, as to the reality of the risen Lord and the love of the Father revealed through him (cf. 2 Cor 3:18; Col 1:27-2:3; Eph 1:15-19).

Revelation as Realization of the Plan

Paul further suggests in 1 Corinthians 2:9-12 that the hidden salvific plan of God, 'what God has prepared for those who love him', is *revealed* to believers by being *given to* or realized within them. Implicit in this affirmation is Paul's view that the Spirit completes the work of redemption by imparting to the individual believer the divine life and love poured out on the cross (cf. Rom 5:5). The Spirit does not merely bestow knowledge of God's secret plans, but empowers the believer to personally assimilate the redemptive grace released by Christ's passion and resurrection. The past event of Christ's self-gift on Calvary becomes a present,

---

[16] Dunn analyzes this feature of Paul's teaching in *Jesus and the Spirit*, 212–25.

[17] Dunn, *Jesus and the Spirit*, 213.

[18] Dunn, *Jesus and the Spirit*, 213.

[19] In support of this thesis Dunn notes Paul's use of 'our' rather than 'my' in 2 Corinthians 4:6 (*Jesus and the Spirit*, 413 fn. 74).

experienced reality bringing a person into deliverance from sin and fellowship with God. This personalization of redemption is the specific role of the Spirit in Pauline soteriology. In other contexts, Paul expresses this idea by associating the Spirit with the work of sanctification[20] and by declaring that the Spirit 'bears witness' to believers regarding the reality of their adoptive sonship acquired through the cross (Rom 8:16; Gal 4:6).

For Paul, those who accept the Spirit's revelation do not merely acknowledge *that* Christ is Lord and Savior, but come to know him *as* Lord and Savior by entering into a relationship with him and experiencing his power at work in their lives (cf. 2 Cor 4:5f; Phil 3:8). Likewise, believers do not merely assent to the doctrine that God is Father but experience a new relationship with him *as* Father through the Spirit's interior testimony (Rom 8:16; Gal 4:6). They are not merely informed that their sins are forgiven and the power of sin conquered, but experience that forgiveness and freedom.[21] As Paul attests of his own experience in Philippians 3:4-11, the self-revelation of the living God is inherently transformative, involving a reorientation of one's whole 'self-understanding, world-view and life-style', placing everything in an entirely new perspective.[22] The world comes to be seen in its true status as created by God in Christ, graciously redeemed by him, and destined for a transfigured existence in heaven. Since even those who have received the grace of Christ still have minds in need of purification from the intellectual and moral outlook imbibed from the world, this mental reorientation is a gradual process requiring active cooperation (cf. Rom 12:2; Col 2:8; Eph 4:22-24). Paul refers to this process as 'renewal of the mind' (Rom 12:2; Eph 4:23) or having 'the mind of Christ' (1 Cor 2:16; Phil 2:5).[23] This process can, however, be obstructed, which Paul identifies as the cause of the defects in the Corinthians' communal life (1 Cor 2:14). The Corinthians have not adequately appropriated the Spirit's revelation; that is, they have failed to interiorize fully the mystery of salvation, mediated by the Spirit, as a consciously experienced reality.

For Paul, revelation in the senses described above always remains subordinate and anticipatory to the ultimate revelation that will take place at the parousia, 'when the Lord Jesus is revealed from heaven with his mighty angels in flaming fire' (1 Thes 1:7). Paul can even refer to the second coming as simply 'the revelation of our Lord Jesus Christ' (1 Cor 1:7).[24] He thereby indicates that revelation in this world retains an obscure and provisional character, which will eventually give way to the

---

[20] Cf. 1 Cor 6:11; 12:13; 2 Cor 3:18; 5:5; Rom 7:6; 8:1–14; 15:16; Gal 5:16–25; Eph 3:16f; 2 Thes 2:13; Tit 3:5.

[21] Cf. Rom 5:1; 6:5–23; Gal 5:1; 6:22–25.

[22] Dunn, *Jesus and the Spirit*, 213.

[23] As Dunn describes it, 'renewal of the mind' signifies for Paul 'that fundamental reshaping and transformation of inner motivations and moral consciousness (*nous*) which he elsewhere thinks of as the writing of the law in the heart, and as the work of the eschatological Spirit (2 Cor 3:3)' (*Jesus and the Spirit*, 223).

[24] The parousia is referred to with the related terminology of 'appearing' in the Pastoral Letters (1 Tim 6:14; 2 Tim 4:1, 8; Tit 2:13), and of 'manifesting' in Hebrews 9:28.

clarity of direct vision (1 Cor 13:9-12). At the eschaton not only will the person of Christ be fully manifested, but also the glory of all those who are inseparably united with him (Rom 8:18f; Col 3:4).[25]

Knowledge in Paul

As noted above, Paul identifies knowledge as the human response to God's revelation.[26] Knowledge appears in verbal form seven times in 1 Corinthians 2:6-16, where its object is, respectively, 'the wisdom of God' (twice), 'the things of man', 'the things of God', 'the things bestowed on us by God', 'the things of the Spirit of God', and 'the mind of the Lord'. Apart from 'the things of man' in v. 11, all these are expressions for the one all-encompassing mystery of God's plan for salvation in Christ. These statements are the correlate on the human side to the assertion that the mystery is 'revealed by the Spirit' (v. 10). The knowledge in view is thus a revelatory knowledge, a knowledge that proceeds from revelation. Some questions to pursue are: What are the characteristics of this knowledge? How does it relate to revelation? What, if anything, is distinct about it other than its supernatural content? Finally, what does it have to do with what is usually regarded as the Pauline correlate to revelation, faith?

Before addressing these questions, a word is in order on the Old Testament as the most significant source of Paul's epistemic vocabulary and concepts. Paul's use of *ginōskō* and *oida* reflects the Hebrew verb *yāda*ʿ, which in the Septuagint is normally rendered with one of these two Greek verbs. In contrast to the Greek emphasis on knowledge as theoretical comprehension of reality, or discovery through observation, *yāda*ʿ connotes concrete personal experience. To 'know' can be applied to such widely varied experiences as childlessness, sickness, sin, divine retribution, war, peace, good and evil, and sexual intercourse.[27] To know an

---

[25] The terminology of revelation also is used in certain more narrow and specific senses, which will not be treated here. For instance, a revelation can be an inspired utterance (1 Cor 14:6, 26, 30), or interior guidance regarding a particular course of action (Gal 2:2; 2 Cor 12:9; Phil 3:15), or a mystical communication (2 Cor 12:1, 7).

[26] As with 'revelation', Paul also uses 'knowledge' in certain extended, almost technical senses, which are secondary to and dependent on the primary sense described below. In 1 Corinthians 8, *gnōsis* has an specific sense obviously defined by the Corinthians' own particular concerns, and reflecting a Greek background. In their claim that 'all of us possess knowledge' (8:1), knowledge refers to a theoretical grasp of a particular theological truth and its ethical application – in this case, the fact that idols have no real existence, and that therefore it is permissible to eat food consecrated to them. While not disputing their theoretical claim, Paul challenges their ethical application. Such 'knowledge' merely 'puffs up', in contrast to the knowledge animated by *agapē* which alone builds up the church (1 Cor 8:1). In 1 Corinthians 12–14, knowledge has yet another meaning as a Spirit-inspired utterance in the church assembly, imparting insight into the practical consequences of revealed truth (1 Cor 12:8; possibly 1 Cor 1:5; 13:2; 14:6; 2 Cor 8:7).

[27] Cf. Gen 2:9; 4:1; Num 31:18; Jdg 3:1; Is 47:8; 53:3; 59:8; Jer 16:21; Wis 3:13.

individual, in particular, means 'to participate in a personal relationship admitting a variety of form, embracing many stages.'[28] More significantly, *yāda*ᶜ is one of the principal ways of expressing God's covenant relationship with his people. God sovereignly chooses (*yāda*ᶜ) human beings (Gen 18:19; Jer 1:5; Amos 3:2), giving rise to a concomitant human responsibility to acknowledge (*yāda*ᶜ) God and serve him alone (Hos 13:4). To know the Lord, or to be known by him, involves both understanding his will and acting accordingly.[29] This theme becomes interwoven with that of spousal union, particularly in Hosea (Hos 2:20; 6:6; 13:4).[30] God's people are, however, characterized more often by ignorance than by knowledge of him, which ultimately becomes a cause of their ruin (Hos 4:6).

The historical experience of persistent failure to know the Lord eventually led to the notion in the prophetic tradition that only a conversion of heart, effected by YHWH himself, will make possible the true knowledge that he requires.[31] This notion is central to Jeremiah's new covenant prophecy (Jer 31:31-34), and is further developed by Ezekiel and Deutero-Isaiah, who foretell that both God's punishments and his mighty deeds of salvation will bring about a new and definitive knowledge of him through the interior presence of his spirit (Ezek 37:13f; cf. 35:9; 39:29), which will extend not only to Israel but to all nations.[32] The prophetic writings express the increasing conviction that God and his transcendent ways remain opaque to human beings without an interior principle of understanding provided by God himself. The promise of a new, perfected form of knowledge of God becomes a central aspect of messianic and eschatological hope. This promise, and its fulfillment in Christ, forms the backdrop to all Paul's statements about knowledge.

Knowledge as Relationship

In 1 Corinthians 2:9-10, Paul conflates two Old Testament texts in his quotation: 'As it is written, "What no eye has seen, nor ear heard, nor the heart of man conceived, what God has prepared for those who love him", God has revealed to us through the Spirit.' These texts are Isaiah 64:4, part of a plea for a divine epiphany; and Deuteronomy 29:4, a reproach for spiritual obtuseness. By affirming that God has now revealed these previously unperceived things through the Spirit, Paul indicates that the desired epiphany of Isaiah 64:4 has occurred and, simultaneously, the obtuseness of Deuteronomy 29:4 has been healed, in Christ crucified, risen, and revealed to the Church through the Spirit. The knowledge bestowed by the Spirit has overcome the spiritual blindness of the old covenant, in which the people could not penetrate through God's deeds to an understanding of God himself. This new

---

[28] J. Corbon and A. Vanhoye, 'Know', *Dictionary of Biblical Theology* (New York: Seabury, 1973²), 296–298.

[29] Jer 22:16; cf. Ex 33:17; Ps 147:19f.

[30] Cf. Job 18:21; Is 1:3; 5:13; Hos 4:6; 5:4; Mal 2:7f.

[31] Cf. Jer 24:7; Ezek 36:26f; Deut 29:4; 30:6.

[32] Cf. Ezek 36:23; 37:28; Is 11:9; 43:10; 49:26.

revelatory knowledge culminates in our having a share in the 'mind of Christ', giving us a way of access to the previously inaccessible thoughts of God (1 Cor 2:16, citing Is 40:13). Paul is hereby indicating that through the eschatological gift of the Spirit, the interior principle of understanding promised by Jeremiah has at last been given, leading to a knowledge of God that was formerly impossible. This is an elaboration of his earlier declaration that 'since ... the world did not know God through wisdom, it pleased God through the folly of what we preach to save those who believe' (1 Cor 1:21). Here Paul places 'not knowing God' in opposition to 'being saved', so that knowing God is equated with being saved. This does not mean that 'to know God' exhausts the meaning of 'to be saved' or that salvation is essentially a noetic reality, but simply that knowledge of God is an intrinsic dimension of salvation.[33] Paul is announcing that as foretold by the prophets, God has come to be recognized for who he is through his mighty act of deliverance, now understood to be forgiveness of sin and new life in Christ.

This soteriological perspective is a fundamental point of reference for Paul's teaching on knowledge of God. For Paul, salvation is a release from the ignorance or estrangement from God which is the principal consequence of sin (cf. Gal 4:8f; Rom 8:7; Col 1:21; Eph 2:12); to be saved is thus to enter into a personal relationship with God. To become a Christian can be described simply as to 'come to know God, or rather to be known by God,' whereas the former condition of Jews and pagans alike was that of not knowing God (Gal 4:8f; cf. Rom 10:2; 1 Thes 4:5). Unbelievers can even be defined as 'those who do not know God,' which is equivalent to 'those who do not obey the gospel of our Lord Jesus' (2 Thes 1:8). The gentiles are 'darkened in their understanding, alienated from the life of God because of the ignorance (*agnoia*) that is in them, due to their hardness of heart' (Eph 4:18). These statements imply a kind of knowledge very different from the Greek idea of knowledge as theoretical speculation. Rather, it is much closer to the Old Testament idea of personal acquaintance with another.[34] To come to know God is to become personally familiar with him, interacting with him and letting oneself be acted upon by him. It is to recognize God *as* God, again in the dual sense of perception and acknowledgement (cf. Rom 1:28). This personalistic perspective does not imply, however, that doctrinal truth is insignificant where knowledge of God is concerned. On the contrary, Paul emphasizes the inseparability of doctrinal and personal knowledge in the rebuke of 1 Corinthians 15:34, where he charges that the denial of the resurrection by some demonstrates that they 'have no knowledge of God'. Their rejection of a central tenet of the gospel shows that they have scarcely a minimal acquaintance with God and his ways.

The personal character of knowledge of God is accentuated by Paul's use of reciprocal formulae. In a striking turn of logic, he admonishes the Corinthians that

---

[33] Fee, 'Toward a Theology of 1 Corinthians', in D.M. Hay (ed.), *Pauline Theology*, II: *1 and 2 Corinthians* (Minneapolis: Fortress, 1993), 40, aptly comments that for Paul, 'Salvation finally has to do with being known by and knowing God (1 Cor 13:12).'

[34] Dunn, *Jesus and the Spirit*, 218.

'If any one imagines that he knows something, he does not yet know as he ought to know. But if one loves God, one *is known* by him' (1 Cor 8:2f; emphasis added). In other words, true knowledge of God is not a matter of the philosophical (or theological) erudition boasted by some Corinthians; in fact, to assume that it is is already to display one's ignorance. Rather, it is a personal familiarity by which one is moved to reciprocate God's love.[35] Since God obviously 'knows' all his creatures perfectly in an epistemic sense, the special divine 'knowing' reserved for those who love him must refer to a relational intimacy. Human knowledge of God, in turn, can only occur by opening oneself to God and allowing him access to one's inmost self – an act that engages the whole person, including the will and emotions. Later in the letter Paul applies this reciprocity to the perfected knowledge of the eschaton: 'Now I know in part; then I shall know fully, even as I have been fully known' (1 Cor 13:12). In Galatians, he again equates our knowing God with God's knowing of us: 'Now that you have come to know God, or rather to be known by God …' (Gal 4:9).[36] The kind of knowledge to which these statements testify is gained only by entering into some form of communion with the other. Its closest analogy is knowledge of another human being, in which knowing the other is in a certain sense conditional on and proportionate to allowing oneself to be known.[37] Moreover, in personal knowing (*connaître* rather than *savoir*), the object of knowledge always retains something of the mystery of personal interiority, and so can never be reduced to an objective, identifiable content.[38] It involves an element of trust and of self-surrender, committing oneself even while recognizing that one will never be able to mentally 'grasp' or exhaustively comprehend the one who is known. This explains why Paul, echoing Jesus' own teaching (cf. Mt 11:25f), insists that according to God's deliberate intention, 'the world did not know God through wisdom' (1:21). A knowledge founded on autonomous reason evades the risk of self-engagement which is the *sine qua non* of personal knowledge.

---

[35] The converse movement of this dialectic, where love leads to knowledge, appears in Philippians 1:9: 'it is my prayer that your love [for God and one another] may abound more and more with knowledge and all discernment.'

[36] For other New Testament expressions of this reciprocal knowledge see Mt 11:27 par. Lk 10:22; Jn 10:14f; 17:25.

[37] Recent work in personalistic philosophy could contribute much to a better understanding of the interpersonal notion of knowledge which is implicit in Paul. See F.J. van Beeck, 'Divine Revelation: Intervention or Self-Communication?' *TS* 52 (1991), 199–226, for an illuminating phenomenological analysis of human communication as not only the best analogy for divine revelation but its 'indispensable anthropological infrastructure' (208). For a defense of the view that relationship is the most basic order of knowledge, see D.L. Schindler, 'God and the End of Intelligence: Knowledge as Relationship', *Communio* 26 (1999), 510–40.

[38] As van Beeck points out, 'Divine Revelation', 209, even human communication 'involves more than things communicated; communication is not a mere transfer of "matter" between and among people … what is required on the part of both is an interpersonal context – an awareness of mutual presence, of actively and receptively being with one another.'

Knowledge as Participatory

As noted above, Paul indicates in 1 Corinthians 2:6-16 that those who 'know the gifts bestowed on us by God' (v. 12) know them by existentially 'receiving' them (cf. v. 14). That is, the gift of redemption is progressively realized in believers as they come to a more profound epistemic grasp of God's love as manifested in the sacrifice of his Son.[39] Conversely, the mystery is truly understood to the degree that it has been appropriated through conversion. Thus a further characteristic of knowledge for Paul is that it intrinsically involves existential participation in what is known. Participatory knowledge underlies the realized eschatology of 1 Corinthians 2:6-16. The believer who consciously appropriates the Spirit's revelation begins to experience proleptically 'what God decreed before the ages for our glory'; that is, to have an assurance about, and foretaste of, his eternal inheritance as a child of God.

As in the Old Testament, in many Pauline texts 'experience' could be substituted for 'know' without any distortion of meaning: 'that we might experience (*oida*) the things bestowed on us by God' (1 Cor 2:11); 'experiencing (*oida*) the fear of God' (2 Cor 5:11); 'you heard and experienced (*epiginōskō*) the grace of God' (Col 1:6); 'that you might experience (*ginōskō*) the love of Christ which surpasses knowledge' (Eph 3:19). However, Paul's treatment deepens and interiorizes the Old Testament concept. Knowledge of God is not only an experience of his salvific deeds – whether in the history of Israel or in the circumstances of one's own life – and the response of grateful acknowledgement and worship. It is now an awareness of the power of those acts within one's inmost depths, bringing about an increasingly intimate communion with God (2 Cor 3:18; Gal 2:20; Phil 3:8-10).[40] God's self-disclosure lights up the human heart, as the risen life of Jesus becomes a conscious reality (2 Cor 4:6).[41] The believer experiences not only the efficacy of the cross freeing him from sin, but the interior presence of the crucified and risen Lord. This awareness of Christ within is not limited to the event of conversion but is a permanent conviction; Paul knows existentially that 'It is no longer I who live, but Christ who lives in me, and the life I now live in the flesh I live by faith in the Son of God' (Gal 2:20; cf. Col 1:27).

Clearly Paul's experiential statements are rooted in his own personal life, both his initial encounter with Christ on the Damascus road and his subsequent ministry. But as noted above, the Apostle never suggests that such personal knowledge of Christ is

---

[39] This fundamentally Pauline notion is expressed in a fourth-century Easter homily: 'As far as we are concerned, Christ's immolation on our behalf takes place when we become aware of this grace and we understand the life conferred on us by this sacrifice.' Pseudo-Chrysostom, *Sermo in sanctum pascha*, I, trans. P. Nautin, Sources Chrétiennes 36 (Paris: Cerf, 1953), 1, 7.

[40] There are antecedents to this interiorized notion of experience in the Old Testament, although they are relatively infrequent and inchoate. They occur particularly in the notion of 'beholding' God expressed in the Psalms (Pss 11:7; 27:4; 63:2).

[41] This text alludes to the fulfillment of the prophetic oracle of Isaiah 40:5: 'And the glory of the Lord shall be revealed.'

a unique prerogative of himself or of the apostles in general.[42] If such knowledge were not in principle available to every believer, the rebuke and implied challenge in 1 Corinthians 2:13-3:4 would be pointless. As Stuhlmacher remarks, 'Paul applies to the Corinthians the very same cognition that brought illumination to him on the Damascus road.'[43] While such experiential awareness can be greater or lesser, and is certainly meant to increase, its complete absence from a Christian life is the aberrant situation characterized as that of the 'unspiritual person' (1 Cor 2:14). In 2 Corinthians the Apostle again challenges his disciples, relying on the assumption that it is just as possible for them as for him to consciously discern the indwelling of Christ (2 Cor 13:5). The whole point of Philippians 3:7-15, similarly, is to urge his addressees to seek the depth of knowledge that he himself has acquired.

The participatory quality of knowledge of God underlies the close bond between Pauline epistemology and Pauline ethics.[44] In 1 Corinthians 1:18-2:5, Paul draws a connection between wisdom and power: the true *sophia* of God is the knowledge that brings life-transforming power: it is 'not merely a rational acknowledgment; it includes *experiential participation in that salvation-history*, the actual experience of God's saving power in the here and now – the "demonstration of Spirit and power" (1 Cor 2:4).'[45] Knowledge of the mystery of Christ's death to sin and life to God touches a person's life, communicating a divine energy to be conformed to Christ (cf. Rom 6:10; 8:29). This is why throughout his letters Paul repeatedly prays for or commends a growth in 'knowledge' on the part of his addressees.[46] Often in such contexts the verb has no direct object, but seems to refer to a grasp of the divine mystery revealed in Christ which becomes existentially manifest in the life of the believer.[47] For Paul it is inconceivable that a living contact with Christ would not increasingly shape a person's whole personality, leading to a perceptible effect on one's outward conduct. To be 'full of goodness' is inseparable from being 'filled with all knowledge' of God and his saving work (Rom 15:14).

---

[42] Although Ephesians 3:2–5 declares that 'the mystery was made known to me [Paul] by revelation' and 'has now been revealed to his [Christ's] holy apostles and prophets by the Spirit', this occurs within the specific context of a discussion of Paul's apostolic mission to the gentiles. It is subsequent to the prayer that all the Ephesians may receive 'a Spirit of wisdom and of revelation' to know Christ and their glorious inheritance in him (1:15-23). In Colossians 1:26 the mystery is said to be 'now made manifest to his saints', i.e., to all believers.

[43] Stuhlmacher, 'Hermeneutical Significance', 338–39.

[44] Scott construes this relationship in a slightly different but not incompatible way: theological knowledge is structured as a grand narrative, and ethical reasoning 'is for Paul a matter of "emplotting" himself or other human beings within this overarching narrative by correlating the events of the story with his mundane knowledge about himself and others' (*Implicit Epistemology*, 278).

[45] Dunn, *Jesus and the Spirit*, 220. Italics are in the original.

[46] Rom 15:14; 1 Cor 1:5; Phil 1:9; Col 1:9f; Phm 6.

[47] Knowledge is used in this general theological sense in 1 Cor 13:2, 8; 2 Cor 6:6; 10:5; 11:6; Rom 10:2; Col 2:2f; 3:10; Eph 1:17.

The ethical implications of revelatory knowledge help us to pinpoint the deficiency of the Corinthian community whose behavior Paul castigates. Their supposed 'wisdom' (cf. 3:18; 4:10) and 'knowledge' (8:1) have led not to edification of the church but to discord. This shows that despite their high self-evaluation, they are actually woefully deficient in the revelatory knowledge of God that is accompanied by power.[48] In Paul's equivalent expression, they are 'still carnal' (1 Cor 3:3). This stinging rebuke conveys 'the apostle's reproachful sorrow over the fact that the spiritually richly gifted Corinthians had not yet attained (on account of their strife and divisions) this full knowledge, which is there for all believers by virtue of the Spirit.'[49] The deficiency is illustrated in several of the specific ethical problems discussed in the letter. If the Corinthians had, for instance, grasped with spiritual insight that they are God's temple and that God's Spirit dwells in them (1 Cor 3:16), they could not possibly have continued to compete jealously and fight with one another, and so desecrate the divine dwelling place. If they had been animated by the pervasive conviction that all things belong to them, and they belong to Christ (1 Cor 3:21-23), their lives would have radiated a profound trust and dependence on God that would have quelled the impulse to boast. If they had understood spiritually what it means that the apostles are 'servants of Christ and stewards of the mysteries of God' (1 Cor 4:1) they would have accorded them proper respect for the sake of Christ rather than idolizing or dishonoring them. If they had recognized the presence of the Lord in the Eucharistic supper, they would not have humiliated one another and so profaned his body and blood (1 Cor 11:20-29).[50]

Paul's exhortations persistently express the conviction that revelatory knowledge leads intrinsically to good works; conversely, ignorance leads to sin.[51] This relationship is stated in its strongest form in 1 Corinthians 2:8, where the most heinous sin, crucifixion of the Lord of glory, is attributed precisely those who 'did

---

[48] As Veronica Koperski points out, Paul's procedure is perfectly tailored to the needs of the church in Corinth. Comparing 1 Corinthians 1–2 with Philippians 3:3–21, she notes that 'in Corinth it appears that the enthusiasm over the power of the resurrection has led to a neglect of awareness of the power of God at work in the midst of apparent weakness and folly. In Philippians the problem seems to be more that the resurrection power does not seem to be experienced at all, with perhaps the exception of the "perfect" in Philippians 3:15. The Corinthians are certain God's power is at work, but they are mistaken as to the situation in which it works; they need to understand that it works precisely in weakness. The Philippians also need to understand that power works in weakness, but apparently the more basic problem is to keep them from giving in to discouragement.' Koperski, 'Knowledge of Christ and Knowledge of God in the Corinthian Correspondence', in R. Bieringer (ed.), *The Corinthian Correspondence*, BETL 125 (Leuven: Leuven University Press/ Peeters 1996), 383.

[49] Stuhlmacher, 'Hermeneutical Significance', 333.

[50] Paul deliberately uses the same word 'body' (*sōma*) for the Eucharist in 11:24–29 and for the Church in 12:12; in 1 Corinthians 10:16f the connection is even more explicit.

[51] Cf. the similar line of reasoning in Romans 1:21–25. Both passages imply that the reverse order also holds true: sin leads to ignorance of God. Otherwise there would be no way to impute culpability to the ignorance.

not know' God and his plan. Conversely, Paul presents the true wisdom of God as resulting in heartfelt worship of God and harmonious ecclesial fellowship. Those who have interiorized the Spirit's revelation lead a life manifesting the mind of Christ through mutual love and service.

The Role of the Holy Spirit

The irreducibly personal nature of knowledge of God accounts for the key role Paul attributes to the Holy Spirit in the interplay of divine and human knowledge.[52] A close examination of his argument in 1 Corinthians 2:9-12 shows that this is not simply a matter of the Spirit's imparting revelation in the 'downward' movement from God to man. The Spirit also empowers the human mind to reach 'upward' to God in an act of knowledge that it could not achieve on its own: 'we have received ... the Spirit from God, *that we might understand*' (1 Cor 2:12).[53] Such divine–human intercommunication is possible only by the Spirit's mediation, without which the human mind is perpetually thwarted in its attempts to attain the mind of God (1 Cor 1:20f). Paul is alluding to the principle, common in the ancient world, that 'like is known by like.' In this case the object of knowledge is infinitely incommensurate with human cognitive powers, but the Spirit who 'searches the depths of God' can allow human beings to participate in his own divine knowledge of God. The Spirit becomes the hermeneutical key enabling the human mind to adequately interpret what is revealed in the crucifixion of Jesus; that is, to look into the depths of divine love through the kenosis of God's Son. Even more, we can infer that since the Spirit dwells in the believer, he searches the depths of God *from within the believer* and thus invites the believer into the intra-Trinitarian communion. Thus understood, the Spirit's communication of divine truth is indistinguishable from his communication of divine life.

The importance Paul ascribes to the Spirit's epistemic role, opening the believer's mind to otherwise inaccessible realities, is evident throughout his correspondence. Just as the Corinthians' initial reception of the good news was made possible by a 'demonstration of Spirit and of power' (1 Cor 2:4), so the evangelization of the Thessalonians was effected by the Spirit bringing 'power' and 'full conviction' (1 Thes 1:5). This implies not merely that the Spirit caused visible miracles or

---

[52] Scott, *Implicit Epistemology*, 49, notes the importance of the Spirit's epistemic role, but sees this role as essentially remedial; that is, Paul's hearers cannot comprehend the message of the gospel 'unless they first overcome certain moral vices which consistently distort human intellectual standards. It is the Spirit who plays the key role in this epistemic process, by healing the human moral constitution so that the internal coherence and rational implications of the gospel can be recognized.' While this is an important insight, it does not do full justice to the Spirit's mediation in human knowledge of God even apart from moral failings, as argued below.

[53] In the words of P. Gooch, the Spirit bridges the 'epistemic gap' between God and man (*Partial Knowledge*, Philosophical Studies in Paul [Notre Dame, IN: Notre Dame, 1987], 36–37).

charismatic phenomena confirming the credibility of the message, but that he brought about an interior conviction disposing the listeners to recognize its truthfulness. Likewise, Paul advises the Corinthians that 'No one can say "Jesus is Lord" except by the Holy Spirit' (1 Cor 12:3); that is, only by the Spirit is Christ's sovereignty over all things grasped as a vital truth. The Spirit's illumination is equally indispensable for removing the 'veil' of human incomprehension so that Christ may be recognized in the prefigurations of the old covenant (2 Cor 3:16f). The Spirit bestows a living awareness of our adoptive sonship (Rom 8:15-17; Gal 4:6) and gives the inner 'strength' necessary to comprehend the immeasurable scope of divine love (Eph 3:16-19). In an another text that alludes to the 'like by like' principle, Paul explains that the Spirit enables one to interiorly 'see' or become consciously aware of the splendor and truth of God's self-revelation in Christ: 'And we all, with unveiled face, beholding the glory of the Lord, are being changed into his likeness from glory to glory; for this comes from the Lord who is the Spirit' (2 Cor 3:18).[54] Here 'likeness' to Christ is not only a prerequisite but also a result of knowing him, suggesting that knowledge and likeness increase in a dialectic relationship. All of these assertions confirm in various ways that revelatory knowledge involves an ongoing work of the Spirit, empowering the human mind to transcend its natural capabilities in order to receive and reciprocate the divine self-communication.

A Twofold Mode of Knowledge?

How does this Spirit-bestowed revelatory knowledge relate to ordinary human knowing? In the conflated citation of 1 Corinthians 2:9, Paul refers to that which 'eye has not seen, nor ear heard, nor the heart of man conceived'. By speaking of eye, ear and heart, he sums up in biblical language the sources of knowledge available within the natural sphere, from the highest physical senses to rational intelligence. He does so in order to emphasize that the hidden wisdom of God has not come by these human channels, but only by the Spirit's revelation. That which the human heart has not conceived, and was constitutionally incapable of conceiving, has become the object of revelatory knowledge. Paul thus establishes what Gooch refers to as 'the religious impotence of reason';[55] that is, reason's incapacity to arrive independently at the central content of Christian faith. But based on what was said above regarding the ongoing and personal nature of revelation, we can take this notion a step further. Paul's overarching purpose in 1 Corinthians 2:6-16 is to urge his readers to open themselves more deeply to the continuous revelatory work of the Spirit, so that the divine mystery may become a living source of life for them. He is not merely informing them that an understanding of God's plan, which could never

---

[54] The notion of beholding or 'seeing' the things of God is also expressed in 1 Corinthians 13:12, although the accent there is on the contrast between the relatively obscure mode of vision in this life, 'in a mirror dimly', and that in the life to come, which is 'face to face.'

[55] Gooch, *Partial Knowledge*, 43.

have been generated by human reason, has now been revealed to the apostles, who pass it on to the believers. Rather, he is declaring that the hidden wisdom of God continues to transcend the grasp of reason and to surpass anything that human thought can sustain on its own. Because it involves an irreducible, personal mystery, the object of knowledge is not only previously unknown to sense and intellectual cognition, but *per se* beyond the power of human faculties. It thus requires a permanent disposition of openness to and reliance on the Spirit. This suggests that the revelatory knowledge Paul is referring to is different in kind, not just in origin, from natural knowledge. It is a spiritual perception by which the Spirit, through a gift of grace, elevates the human mind to a share in his own personal 'acquaintance' with God. That which 'the heart of (natural) man has not conceived' still cannot be conceived without the Spirit.

This raises the question as to whether, in knowledge of the divine mystery, there is any room for the natural functioning of the mind. Is Paul referring to a form of charismatic illuminism or a separate spiritual 'track' of knowledge appropriate to divine matters, in which reason and sense perception have no role? [56] An attentive consideration of his statements shows that such is not the case. Although the divine mystery permanently transcends human understanding, Paul nowhere gives any indication that it precludes the need for human understanding. Both his writings and his life testify to the urgency of preaching and teaching the gospel in a form that appeals to human intelligence.[57] Of his own ministry he affirms, 'By the open statement of the truth we would commend ourselves to every person's conscience in the sight of God' (2 Cor 4:2), and he asks rhetorically, 'How are people to call upon him in whom they have not believed? And how are they to believe in him of whom they have never heard? And how are they to hear without a preacher?' (Rom 10:14). The necessity for the active cooperation of the mind is equally apparent in 1 Corinthians 2:13, where Paul indicates that the Spirit's revelatory action takes place precisely through, not apart from, the normal channels of human communication with all their attendant linguistic, intellectual and cultural forms. Moreover, Paul's very act of communicating divine truth by writing a letter, using all the tools of logical and rhetorical persuasion at his disposal, presupposes that the addressees will actively engage their minds in hearing and interpreting it. All this indicates that for Paul, knowledge acquired by ordinary human means is not circumvented but elevated and integrated into the revelatory knowledge bestowed by the Spirit.

As noted above, the central content of divine revelation is the 'mystery,' i.e., God himself as communicated in Christ crucified and risen. Thus, although the content of the knowledge of 'spiritual' Christians may be identical with that of 'immature' Christians (that is, the *kerygma*), it is known in a different way, as is manifested by their lives which either do or do not manifest increasing conformity to Christ. A

---

[56] For a thorough discussion of this question see Scott, *Implicit Epistemology*, 44-68.

[57] As noted above, Paul's teaching on charismatic phenomena differs from the classical Greek view in that the mind is engaged, not supplanted, in the Spirit's inspirational activity (1 Cor 14:15; cf. 14:6, 19).

mature knowledge, which is more adequate to the deeper dimensions of divine reality,[58] might be called spiritual or mystical as opposed to the merely rational. The use of the adverb 'spiritually' (*pneumatikōs*) in 1 Corinthians 2:14 reaffirms that a spiritual person apprehends the same objects as a natural person, but apprehends them differently.[59] They are only recognized *as* gifts of the Spirit of God through Spirit-inspired knowledge. This principle applies primarily, of course, to the 'foolishness' of a crucified Messiah, but secondarily to other gifts of God which may come in 'distressing disguise,' for instance trials and temptations (2 Cor 12:9f), hardships (2 Cor 4:16f), or weak and troublesome members of the body of Christ (1 Cor 12:15-24).

The latter observation enables us to answer the question whether revelatory knowledge applies only to the mystery of Christ, that truth undiscoverable by human reason, or whether it extends to other matters. By affirming that the spiritual person 'discerns all things', Paul indicates that the Spirit's illumination, when actively welcomed, sheds its light on everything the mind apprehends. This is not to say that ordinary matters are now known by special revelation, but that the understanding conferred by the Spirit effects a new hermeneutic that influences one's perception of all reality. Paul challenges the Corinthians in this regard by his repeated refrain, 'Do you not know ...?' by which he reminds them that they ought to be aware of the radical implications of their faith in every aspect of life.[60]

Finally, we have to ask where human philosophical inquiry, subject to such a stringent critique in 1 Corinthians 1:18-2:5, stands in light of revelatory knowledge. This question is best answered by interpreting 1 Corinthians 2:6-16 in juxtaposition with Paul's indictment of pagan ignorance of God in Romans 1:18-32. Whereas in the Corinthians text Paul declares the impossibility of 'knowing God' through human intellectual inquiry (1 Cor 1:21), in Romans he insists that even the most benighted pagans 'knew God' (Rom 1:21). But the inconsistency is only apparent, since the knowledge referred to in Romans is an inferential knowledge limited to 'what can be known about God' (1:19), that is, an awareness of God's invisible power and deity, and of the moral law (Rom 1:20; 1:32). It is attained by reasoning about the things God has created and is thus naturally available to all people 'since the creation of the world' (1:19). It does not reach the mysterious 'depths of God' or his eternally hidden plan for salvation in Christ. From this distinction, we can infer that if philosophy is defined as human inquiry into the meaning of existence and of the cosmos, Paul regards it as a legitimate but ultimately deficient activity. To the degree that it arrogantly ignores its limitations, and thereby closes itself to the Spirit's revelation, the 'wisdom of men' becomes a hindrance to revelatory knowledge and thus reprehensible.

---

[58] See R. Guardini, 'Sacra Scrittura e scienza della fede', in I. de la Potterie et al. (eds.), *L'esegesi cristiana oggi* (Casale Monferrato: Piemme, 1991), 46–48, for insightful reflections on the principle that knowledge must be adequate to its object.

[59] Cf. the equivalent notion, 'in all spiritual wisdom and understanding' in Colossians 1:9.

[60] 1 Cor 3:16; 5:6; 6:2, 3, 9, 15, 16, 19; 9:13, 24.

Another key text where Paul draws a contrast between two forms of knowledge is 2 Corinthians 5:16: 'From now on, therefore, we know (*oida*) no one according to the flesh; even though we once knew (*ginōskō*) Christ according to the flesh, we know (*ginōskō*) him thus no longer.'[61] As in 1 Corinthians, Paul is pointing to a new way of knowing corresponding to a new form of existence, which is specified in the subsequent verse: 'If any one is in Christ, he is a new creation; the old has passed away, behold, the new has come' (2 Cor 5:17). As a persecutor of the Church, Paul previously had a carnal view of Christ, that is, one limited to his own intellectual resources which were still 'veiled' and 'darkened' by sin (cf. 2 Cor 3:15; 4:4). He 'knew' Jesus as merely an itinerant preacher and dangerous messianic pretender; he was blind to Jesus' divine identity and salvific mission. But 'from now on' – a phrase that refers both to Paul's conversion and to the eschatological 'now' inaugurated by the Christ-event – he knows him as Savior and Lord. In the same way, the Corinthians are to put off their 'carnal' understanding of the divine mysteries that belongs to their former life and gain the revelatory knowledge which belongs to the new life in the Spirit. As in 1 Corinthians, Paul emphasizes that such knowledge, though divinely bestowed, fully engages human freedom. To account for the fact that some people refuse to accept the good news, he explains that 'their minds were hardened', 'a veil lies over their heart' (3:14f), and they have been blinded by 'the god of this world' to keep them from seeing the light of the gospel (4:4). These formulations suggest both unintentional deception and willful blindness. Although such people may have heard the gospel proclaimed, they, like the 'rulers of this age' in 1 Corinthians 2:8, fail to recognize the cogency and truth of God's plan. Such understanding can only come about by a 'turning to the Lord'; that is, a free and trusting self-surrender (3:16f). While human beings do not have the power to arrive independently at revelatory knowledge, they do have a choice to allow the Spirit to grant it.

Knowledge and Faith

How, then, does knowledge relate to that more celebrated and studied Pauline theme, faith? The latter is strikingly absent from 1 and 2 Corinthians relative to the other epistles, especially Romans.[62] In fact, it is fair to say that the place taken by *pistis/pisteuō* in Romans is occupied by *gnōsis/ginōskō* in the Corinthian

---

[61] Davies, *Paul and Rabbinic Judaism*, 194–95, has shown that there is no foundation for the claim that this verse is a later Gnostic gloss deprecating the earthly Jesus. See also Koperski, 'Knowledge of Christ', 385. For the Gnostic interpretation see Schmithals, *Gnosticism*, 302–15.

[62] Of the 142 Pauline occurrences of *pistis* (including the Pastorals), only seven are in 1 Corinthians, as compared with 40 in Romans. Of these seven, two refer to a narrower sense of faith as a charismatic gift given only to some for the edification of the body (1 Cor 12:9; 13:2). 2 Corinthians likewise has seven occurrences. The verb *pisteuō* appears nine times in 1 Corinthians (of which two, 9:17 and 11:18, have a non-theological meaning), and twice in 2 Corinthians, as compared with 21 times in Romans and 22 times in the other letters.

correspondence. The approach of scholarship to this disparity has generally been to take faith as the paradigm, and knowledge as a side issue whose prominence in 1 and 2 Corinthians is due to that community's aberrant preoccupations. Such a reluctance to treat *gnōsis* in its own right may be partly owing to the damaging effects of Gnosticism (which claims Paul as one of its chief sources) on Christian life from the earliest centuries of the Church. But we may legitimately ask whether the Gnostic threat has not led to an unwarranted downplaying of certain elements that Paul himself considered important in his theology.

Although faith is not mentioned in 1 Corinthians 2:6-16, it does occur in the immediately preceding unit, where Paul explains that his manner of preaching was such that the Corinthians' faith 'might not rest in the wisdom of men but in the power of God' (2:5). It reoccurs in verbal form in 3:5, where Paul and Apollos are described as 'servants through whom you believed (*episteusate*)'. Earlier, in the wisdom antitheses of Chapter 1, Paul states that since 'the world did not know God through wisdom, it pleased God through the folly of what we preach to save those who believe (*pisteuontas*)' (1 Cor 1:21). In these texts faith appears with its typical Pauline meaning as the obedient and trusting acceptance of God's gift of grace in Christ, which is the immediate goal of apostolic preaching although it is produced by God and not by the preaching itself. As the proper response to an encounter with Christ through the gospel proclamation, faith is what distinguishes 'those who are perishing' from 'those who are being saved' (1:18).[63] Faith thus seems to be a more basic and fundamental reality than the mature knowledge described in 1 Corinthians 2:6–16.[64] It involves not a plumbing of the depths of God but an acceptance of the divine 'foolishness' of the cross even before its full implications are understood. Whereas knowledge is an indicator of relative maturity among Christians, faith marks the divide between Christians and non-Christians.[65]

But although Paul associates knowledge rather than faith with Christian maturity, he never states or implies that faith is a lesser reality eventually replaced by knowledge. There is no suggestion that the spiritual person, who knows experientially the gifts bestowed by God, need no longer rely on faith. In fact, in an eschatological context Paul asserts the very opposite, declaring that 'knowledge passes away' whereas faith 'remains' (1 Cor 13:8, 13). In other contexts, faith and knowledge are paired as Christian qualities equally expected to grow in the life of

---

[63] This distinction is also implicit in 1 Corinthians 14:22; 15:11.

[64] For Paul, as for the Bible in general, the very notion of faith already implies at least a minimal degree of knowledge (cf. Rom 10:14). In order to believe one must have at least a rudimentary understanding of the object of belief, i.e., the existence of God and his plan of salvation. But such initial comprehension is not the same as the mature knowledge referred to in 2:6–16.

[65] This helps explain why, for all their deficiencies in knowledge, Paul does not say the Corinthians are lacking in faith. The absence of such statements in Paul is in marked contrast to the sayings of Jesus, for whom his disciples' lack of faith was a frequent subject of reproach: cf. Mt 8:10b; 19:20; Mk 4:40; 9:24; Lk 17:6; Jn 4:48.

the believer.[66] Paul expresses his hope that the Corinthians' faith increase (2 Cor 10:15; cf. Phil 1:25), and exhorts them not to grow out of their faith but to 'stand firm' in it (1 Cor 16:13; 2 Cor 1:24). How is this paradox to be explained? It can only make sense in light of the irreducibly personal and relational character of Pauline knowledge of God as noted above, to which human relationships are the closest analogy. Even in the case of a human relationship, knowing another can never exhaust the mystery of the other. In fact, as van Beeck observes, interpersonal knowledge paradoxically increases the mystery: 'persons we have come to know really well are often more mysterious to us than others whom we know only superficially.'[67] Knowledge of another person – and preeminently of a divine Person – thus involves a dialectic of mystery and intelligibility, such that increasing knowledge entails an increasing wonder and deference before the mystery of the other. It is a kind of knowledge which proceeds by trust, in which further knowledge always entails a corresponding deepening of trust.[68] Such a description is *a fortiori* true of knowledge of the invisible God, who reveals himself by his saving acts and invites human beings to respond with trusting acceptance. This observation suggests that for Paul *gnōsis and pistis are in fact the same reality considered under different aspects.* Knowledge of God is a personal acquaintance with God and his ways considered as experiential contact; faith is that same acquaintance considered in light of its necessary concomitant of obedient trust. As von Balthasar remarks in his illuminating treatment of the subject, faith is united with knowledge 'in one and the same total human act'.[69]

Paul defines the spiritual (*pneumatikos*) or mature Christian, in contrast to the unspiritual (*psychikos*) or infant Christian, as one who 'knows' the things of God because he actively appropriates the Spirit's interior revelation (1 Cor 2:14f). Knowledge of God is presented as a gauge of Christian maturity, not merely as another way of referring to the faith which belongs to all Christians. This suggests that faith, as the foundational act of trusting in God's revelation, is meant to blossom into knowledge, as a deepening familiarity with God and participation in the mystery of salvation. At the same time, the perdurance of mystery guarantees that knowledge does not preclude or even diminish faith. In short, faith and knowledge of God do not stand in an inverse relationship but are directly proportionate to each other. As von Balthasar remarks, for Paul 'The highest Christian experience and *gnōsis* can

---

[66] Cf. Phm 6; Eph 4:13; Tit 1:1. This pairing also occurs where faith and knowledge are charismatic gifts: 1 Cor 12:8f; 13:2; 2 Cor 8:7.

[67] Van Beeck, 'Divine Revelation', 211.

[68] Cf. John Paul II, *Fides et Ratio* (Vatican City: Libreria Editrice Vaticana, 1998), §13–14: 'the knowledge proper to faith does not destroy the mystery; it only reveals it the more ... Revelation has set within history a point of reference which cannot be ignored ... Yet this knowledge refers back constantly to the mystery of God which the human mind cannot exhaust but can only receive and embrace in faith. Between these two poles, reason has its own specific field ...'

[69] H.U. von Balthasar, 'Pistis and Gnōsis', in *The Glory of the Lord: A Theological Aesthetics*, I: *Seeing the Form*, E. Leiva-Merikakis (tr.) (San Francisco: Ignatius, 1982), 133.

never surpass faith, but only strengthen it and demonstrate its rightness.'[70] This interrelationship is confirmed by other Pauline texts. In Philippians, the Apostle declares that he knows Christ (3:8) and has faith in him (3:9), yet strives toward a deeper participatory knowledge: 'that I may know him and the power of his resurrection, and may share his sufferings, becoming like him in his death ...' (3:10). In Romans, he develops an interplay of knowing, believing and reckoning, in which knowledge leads to greater faith, and conversely, the act of trust involved in 'reckoning' increases the experiential depth of one's knowledge (6:1-11). Knowledge is the full flowering of faith, without ever supplanting it.[71]

Since faith is the distinctively Christian mode of knowledge of God, as the fundamental disposition that God seeks in response to his self-revelation in Christ, it is not surprising that faith has overall priority in Paul as in the New Testament in general.[72] Why, then, is knowledge more prominent in 1-2 Corinthians? The supposition that knowledge is a Corinthian catchword (cf. 1 Cor 8:1) is a plausible but not entirely satisfying explanation. The only setting where knowledge is treated in an unambiguously polemical sense is in the discussion of idol meat in Chapter 8. Paul's insistence on the futility of knowledge without love (13:2) is matched by an equal insistence on the futility of faith without love (13:2). In virtually every other context, *gnōsis* is commended, exhorted, defended, and praised.[73] A more convincing explanation is that Paul recognizes that although the Corinthians have in certain ways a vibrant faith (as manifested particularly in their exercise of spiritual gifts), their knowledge of God remains at a shallow and superficial level. Their characteristic weakness is not that of seeking justification by works apart from faith

---

[70] Balthasar, *Glory*, I, 227.

[71] The notion of *gnōsis* as the perfection of *pistis* was developed by Clement of Alexandria (*Stromata*, ET. *Miscellanies*, ANF, II, 7, 55, 5; 3, 41, 1) and Origen (*Commentaria in Evangelium Joannis*, ET. *Commentary on John*, ANF, X, 32, 20–21), following earlier Fathers. See Louis Bouyer, *The Spirituality of the New Testament and the Fathers*, M.P. Ryan (tr.) (New York: Desclee, 1963), 211–36. For these thinkers in the Alexandrian school, Christian maturity entails moving beyond a purely external relationship with the doctrines of faith, received on authority, to an interior actualization of these mysteries so that they unfold before one's inner 'vision'. Knowledge never outgrows faith but rather fulfills it: 'There is no knowledge without faith, and there is no faith without knowledge' (Clement, *Stromata*, 5, 1, 3). See Balthasar, *Glory*, I, 137–138.

[72] This is the case despite the numerical priority of the vocabulary of knowledge (depending on how the words are counted), because terms for knowledge are more often used in an ordinary, non-theological sense than terms for faith.

[73] Cf. 1 Cor 1:5; 12:8; 14:6; 2 Cor 2:14; 4:6; 6:6; 8:7; 10:5; 11:6. In 1 Corinthians 13 the limitations of *gnōsis* are noted but not in a polemical tone: although '*gnōsis* passes away' (13:8), in the end 'I shall fully know (*epignōsomai*)' (13:12). Outside the Corinthian correspondence, *gnōsis* appears in a polemical context in Romans 2:20, where self-righteous Jews are chided for thinking they 'have in the law the embodiment of knowledge and truth', and 1 Tim 6:20, where the young pastor is urged to avoid 'what is falsely called knowledge.' All other instances are unequivocally positive: Rom 11:33; 15:14; Phil 3:8; Col 2:3 and Eph 3:19.

(as is implied, for instance, of the Galatian and Roman Christians). Rather, it is a failure to enter more deeply into the mystery of Christ's death to sin and communion with God, due to their self-satisfied complacency.

Perhaps the most obscure of Paul's claims on the relationship of knowledge and faith are the eschatological statements mentioned above, that in the end knowledge 'will pass away' whereas faith 'remains' along with hope and love (1 Cor 13:8, 13).[74] In what sense does faith remain, and how does this square with his distinction between 'faith' as characteristic of the present life and 'sight' as characteristic of the life to come (2 Cor 5:7)? This dilemma is resolved by understanding faith in Paul's terms as the trust and surrender appropriate to personal knowledge. Although such trust is a manifest requirement of discipleship on earth with all its trials and obscurities, it is not necessarily precluded even by the direct vision of heaven. A further question concerns what kind of 'knowledge' is to vanish away. Is Paul referring merely to the charismatic gift of 12:8 and 14:6,[75] or to earthly knowledge in general? His ensuing comments indicate that although he began with a reference to the spiritual gifts, he has moved to a more encompassing consideration. Our present knowledge, though not invalid, is 'partial' or 'imperfect' (vv. 9 and 12), and will in the end give way to 'full knowledge' (*epignōsis*, v. 12).[76] Such a transformation involves the obliteration not of the element of faith, but of the incompleteness and imperfection of earthly knowledge. What we know now through the Spirit's interior revelation will be consummated in a personal knowing as perfect as God's knowledge of us.

Conclusion

This study has challenged the common assumption that knowledge is a relatively insignificant theme in Pauline theology. A close look at the data has, in fact, led to the opposite conclusion – that for Paul, knowledge of God is an immensely important dimension of salvation and of the Christian life. For Paul, to know God is to respond to his disclosure within the world of the inmost divine mystery through the person and life of Jesus Christ. The Holy Spirit has an essential role in this process, as the hermeneutical key enabling the human mind to apprehend the depths of divine love revealed in the crucifixion of Jesus. Such knowledge is received only through revelation by the Spirit and thus can be termed a *revelatory knowledge*. Through it God's plan of salvation is no longer just a historical fact or doctrinal truth but something one knows consciously and participates in. The believer experiences the efficacy of the cross freeing him from sin, becomes aware of the presence of

---

[74] The repeated use of the verb *katargeō* (vv. 8, 10, 11) associates knowledge with the structures of 'this age' which have been doomed to inevitable destruction by Christ's victory on the cross (cf. 1:28; 2:6; 6:13; 13:8, 10f; 15:24, 26).

[75] As Fee, for instance, contends in *First Corinthians*, 642–43.

[76] As Gooch has shown in his penetrating study of the passage, Paul describes the incompleteness of the knowledge in three ways, each of which helps to clarify his meaning: it is 'childish', indirect ('in a mirror'), and 'puzzling' (*Partial Knowledge*, 145–54).

Christ within him, and is brought into a living communion with the triune God, in transcendent fulfillment of the Old Testament promises. This knowledge has immediate ethical consequences, since genuine knowledge of God leads to a transformed life (cf. 2 Cor 3:18). It is attended by the power to serve, to repent, to forgive, to love, to edify the body, and to live the new life in the Spirit in all its ramifications, as detailed throughout Paul's letters. Knowledge of God is, so to speak, the flower, of which a communal life of mutual love and unity is the fruit.

Bibliography

Balthasar, H.U. von, *The Glory of the Lord: A Theological Aesthetics*, I: *Seeing the Form*, E. Leiva-Merikakis (tr.) (San Francisco: Ignatius, 1982)

Beeck, F.J. van, 'Divine Revelation: Intervention or Self-Communication?' *Theological Studies* 52 (1991), 199–226

Bouyer, L., *The Spirituality of the New Testament and the Fathers*, M.P. Ryan (tr.) (New York: Desclee, 1963)

Bultmann, R., *Faith and Understanding*, L. Smith (tr.) (Philadelphia: Fortress, 1987)

_____, 'ginōskō,' *Theological Dictionary of the New Testament*, I, 689–719

Clement of Alexandria, *Stromata*, ET. *Miscellanies*, ANF, II

Conzelmann, Hans, *1 Corinthians*, Hermeneia, J.W. Leitch (tr.) (Philadelphia: Fortress, 1975)

Corbon, J., and A. Vanhoye, 'Know,' *Dictionary of Biblical Theology* (New York: Seabury, 1973²), 296–98

Davies, W.D., *Paul and Rabbinic Judaism. Some Rabbinic Elements in Pauline Theology* (London: SPCK, 1948)

Davis, J., *Wisdom and Spirit: An Investigation of 1 Corinthians 1.18–3.20 against the Background of Jewish Sapiential Traditions in the Greco-Roman Period* (Lanham, MD: University Press of America, 1984)

Dunn, James D.G., *Jesus and the Spirit. A Study of the Religious and Charismatic Experience of Jesus and the First Christians As Reflected in the New Testament* (Philadelphia: Westminster, 1975)

_____, *The Theology of Paul the Apostle* (Grand Rapids: Eerdmans, 1998)

Dupont, J., *Gnōsis: La connaissance religieuse dans les épitres de Saint Paul* (Louvain: Gabalda, 1949)

Fee, G., *The First Epistle to the Corinthians*, NICNT (Grand Rapids: Eerdmans, 1987)

_____, 'Toward a Theology of 1 Corinthians,' in D.M. Hay (ed.), *Pauline Theology*, II: *1 and 2 Corinthians* (Minneapolis: Fortress, 1993), 37–58

Fitzmyer, J.A., 'Pauline Theology,' *New Jerome Bible Commentary* (Englewood Cliffs, NJ: Prentice Hall, 1990), 1382–1416

Funk, R.W., *Language, Hermeneutic, and the Word of God: The Problem of Language in the New Testament and Contemporary Theology* (New York: Harper, 1966)

Gooch, P., *Partial Knowledge*, Philosophical Studies in Paul (Notre Dame, IN: Notre Dame, 1987)

Guardini, R., 'Sacra Scrittura e scienza della fede,' in I. de la Potterie et al. (eds.), *L'esegesi cristiana oggi* (Casale Monferrato: Piemme, 1991), 45–91

Horsley, R.A., 'Wisdom of Word and Words of Wisdom in Corinth,' *Catholic Biblical Quarterly* 39 (1977) 224–39

John Paul II, *Fides et ratio* (Vatican City: Libreria Editrice Vaticana, 1998)

Koperski, V., 'Knowledge of Christ and Knowledge of God in the Corinthian Correspondence', in R. Bieringer (ed.), *The Corinthian Correspondence*, BETL 125 (Leuven: Leuven University Press/ Peeters 1996), 377–96.

Murphy-O'Connor, J., 'The First Letter to the Corinthians', *New Jerome Bible Commentary* (Englewood Cliffs, NJ: Prentice Hall, 1990), 798-815

Origen, *Commentaria in Evangelium Joannis*, ET. *Commentary on John, The Ante-Nicene Fathers*, X

Pearson, B.A., *The Pneumatikos-Psychikos Terminology in 1 Corinthians*, SBLDS 12 (Missoula, MT: Society of Biblical Literature, 1973)

Pseudo-Chrysostom, *Sermo in sanctum pascha*, I, P. Nautin (tr.), Sources Chrétiennes 36 (Paris: Cerf, 1953)

Reitzenstein, R., *Hellenistic Mystery Religions: Their Basic Ideas and Significance*, PTM 15, J.E. Steely (tr.) (Pittsburgh: Pickwick, 1978)

Schindler, D.L., 'God and the End of Intelligence: Knowledge as Relationship', *Communio* 26 (1999) 510–40

Schmithals, W., *Gnosticism in Corinth: An Investigation of the Letter to the Corinthians*, J. Steely (tr.) (Nashville: Abingdon, 1971)

Scott, I.W., *Implicit Epistemology in the Letters of Paul. Story, Experience and Spirit*, WUNT 205 (Tübingen: Mohr Siebeck, 2006)

Scroggs, Robin, 'Paul: ΣΟΦΟΣ and ΠΝΕΥΜΑΤΙΚΟΣ,' *New Testament Studies* 14 (1967) 33–55

Stuhlmacher, P., 'The Hermeneutical Significance of 1 Cor 2:6–16', C. Brown (tr.), in G. Hawthorne and O. Betz (eds.), *Tradition and Interpretation in the New Testament. Fs. E. Earl Ellis* (Grand Rapids: Eerdmans, 1987), 328-47

Wilckens, U., *Weisheit und Torheit. Eine exegetisch-religionsgeschichtliche Untersuchung zu 1 Kor 1 und 2*, BHT 26 (Tübingen: Mohr/Siebeck, 1959)

Wilson, R. McL., 'Gnosis at Corinth,' in M.D. Hooker and S.G. Wilson (eds.), *Paul and Paulinism. Fs. C.K. Barrett* (London: SPCK, 1982), 102–14

Part II

Theological and Philosophical Reflections

CHAPTER 8

'Incline Your Ear So That You May Live': Principles of Biblical Epistemology

Murray Rae

Knowledge of God is not, first of all, the fruit of human industry, but rather of attentiveness. This biblical conception of how we may attain knowledge of God contrasts with the prevailing view of Modernity that knowledge is mastery. As Francis Martin points out in this volume, the pervasive view of the modern mind is that 'the thinking subject is dominative in the act of knowing.'[1] Immanuel Kant represents well the modern view. The individual subject, possessed of the capacity to think rationally, takes hold of the world and determines the categories according to which it is to be conceptually rendered. Even space and time, commonly regarded as fundamental categories of created existence, are conceived not as divinely established conditions of the created order, but as creations of the human mind established for the sake of the rational subject's own ordering of the world. Although the mind's capacity to receive impressions is a necessary condition of knowledge for Kant, the world is known by virtue of being assimilated to an order of our own making. This, as Martin again points out, is exactly the opposite of the epistemology prominent in the Christian theological tradition according to which knowledge comes about as the knowing subject is assimilated to what is known. Martin quotes Thomas Aquinas who writes, 'True (*verum*) expresses the correspondence (*convenientia*) of being to the knowing power (*intellectus*), for all knowing is produced by an assimilation of the knower to the thing known, so that assimilation is said to be the cause of knowledge (*assimilatio dicta est causa cognitionis*).'[2] Elsewhere Aquinas speaks of the knowing subject being *conformed* to the object that is known.

The investigations of this volume reveal a striking consistency amongst the biblical authors in adhering to the epistemology here represented by Aquinas. Human knowing does not arise through domination but through attentiveness to the object. Such attentiveness conforms the knower to what is known rather than the other way around. The result is that the knower is not left as she was but is transformed through the knowing process. The knower is made a new person under the impact of the new relation with the object established through attentiveness. In

---

[1] Martin, 'Psalms', 43.
[2] Martin, 'Psalms', 45.

the special case of knowledge of God, this transformation is nothing less than the gift of new life. In what follows I shall trace the epistemological features of this attentiveness and transformation as they are brought to light in the essays of this volume.

Revelation

The presupposition of an attentive epistemology is that the object to be known somehow gives itself to be known. Martin cites Jacques Maritain's claim that there is a 'basic generosity of existence'.[3] While one cannot attribute intention to all of the natural world, it is clearly the case in the knowledge of persons that we rely to a large extent on their giving themselves to be known. The rich knowledge of another that comes through conversation, intimacy and love depends upon the hospitality and the generosity of the other. In this case, knowledge is received as gift. It cannot be coerced. That is especially true of the knowledge of God for whom there can be no question of either an unwitting self-disclosure or of our taking hold of God against God's will. Knowledge of God is always *revealed* knowledge. There is no means available to us of knowing God other than by heeding the counsel offered in Isaiah: 'Incline your ear, and come to me; listen, so that you may live' (Is 55:3). The three features of Isaiah's 'epistemology' recur again and again in the biblical materials surveyed in this volume. First, knowledge of God comes through attentiveness to what is given; it is not of our own making. Second, it is given in relationship; it depends upon our response to the One who says, 'Come to me.' And third, both attentiveness to God and relationship with him are the constituents of new life, indeed, of the only true life there is.

   The theme of attentiveness to God's giving of himself is characteristic of the Old Testament literature. Ryan O'Dowd observes that knowledge in the biblical wisdom literature is understood to be contingent upon a religious encounter with Yahweh. 'Wisdom acts after, and because of, a divine encounter – not before it.'[4] Likewise, in the Pentateuch, divine speech is understood to be the condition and presupposition of all human speech about God. Thus in Deuteronomy when, as O'Dowd again explains, the momentum of the previous four books (Genesis to Numbers) is shifted away from the divine and toward human speech, the words of Moses are a response to all that God has said and done.[5] O'Dowd draws on the work of Walther Zimmerli and Lyle Eslinger to suggest that the revelation of Yahweh and the manifestation of the divine name is the central theme of the Exodus, and it is this self-disclosure of Yahweh that yields knowledge of him.[6] Francis Martin likewise summarizes the epistemology of the Psalms: 'Our journey back to truth begins by recognizing that truth is most often found in a relationship of trust in another that leads us to a

---

[3] Martin, 'Psalms', 45.

[4] O'Dowd, 'Wisdom', 67.

[5] O'Dowd, 'Deuteronomy', 5.

[6] O'Dowd, 'Deuteronomy', 6.

movement of self-giving and of commitment to the truth which the other has shown us.'[7] The theme is continued in the New Testament. Mary Healy, for instance, notes Paul's insistence that 'in human knowledge of God, it is always God who takes the initiative by revealing himself.'[8] The Johannine epistemology, elucidated by Cornelis Bennema, involves 'a human response of belief to [the] divine initiative ...'[9] and in Luke-Acts Thomas Stegman discovers what he calls a 'prayer epistemology', an epistemology that consists in 'a quiet, reverent posture of openness before God in order to listen to the divine Word ...'[10]

The consistency of the biblical testimony to the primacy of revelation should come as no surprise, and yet the epistemic practices that the primacy of revelation requires are easily forgotten, especially among those of us who seek theological knowledge under the auspices of the modern academy. We need to be constantly reminded, therefore, that theological knowing is inseparable from the life of obedience and faith. It is fostered through worship and prayer – those practices by which we submit ourselves to the Word and Spirit of God – and it is borne of humility before the Word. Theological knowing, furthermore, is always the fruit of grace. It is not attained through our own intellectual prowess but is given to those who are humble and contrite in heart. Those who attend to the message of the cross rather than to human wisdom attain the true knowledge of God (c.f. 1 Cor 1:18-31).

The primacy of revelation in theological knowing is one of the reasons, I think, that we do not often discover an explicit epistemology in the biblical writings. Several of the authors in this volume point out that in consideration of the particular texts they have been assigned, their task has required them to draw out from the ways in which the biblical author speaks of God what Gregory Vall describes as 'a nascent epistemology of faith'.[11] Similarly, Cornelis Bennema remarks that if we are to enquire after a Johannine epistemology we must *infer* it from the texts.[12] The lack of explicit epistemology in the biblical writings reflects the fact that we do not first establish the epistemological rules by which we may come to know God and then set out upon the task of making God known. God is prevenient, also in our acts of knowing;[13] the summons to obedience precedes theological inquiry and reveals the curious modern insistence upon setting aside revelation in order to establish an epistemology of our own to be a form of unbelief. The biblical writers are prompted to enquire after God because God has addressed them. They have already been arrested by the compelling authority of divine revelation and are constrained therefore, to proclaim what they have seen and heard. The question of how we may know God is therefore subordinated to the more urgent question of how those who have seen and heard are being called to respond. That is infuriating for the skeptic

---

[7] Martin, 'Psalms', 50.

[8] Healy, 'Pauline', 137.

[9] Bennema, 'Johannine', 108.

[10] Stegman, 'Luke-Acts', 105.

[11] Vall, 'Prophetic', 24.

[12] Bennema, 'Johannine', 107.

[13] On which, see J. Webster, *Confessing God* (London: T&T Clark, 2005), 19.

who wants to be assured that the word heard is really God's word and not just a projection of human wishful thinking, values, or high ideals,[14] or, indeed, that the hearing of this word is not merely a delusion. Yet the demand for justification of one's belief implies the existence of an authority other than God – commonly human reason – to which divine revelation is answerable. The Bible permits no such strategy, although it does suggest, as we shall explore further below, the possibility of a relation between revelation and reason that is other than antagonistic. Does this lack of concession to modernist epistemological predilections render theological claims especially problematic? That might be the case if the modern version of rationalistic epistemology were self-evidently superior and uncontestable, but it is neither. What we have in the contrast between modern rationalistic claims about what counts as knowledge and the biblical testimony to the self-disclosure of God, is a clash of world-views that cannot be resolved by appealing to the authority of one or the other. Commitment to either authority is a matter of trust and faith, an independent justification of which cannot be supplied. Our basic epistemological commitments, whatever they may be, have an irreducibly fiduciary character. It is to the merit of the biblical writers, therefore, that they implicitly and sometimes explicitly recognise that fact.

The fiduciary character of all human knowing does not commit us to fideism if by fideism we mean a determined resistance to all reasoned consideration of the claims of faith. All fields of human epistemic endeavor, theology included, are bound to establish practices for the clarification and testing of competing claims, chief among which will be the participation of those who claim to know X, Y or Z in communities of inquiry about the subject matter in question. We inhabit those communities of inquiry and participate in the practices handed on through the traditions of those communities, all the while trusting that such habitation leads us to discover more and more of the way reality is constituted. Beyond the specialist communities of physicists, literary critics, botanists, and so on, to which we may belong, or whose discoveries we may learn something of, each of us inhabits wider spheres of inquiry that are characterized by particular beliefs about the nature of the world, its origin and purpose, the meaning of our own lives, and the responsibilities to which we feel ourselves called. These too are fiduciary frameworks. We cannot live without them, nor detach ourselves from them. So long as they continue to have explanatory power we go on indwelling them, letting them shape, both intentionally but often unwittingly, the complex of thought and action that constitutes our lives. Only when the worldview we inhabit is challenged by the disclosure of new aspects of reality that cannot easily be accommodated within it does the possibility of *metanoia* or conversion emerge. In this case, and under the impact of reality itself, we may be converted to a new way of seeing and understanding and thus be led to a deeper and more coherent knowledge of the world. The epistemologists of Modernity, by

---

[14] This, of course, is the Feuerbachian charge, echoed variously by theological non-realists of our own time.

contrast, held detachment and objectivity to be the cardinal epistemic virtues and sought knowledge 'without our being altered or matured in the process'.[15]

The clash between the gospel and the wisdom of the world is not a new one, of course. In his correspondence with the church in Corinth Paul contrasts the 'foolishness' of the gospel with the wisdom of the world. Commenting on this passage, Mary Healy explains, 'A knowledge founded on autonomous reason evades the risk of self-engagement which is the *sine qua non* of personal knowledge.'[16] Thomas Stegman finds the author of Luke-Acts to be similarly ambivalent about the value of human reason. While 'Luke seems to sound an optimistic note about the possibility that natural theology can lead people to acknowledge and worship God', Stegman explains, 'there are clues in both [Acts 14 and 17] that militate against such optimism. In Acts 14:16 Paul adverts to God's allowing the Gentiles of previous generations "to go their own ways"; they in fact did *not* succeed in finding their way to the one true God.'[17] In Acts 17 Paul contrasts the 'times of ignorance' with the present era in which God, through the resurrection of Jesus Christ, has revealed his will and calls us to account. The New Testament writers generally follow Paul in announcing what has been disclosed in Christ rather than by seeking to build a theology upon the foundations of human reason, and yet, taking Paul especially as exemplary, reason, under the tutelage of faith, may play a part in tracing the theological, ethical and ecclesial implications of divine revelation. The knowledge yielded by faith is not inherently irrational or anti-rational, therefore, but it does stand opposed to that form of rationality that presumes to find a criterion of theological truth located elsewhere than in the one Logos of God made flesh in Jesus Christ.

Returning to the theme of revelation, which is the starting point and condition of all theological knowing, it is a basic axiom of biblical theology that God and the creation are ontologically distinct. This means that the establishment of an epistemic relation between God and creatures involves a process of mediation. God is not another 'like us'. He is not part of the furniture of the world, as Karl Rahner has put it, and is not available to be known, therefore, by virtue of his being one with us as a cohabitant of the created order. Kant understood this much but erred in supposing that God must therefore remain unknown, except as a necessary condition of our moral experience. The consistent proclamation of the biblical writers is that the God who is other than us makes himself known through Word and Spirit. The New Testament is an extended expression of the further confession that by the power of the Spirit the Word becomes flesh and dwells among us, full of grace and truth. This is the fundamental claim of any *Christian* epistemology. God makes himself known by declaring his Word in human form, a form, that is, that through the Spirit's prompting we can both apprehend and understand. The mediation of Jesus Christ,

---

[15] The point is taken from D.H. Knight, *The Eschatological Economy: Time and the Hospitality of God* (Grand Rapids: Eerdmans, 2006), 182.

[16] Healy, 'Pauline', 144.

[17] Stegman, 'Luke-Acts', 98.

called Emmanuel in Matthew 1:23, is the means by which God draws his creatures into a redemptive and epistemic relation with himself, thereby safeguarding both his own transcendent otherness and his immanent availability.

Although we cannot here enter in any detail upon the question of 'Christ in the Old Testament' we may observe that the epistemic logic set out above is maintained through both Testaments. God is known through the mediation of his Word and Spirit. It is to be noted, furthermore, that this mediation takes place not at an abstract philosophical level but through the particularities of history. God engages his people through exodus and exile, through the establishment of a covenant and in the settlement of a land. He makes himself known in the form of a human child, in a cross, an empty tomb, and in the breaking of bread. By these means God makes himself available and draws his creatures into the loving communion that is the purpose of creation itself.

Relational Epistemology

The connection in biblical understanding between knowledge of God and relationship with God is an essential one. Whereas in Modernity, as we have noted, detachment and objectivity are striven after, the biblical writers universally presume that personal relationship with God is the indispensable condition of knowledge. Knowledge is the fruit of worship, discipleship and obedience, and takes place within the context of covenant relationality. In his explication of the epistemological logic of the book of Deuteronomy Ryan O'Dowd explains that the Torah sets out the means by which Israel will be maintained in relationship with God, even after the death of Moses. The family and community laws in Deuteronomy 6:4-9, O'Dowd comments, 'reaffirm that Israel's knowledge of Yahweh is distinctly relational'.[18] Francis Martin's exposition of Psalm 86 confirms the point. The plea of the psalmist, 'Teach me, YHWH, your way' – a plea for knowledge and understanding – is set amidst the confession of a profoundly intimate communion with God. The psalmist commits himself to walk in faithfulness to YHWH just as YHWH has dealt faithfully with him, and it is only within the context of that mutual commitment that he presumes to ask for understanding of God's 'way'.

Drawing elsewhere upon the Wisdom literature, O'Dowd describes the fruits of this faithfulness as 'reflexive knowledge'. 'Wisdom acts after, and because of, a divine encounter – not before it', while the wisdom and knowledge set out in the book of Proverbs, for example, are 'dependent on faithfulness to Israel's God and covenant.'[19] O'Dowd points out, again, the contrast with Kantian epistemology according to which the autonomous knowing subject is called upon to think for herself without recourse to any external authority. The Kantian motto, 'think *for* yourself!', carries with it the implication that one ought also to think *by* oneself. Before Kant, Descartes, sitting alone in order to determine in solitude what may and

---

[18] O'Dowd, 'Deuteronomy', 10.
[19] O'Dowd, 'Wisdom', 67.

may not count as knowledge, epitomized the later Modernist mood. In the biblical literature, however, wisdom and knowledge are understood to be gifts received through encounter with the 'other'. Although Kant was right to draw attention to the responsibility we have as rational human beings to eschew the kind of intellectual laziness that simply carries us along with the crowd, his counsel had the false and damaging implication that in the pursuit of knowledge and understanding we are self-made men and women. The truth is, there is hardly a single shred of our knowledge that is not the fruit of participation in relationships with others. Even those things we *appear* to discover for ourselves depend on the utilization of a conceptual apparatus that is formed in community with others. As Francis Martin points out, 'knowing is always a communal reality ... the very language we need as a medium of thought is a societal possession, a common good.'[20] The relational epistemology assumed and sometimes made explicit by the biblical writers applies not only to our knowledge of God, therefore, but also to all else that we claim to know about the world.

Gregory Vall points out that in Israel's understanding knowledge and communion with the other are virtually synonymous. 'The "knowledge" to which Israel is called', Vall says, '*is* an interpersonal relationship between a free and righteous God and free human moral agents.'[21] Knowing is irreducibly bound up with being in relation as the Hebrew euphemism to 'know' one's husband or wife attests. In her essay on Pauline epistemology Mary Healy draws attention to the relational content implicit in the Hebrew word *yāda'* and points out that Paul's conception of knowledge, rendered through use of the Greek terms *ginōskō* and *oida*, is shaped by the Old Testament understanding.[22] Paul is thus at pains to impress upon the Corinthians that 'true knowledge of God is not a matter of the philosophical (or theological) erudition boasted by some Corinthians ... Rather it is a personal familiarity by which one is moved to reciprocate God's love.'[23]

Congruent though it is with Old Testament epistemology, in the New Testament the relational epistemology becomes more explicitly trinitarian. God's own life is understood to be constituted by the triune relationality between Father, Son and Spirit. The gospel testifies that this divine communion takes the form of a capacious love that creates and redemptively embraces that which is other than God. The creature, who is not divine, is thus drawn into the divine communion of love and is thereby enabled to know God. Cornelis Bennema sets out in this volume the epistemic logic of this divine economy as it is developed in John's Gospel. The 'relationship of life, love, knowledge/truth and glory between the Father and the Son is not exclusive,' Bennema observes.[24] By the power of the Spirit, believers are

---

[20] Martin, 'Psalms', 49.
[21] Vall, 'Prophetic', 32. My emphasis
[22] Healy, 'Pauline', 141-42.
[23] Healy, 'Pauline', 144.
[24] Bennema, 'Johannine', 120.

enabled to participate in this relationship and to enjoy its fruits of life, love and knowledge.

According to John, knowledge of Jesus comes through abiding in Christ. The theme is introduced in the very first encounter between Jesus and the prospective disciples. Hearing the testimony of John the Baptist that Jesus was the Lamb of God, Andrew and another unnamed disciple followed Jesus and asked him, 'where do you abide?' (*pou meneis*) (Jn 1:38). Jesus' response, 'Come and see!' constitutes at once both an invitation to the locality where he is staying and an invitation to accompany him through the course of a ministry in which his identity as the Lamb of God will be more fully revealed. In the course of their discipleship, the disciples will hear the further response, 'I am in the Father and the Father is in me' (Jn 14:10, 11), the promise that the Spirit will abide with and in them (Jn 14:17), and the instruction: 'abide in me as I abide in you' (Jn 15:4). All of these sayings of Jesus have epistemological (and soteriological) overtones. Knowledge of God, Father, Son and Spirit, comes about through abiding with or indwelling Christ, and through the indwelling of the Spirit.[25]

Knowledge as Participation and Indwelling

The concept of 'indwelling' was developed in the twentieth century by Michael Polanyi who, in his book *Personal Knowledge* explains that our efforts to know and understand the world depend crucially upon our dwelling within particular conceptual frameworks of which we are only subsidiarily aware and which cannot be reduced to propositional form.

> When we accept a certain set of presuppositions and use them as our interpretive framework, we may be said to dwell in them as we do in our own body. Their uncritical acceptance for the time being consists in a process of assimilation by which we identify ourselves with them. They are not asserted and cannot be asserted, for assertion can be made only *within* a framework with which we have identified ourselves for the time being; as they are themselves our ultimate framework, they are essentially inarticulable.[26]

Polanyi is concerned especially with the modes of knowing that operate in science, often thought to be archetypical for all our epistemic endeavors. Yet the epistemology developed by Polanyi takes its lead from the Johannine conception of abiding in Christ in which personal commitment and love, rather than detached objectivity, are the indispensable conditions of true understanding. An important corollary of this conception, noted above by Polanyi, is that our ultimate frameworks are inarticulable. Elsewhere Polanyi claims that we know more than we can tell.[27]

---

[25] See again, Bennema, 'Johannine', 121-22.

[26] M. Polanyi, *Personal Knowledge: Towards a Post-Critical Philosophy* (London: Routledge & Kegan Paul, 1958), 60.

[27] M. Polanyi, *The Tacit Dimension* (Garden City, NY: Doubleday & Co., 1966), 4.

Our epistemic navigation of the world relies upon our habitation of frameworks of meaning and understanding that we are only subsidiarily aware of. We indwell them and they shape and facilitate our knowing even though we cannot render them in propositional form. Such is the nature of the Christian's dwelling in Christ. Christian conversion involves a transformation of one's being so that the point of orientation for one's habitation of the world becomes now the person of Jesus Christ, confessed, again in John's gospel, to be the way the truth and the life. 'The believing community', notes Bennema, 'consists of those who "hear" and know Jesus' voice' (Jn 10:3-4, 16).[28] Knowledge is something attained, partly as gift, by those who participate in relationship with Jesus Christ. Polanyi's insight is that the same holds true for all our knowing of the world. All knowledge is personal knowledge. It depends upon our personal commitment to and participation in relationships through which our prior conceptions of the world are transformed. Such a conception of the knowing process subverts what has sometimes been called an epistemology of spatial distance – the Modernist ideal of detached, objective inquiry that keeps the object to be known at arm's length.

An unmistakeable feature of the biblical account of how God may be known is the consistent assumption that knowledge is attained by those who share in a history with God, who commit themselves to walk in the way of the Lord, who respond to Jesus' invitation to discipleship. Knowledge is not attained through detached contemplation but through committed participation in the unfolding of God's purposes for the world. Karl Barth puts the matter well:

> We cannot impress upon ourselves too strongly that in the language of the Bible knowledge ... does not mean the acquisition of neutral information, which can be expressed in statements, principles and systems, concerning a being which confronts man, nor does it mean the entry into passive contemplation of a being which exists beyond the phenomenal world. What it really means is the process of history in which man, certainly observing and thinking, uses his senses, intelligence and imagination, but also his will, action and 'heart', and therefore as whole man, becomes aware of another history which in the first instance encounters him as an alien history from without, and becomes aware of it in such a compelling way that he cannot be neutral towards it, but finds himself summoned to disclose and to give himself to it in return, to direct himself according to the law which he encounters in it, to be taken up into its movement ...[29]

O'Dowd's account of the epistemology operative in the book of Deuteronomy is particularly interesting in this regard. O'Dowd explains that Deuteronomy is a book of memory; it recalls the events of Israel's past which have established Israel as the covenant partner of God, but it recalls those events in such a way as to actualize them anew amongst those who now read Israel's Scripture. 'Deuteronomy's demand for actualization', O'Dowd shows, 'is meant to shape and protect Israel's knowledge

---

[28] Bennema, 'Johannine', 120.

[29] K. Barth, *Church Dogmatics* IV.3 (Edinburgh: T&T Clark, 1961), 183-4.

by grounding it in the ontological realities of her history with God.' The point is confirmed in the Passover Haggadah in which each new generation of Israel's people are encouraged to look upon themselves as though they came forth out of Egypt.

> This tenet strove to make the Exodus from serfdom into freedom a living personal experience. It was in this spirit that the story of the liberation was told and handed down from father to son, the son in turn growing up in the knowledge that he would have to tell 'his' story to his children. The Seder became the symbol of the bond between the individual and the family, and between these two and the people, all united in the telling of the old but ever renewed story.[30]

O'Dowd again observes that knowledge, so far as Israel is concerned, 'is a product of living in the biblical story in accordance with the Torah.'[31] The same principle applies to the knowledge mediated sacramentally in baptism and the Lord's supper. Through these sacramental means God makes himself available to his people. God is known by this means, not primarily as the subject of propositions about him but rather as the believer's companion. He is known in baptism and in the breaking of bread, while those who are baptized and who partake of this bread are participants thereby in the life and the ongoing history of Christ, dying and rising with him, and sharing in his communion with the Father. These are the means by which God makes himself available to us and thereby makes himself known.

Epistemology and Ethics

That knowledge of God is acquired through participation in the unfolding history of God's creative and redemptive purposes for the world means that knowing is bound up with action, with discipleship. Those who walk in the way of the Lord will gain knowledge of him. Mary Healy observes, accordingly, that 'the participatory quality of knowledge of God underlies the close bond between Pauline epistemology and Pauline ethics.'[32] The relation between knowledge and ethics has long been the subject of interest in Western thought, although, as Ryan O'Dowd notes, modern western philosophy has been marked by a 'tendency to divorce ontology and ethics (virtue) from epistemology and wisdom.'[33] How then is the relation between ethics and knowledge to be conceived?

An early candidate for the resolution of this question is that proposed by the Greek philosophers who took it as axiomatic that right action flows from right thinking. Socrates argued, for instance, that if a person knows what is truly good – what is beneficial for the soul – then he or she will inevitably act in a good manner. The reason for this inevitability, in Socrates' view, is that no one will knowingly act

---

[30] 'Introduction' to *The Passover Haggadah*, N.N. Glatzer (ed.) (New York: Schocken Books, 1953), 5.
[31] O'Dowd, 'Deuteronomy', 20.
[32] Healy, 'Pauline', 146.
[33] O'Dowd, 'Wisdom', 65. See also Vall, 'Prophetic', particularly his comment at fn. 3.

in a way that is contrary to his or her own interests. It is in the very nature of the good that when it is known, it is also desired, and when desired it is also exercised. Right action flows from right thinking.[34] Right knowledge is the presupposition of right performance.

In the same way Plato, who devotes a great deal of attention to action, contends that the human capacity to exercise the civic virtues of courage, temperance, wisdom and justice, depends upon our having prior knowledge of the ordering principles of the cosmos, and flows inevitably from our having such knowledge. Difficult though that knowledge may be to attain, one has only to know what is right in order to do it, so that a failure in the realm of moral action is in the first place a failure of intellect. Sin therefore is ignorance, so far as the Greeks were concerned. Those who act wrongly are clearly ignorant of the 'Forms', of the principles by which the world is ordered. With this construal of the relation between knowledge and ethics it will clearly be a form of foolishness to the Greeks to suggest as Paul does in Romans 7 that 'I can will what is right, but I cannot do it ... With my mind I am a slave to the law of God, but with my flesh I am slave to the law of sin' (Rom 7:18b, 25b).

Paul's confession here is clearly founded on an alternative view of the relation between knowledge and ethics, one that denies that right action is determined by intellect alone.[35] We shall return to Paul below, and to the biblical view that he represents. But first, let us examine briefly an alternative resolution of our question that has been influential in the western intellectual tradition, namely that set forth by Descartes. Consequent upon his radical dualism between the *res cogitans* and the *res extensa*, Descartes' quest for knowledge was, in conception, divorced entirely from action in the world. Descartes thought himself to live the life of the spectator, observing the world but not participating in it, generating knowledge in isolation from action, a product of the intellect alone. It is from him that we can trace the modern presumption of dispassionate inquiry that we have referred to earlier. The integration of knowledge and ethics, according to this view, including, in some academic circles, the integration of theology with the life of faith, is condemned as a corruption of the knowing process and of true academic inquiry. The contrary biblical assertion that 'the fear of the Lord is the beginning of knowledge', where to be 'God-fearing' describes a form of life rather than simply an attitude, serves well, not as a refutation of the Cartesian view, but as warrant to consider an alternative conception of the matter.

A contrasting construal of the relation between knowledge and ethics has been promoted in recent years by the liberation theologians of Latin America. Theology, it is claimed, is critical reflection upon praxis.[36] Here we find the opposite of the

---

[34] I have taken the point from R. Tarnas, *The Passion of the Western Mind* (New York: Ballantine Books, 1991), 33-4.

[35] The point is supported by Thomas Stegman's discussion of the epistemology of Luke-Acts. According to the Lukan construal of things, 'Knowledge alone does not suffice to produce proper behaviour' (Stegman, 'Luke-Acts', 103).

[36] This is the description of theology offered by Gustavo Gutiérrez in *A Theology of Liberation* (Maryknoll, N.Y: Orbis Books, 1973).

position we have seen in Socrates and Plato. Right action is no longer the consequence of right knowledge but right knowledge is thought to emerge through reflection upon right action. As a description of the theological task this is mistaken, I think, principally because it is upon *human* action that the theologian is supposed to reflect – upon, that is, the very action that the Bible supposes to have been corrupted by sin. And yet, Liberation Theology offers a salutary protest against the Cartesian disengagement of knowledge and ethics and quite properly resists the assumption that we can know the truth of the divine economy and being while keeping our distance from both. Prompted by criticism from outside, liberation theologians have subsequently qualified the description of theology as 'critical reflection upon praxis' by adding the phrase, 'in the light of the gospel'.[37] That modification potentially subverts the original proposal by implying that attentiveness to the gospel rather than praxis is the first step of the theological task. Gustavo Guttiérez, however, though himself proposing the modification, continued to insist that theology was a second act. Praxis must come first. I suggest, however, that there is a reciprocal relationship between knowledge and action. It is true that we learn through doing, rather than through detached reflection, but, equally, our action in the world is shaped and reshaped by all that is learned along the way. This indeed seems to be the biblical pattern. The Bible tells the story of the formation and education of a people. Such *paideia* takes place as God guides his people through the parted waters of the Red Sea and accompanies their wanderings through the wilderness to the Promised Land, and again in their exile from and return to Jerusalem. This long history of Israel is replicated in the life of Jesus who invites our participation in his own journey through the waters of baptism, into the wilderness and on to Calvary, an exile once more from Jerusalem's city walls. Again, the formation and education of a people is underway. Those who follow Jesus on this road are being shaped as stewards and witnesses of God's purpose for the world, and precisely through that process, learn the skills of covenant relationality with God.

John Calvin proclaimed in his *Institutes of the Christian Religion* that 'all right knowledge of God is born of obedience.'[38] The advantage of this expression over those of both the Greeks and the Latin Americans is that it returns us to the biblical insistence that knowledge is the fruit of relationship. It conceives the action in which theological inquirers are necessarily to be involved as obedience to the Lord, and – necessarily therefore – proceeds from attentiveness to the Word of God.

Here we may take a further example from the New Testament. The four evangelists' depictions of the calling of the disciples have in common the pattern of immediate response to Christ's command. None of the accounts allow to the

---

[37] This is the position of Gutiérrez ten years on as summarised by R.M. Brown in the Preface to Gustavo Gutiérrez's *The Power of the Poor in History* (London: SCM Press, 1983), vii. For a picture of Guttiérez on the way to this revised position see his, 'Liberation Praxis and Christian Faith' in *Frontiers of Theology in Latin America*, R. Gibellini (ed.) (London: SCM Press, 1980), 1-33, especially 22-4.

[38] J. Calvin, *Institutes of the Christian Religion*, J.T. McNeill (ed.), F.L. Battles (tr.), Library of Christian Classics, vols 20 and 21 (Philadelphia: Westminster Press, 1960), I.vi.2.

disciples the opportunity for clarification of precisely what the command entails, who it is that makes the command, or what the theological justification might be for such an action. It is in the course of following Jesus that these things begin to become clear. What they know at the point of encounter with Jesus is only the authority of the one by whom they are addressed. The faith with which they respond *seeks* understanding; it does not proceed from a comprehensive knowledge of who Jesus is. A deeper knowledge and understanding emerges as they accompany Jesus on the road. The account of the journey to Emmaus in Luke 24 is especially apposite in this respect. We could speculate, of course, about how the disciples had perhaps met Jesus prior to the call to discipleship. We might suppose that the story-telling of the evangelists compresses into one dramatic encounter a process that took place over some time, thus allowing to the disciples time to think it over, to consult with the professors of theology, and with other intellectuals of the day. Was it a good idea, this following of Jesus? Was it theologically sound? Could it be justified – intellectually? Right thinking leads to right action, the Greeks would have said. But according to the gospel writers, the course of action to which the disciples are called must rest, not on a fully developed understanding of what will be involved, but solely on the authority of the one who invites their obedience. Only in following him will knowledge and understanding emerge. This is a line of thought that has been relentlessly explored by Søren Kierkegaard. Venture the decisive act, Kierkegaard says, by which he means that the Christian must act in obedience to and imitation of Jesus Christ. Without obedience, Kierkegaard further contends, faith does not exist, and without faith there is no knowledge of God. It is when the How – the life of faith – is scrupulously rendered, Kierkegaard maintains, that the What – the understanding of the intellect – is also given.[39] Kierkegaard himself offers the following analogy: the life of faith, he says, is like learning to swim. Whoever remains at the poolside, never venturing into the water, may well claim to know how to swim, but only the act of swimming itself can possibly give warrant for such a claim and thus secure the claim as a legitimate expression of what one knows. This relation between the means and the content of theological knowledge is remarked upon by Ryan O'Dowd who notes the development in Deuteronomy of the principle that '*how* and *what* one knows is tied to the ethics of obedience. There is an inherent virtue required to "know" this God.'[40] Gregory Vall notes the same conviction in the prophetic literature: 'Knowledge of God cannot abide in the intellect', Vall says, 'if it is not acted upon in the concrete historicity of the body.'[41]

Kierkegaard's analogy describes well what it means to have knowledge of God. Only he or she has justification for speaking about the love of God, for instance, or about forgiveness, or about the activity of the Spirit, who participates in that form of

---

[39] S. Kierkegaard, *Journals and Papers*, H.V. Hong and E.H. Hong (eds. and trs.) (Bloomington: Indiana University Press, 1967-78) 4/4550, X2 A 299 (1849).
[40] O'Dowd, 'Deuteronomy', 8.
[41] Vall, 'Prophetic', 25, fn.3

life that these actions of God give rise to. Commenting upon Kierkegaard, Arnold Come writes:

> ... most theologians, most preachers and teachers of the Christian tradition and community, forget and neglect to call into play this absolute requirement of Christian conceptual definition. They teach all about God but forget that God is a living reality who must be dealt with personally if one is to speak of God knowingly. They do not know how to wait in silence for the living God to speak and to reach out and grasp them 'spiritually' at the core and depth of their beings as persons, as self-conscious, free, responsible selves, and to do this at the 'objective' place where this God promises to meet them, namely, in the 'word' of the New Testament and in the 'sacrament' of the Lord's table.[42]

Debate about whether it really is 'most' theologians who are guilty of this forgetfulness need not detain us here. The point to be noted is that knowledge and ethics, Christian conceptual formation and the life of faith, are integrated in such a way that one simply cannot have one without the other.

My point here has been that one cannot have knowledge of God without participating in the life of faith, but is it also true to say that one cannot participate in the life of faith without being knowledgeable? In that case 'knowledge' will mean something other than intellectual mastery. There is undoubtedly a need for conceptual clarity in theological knowing and for the diligent utilization of our intellectual gifts in pursuit of such clarity, but on this Kierkegaardian and biblical account knowledge is not synonymous with conceptual clarity and sophistication. Those who participate in the life of faith, even those with very limited conceptual gifts, can legitimately claim to *know* that their redeemer lives. Their participation in the life of faith is itself a form of knowing. They *know* both whom they have believed and the truth that sets them free.

Knowledge of God does not consist in the accumulation of true propositions about God by the person who otherwise remains unchanged. It consists rather in the formation of persons who share a life in communion with God. Gregory Vall draws attention to the transformative nature of this knowledge in his account of the widow of Zarephath's encounter with the prophet Elijah. The knowledge the widow attains, Vall explains, 'is the sort that is acquired only when one's heart has been transformed by a personal experience of the prophetic word.'[43] Mary Healy likewise observes that '[t]he historical experience of persistent failure to know the Lord eventually led to the notion in the prophetic tradition that only a conversion of heart, effected by YHWH himself, will make possible the true knowledge that he requires.'[44] The notion of knowledge for its own sake,[45] sometimes advocated by the

---

[42] A. Come, *Kierkegaard as Theologian: Recovering My Self* (Montreal: McGill-Queens University Press, 1997), 44-45.

[43] Vall, 'Prophetic', 27.

[44] Healy, 'Pauline', 142.

[45] See the comments of Cornelis Bennema on this matter. ('Johannine', 127)

modern academy and having a certain legitimacy in its place, is thus foreign to the biblical understanding which regards knowledge of God as a constituent of the divine work of transforming hearts and minds and of fashioning, thus, a community to be his people. The single ironic exception to this is the book of Ecclesiastes, but as Ryan O'Dowd points out, the quest for wisdom and understanding for its own sake ends always in vanity or meaninglessness (*hebel*).[46]

The Pneumatological Mediation of Knowledge

To speak of knowledge as a product of the divine economy by which God is forming and sustaining a people to live in communion with him is to recognise that the knowing process is to be conceived not *merely* as human action but also as the action of God. All theological knowing takes place in dependence on the Spirit. Bennema shows that it is the Spirit, according to John's gospel, who 'will guide you into all truth' (Jn 16:13). Paul too explains, as Mary Healy points out, that 'God has revealed [these things] to us through the Spirit' (1 Cor 2:10), and further: 'We have received the Spirit from God, that we might know the things bestowed on us by God' (1 Cor 2:12). 'Whenever the gospel is announced', Healy observes, 'the Spirit is present, imparting understanding and bringing the truth to life.'[47] In Luke-Acts, the Holy Spirit constitutes what Thomas Stegman calls 'a unifying thread' in Lukan epistemology. 'The Spirit is both the source of inspiration of Scripture (Acts 1:16) and the means of properly understanding it.'[48]

The pneumatological account of knowledge apparent in the New Testament is much less explicit in the Hebrew Scriptures. Nevertheless, while a general outpouring of God's Spirit upon the people was considered to be a future reality (see Joel 2:28) the wisdom and understanding of particular leaders and prophets of Israel was attributed to the present anointing of God's Spirit. The Spirit is the source of the wisdom of Joseph (Gen 41:38) and of David (2 Sam 23:2), for example, and is the one who inspires Balaam's oracle (Num 24:2). In the book of Job 'the breath of the Almighty' gives rise to understanding (Job 32:8), and Daniel 5:11 attributes Daniel's ability to interpret dreams and signs to his being endowed with a divine spirit. Zechariah 7:12 claims that both the law and all the words of the Lord are sent by his Spirit. These texts reveal that in the Old Testament too, the authority and truth of theological utterance is thought to rest on the reality of the Spirit's presence.

The logic of this pneumatological epistemology deserves careful attention. In contrast with the common assumption that knowledge is a product of the individual human intellect, the biblical view is that knowledge is a fruit of the divine economy. It arises because God is at work nurturing and maturing a people to be his covenant partner and to be the bearers of his Word. Both the context and the content of theological knowing are the creative and redemptive action of God. To put it in

---

[46] O'Dowd, 'Wisdom', 80.

[47] Healy, 'Pauline', 139.

[48] Stegman, 'Luke-Acts', 104.

terms recently elucidated by Reinhard Hütter, we may say that the practice of Christian theology is a participation in the *poiemata* of the Holy Spirit,[49] a participation, that is, in God's work of shaping a community and maturing a people. More specifically, theological knowledge is received as gift by those who are gathered into the ecclesia and who participate thus in the ecclesial acts of baptism, the Lord's Supper, proclamation and hearing of the Word, prayer and praise, discipleship and service. These practices are the means by which the Spirit nurtures, and sanctifies, and guides the people of God into the truth and understanding that they need in order to be God's people. Colin Gunton has put it this way: 'Being "in Christ" involves a form of personal knowledge of God realized by participation in the worship and life of the Church.'[50]

Thomas Stegman thus suggests, drawing upon the epistemology of Luke-Acts, that along with prayer, 'the pious practices of fasting and almsgiving help to make one more amenable to receiving insight into God's will.'[51] This is consistent with the claim explored above that knowledge of God is contingent upon one's participation in the life of faith. To that insight we now add the further claim that such participation is itself the work of God's Spirit who gathers us into the *koinonia* of the divine life.

I have attempted to support here the contention made by several contributors to this volume that in the case of the knowledge of God, at least, knowledge and praxis belong together. One cannot say simply, however, that right thinking leads to right action as did the Greeks, nor simply that right action leads to right thinking as have liberation theologians in recent years. Both of these formulations are half-truths brought together in theology by the recognition that knowledge is an aspect of that form of life which is Christian discipleship. This integration of knowledge and ethics has a name. It is simply 'faith'. That the word 'faith' is sometimes used interchangeably with belief, a particular commitment of the intellect, and at other times as a characteristic of particular actions, as, for example, when we speak of 'acts of faith', is testament to the dual aspect of the word faith itself. Faith is a matter of both knowledge and action, integrated in such a way that neither takes priority but both are given together.

As I have said above, therefore, the action with which we are concerned in theology is not to be construed merely in terms of human capacities and accomplishments, but principally in terms of the power of the Holy Spirit. Here we must make one further comment by way of clarification. How can it make sense to speak of an action, in this case the action of theological formulation, as both human and divine? We are not claiming for the theologian that like Christ himself he or she too is both fully human and fully divine, and yet the matter must be construed, as

---

[49] R. Hütter, *Suffering Divine Things: Theology as Church Practice,* D. Stott (tr.) (Grand Rapids: Eerdmans, 2000) 144 and passim.

[50] C. Gunton, *Intellect and Action: Elucidations on Christian Theology and the Life of Faith* (Edinburgh: T&T Clark, 2000), 63.

[51] Stegman, 'Luke-Acts', 103.

well as pneumatologically, also christologically. It is Paul who claims that the life of the Christian is one in which 'it is no longer I who live but Christ who lives in me' (Gal 2:20). Thus the act of theological inquiry is not an undertaking of the 'old person', as it were, not of the 'person of flesh', but of the new person in Christ. It is an action of the person that the knowing subject has become under the transforming impact of God's Word and by the enabling of God's Spirit.[52] Knowledge of God is therefore to be understood as a human action that can only be accounted for as also an action of God.

Epistemology and Sin

The divine work of gathering and forming a people encounters, in this fallen world, the resistance of human obstinacy and sin. Because we are alienated in our minds from the truth and estranged from God, the self-disclosure of God and the formation of a community to be his people, is, simultaneously, an act of forgiveness and reconciliation. That there is a limitation and, indeed, an alienation of some kind to be overcome is implicit in the observation made by all the contributors to this volume that knowledge of God involves the transformation of the knowing subject. We are 'made new' by being brought into a knowledge of the truth. The theme is explored by Cornelis Bennema in his study of Johannine epistemology. 'John's evaluation of the human epistemic condition,' Bennema explains, 'is a pessimistic one: the world is enveloped in an epistemic darkness and hence its people reject the Logos-Light.'[53] The plight of humanity is expressed in the concept of 'blindness', an affliction from which we cannot save ourselves. We stand in need rather of a new birth from above, a birth of water and Spirit.[54] John makes it clear that this epistemic and spiritual blindness – as distinct from physical blindness – is the result of sin, and can be dealt with only in tandem with forgiveness. As the light who comes into the world, Jesus imparts truth and gives life. 'The truth will set you free', Jesus says (Jn 8:32). Our alienation from the truth is evidently an ontological problem; it constitutes a form of bondage that precludes our participation in abundant life. John therefore has Jesus explain that '... this is eternal life, that they may know you the only true God, and Jesus Christ whom you have sent' (Jn 17:3). Knowledge of God and of Jesus Christ are constitutive of eternal life, that fullness of life that is God's purpose for the creature and that is denied to us on account of sin. The message of the gospel is that life and knowledge are made available through Christ, and specifically, for John, through what Jesus accomplishes on the cross. There it is that the work of revelation and reconciliation comes to its climax. The glory of God stands fully revealed at Calvary in the suffering and reconciling love of Christ. Those who, by the Spirit's

---

[52] The point is drawn from K. Barth, *Evangelical Theology: An Introduction,* G. Foley (tr.) (London: Weidenfeld and Nicolson, 1962), 101.

[53] Bennema, 'Johannine', 110-11.

[54] Bennema, 'Johannine', 112.

enabling, see the glory of God at Calvary are those who know the truth that sets them free.

The link between ignorance and sin is noted also by Paul. 1 Corinthians 2:8 attributes the crucifixion of the Lord of glory to the ignorance of those who did not know God's plan. As Mary Healy points out, however, the causative relation is reciprocal. In Romans 1:21-25 Paul declares that sinfulness results in foolishness and produces a darkening of the mind.[55] Paul's understanding is, of course, thoroughly rooted in the Hebrew Scriptures. Francis Martin's study of Psalms 86 and 51 reveals the Hebrew writer's acknowledgement that learning the ways of the Lord depends first upon the forgiveness of YHWH and the renewal within the suppliant of a pure heart. What is true for the individual applies also to God's people as a whole. It is noteworthy that the psalmist cannot set himself right before God. He pleads with the Lord to create in him a pure heart and to renew a steadfast spirit within him (Ps 51:12). The path to knowledge and understanding involves openness to the therapeutic work of God that heals the alienation of our minds and the impurity of our hearts.

If knowledge involves a correspondence of thought and being, the conforming of our thinking to the way reality is constituted, and if, further, as is proclaimed in the Bible, God is the creator and sustainer of all being, then our alienation from God will have epistemic consequences. If the order and intelligibility of the universe have their ground in the creative and redemptive purposes of God, then that order cannot be known so long as human beings persist in sin. That seems to be the biblical view. Is it confounded, however, by the evident success of humanity's scientific investigation of the world? The inquiries of human beings across a vast array of subjects have revealed a great deal about the workings of the universe despite the persistent reality of human sinfulness. Two things require to be said in response. The first is that humanity's sinful failure to recognise the theo-logic by which the world is ordered and directed to its true *telos*, has left it bereft of wisdom. We do not know what to make of the knowledge we acquire and are as likely to use it, therefore, for evil ends as for good. Its status as knowledge therefore becomes questionable. Our use of it is not disciplined by a proper conception of its relation to the one in and through whom all things were created and find their purpose (Eph 1:16). In a real and ultimately important sense, therefore, we do not know the true nature of things as we suppose. The second thing to be said, however, is that God in mercy and grace keeps open that future in which we shall see face to face and know even as we are known (1 Cor 13:12). The 'basic generosity of existence' (Maritain) is in fact the generosity of God who does not withhold from his creatures the knowledge and the means by which to live, even though fullness of life and true wisdom and understanding require our repentant return to the one who is the giver of all good gifts (Jas 1:17). Thus, as Douglas Knight says, 'We only really know and act when

---

[55] Healy, 'Pauline', 145, fn.51

we receive our knowledge and action as the gifts that give us our place in the purpose of God.'[56]

Summary Observations

For all the legitimacy of the contemporary concern in biblical studies to maintain a proper appreciation of the diversity of the biblical texts and to hear the distinctive voices of the respective authors, the essays of this volume reveal a notable consistency amongst the authors of the surveyed texts concerning questions of epistemology. Notable too are the contrasts between the conceptions of knowledge and the knowing process evident in the biblical texts and those that are constitutive of the culture of modernity. Whereas the biblical authors characteristically regard knowledge and understanding as gifts of God to be received in humility and exercised in obedience to God's will, modernity typically conceives of knowledge as mastery, promises to free us from the tutelage of another[57] and encourages us to wield knowledge in service of our own ends.

Central too to the biblical epistemology is the irreducible link between knowing and personal formation. The knowing process does not leave us intact but moulds us toward a greater conformity with what is the case. We are works in progress. Our minds and hearts are being shaped by the Spirit of God to a true conformity with Jesus Christ in and through whom all things are created, and who will in due time present the completed creation to the Father. Wherever the truth is learned, therefore, those who learn are being gathered, provisionally and partially as yet, into the life of Christ.

Bibliography

Barth, K., *Church Dogmatics* IV.3 (Edinburgh: T&T Clark, 1961)

————, *Evangelical Theology: An Introduction,* Grover Foley (tr.) (London: Weidenfeld and Nicolson, 1962)

Brown, R.M., 'Preface' to Gustavo Gutiérrez's *The Power of the Poor in History* (London: SCM Press, 1983)

Calvin, J., *Institutes of the Christian Religion,* J.T. McNeill (ed.), F.L. Battles (tr.), Library of Christian Classics, vols 20 and 21 (Philadelphia: Westminster Press, 1960)

Come, A., *Kierkegaard as Theologian: Recovering My Self* (Montreal: McGill-Queens University Press, 1997)

Glatzer N.N. 'Introduction' to *The Passover Haggadah* (New York: Schocken Books, 1953)

Gunton, C., *Intellect and Action: Elucidations on Christian Theology and the Life of Faith* (Edinburgh: T&T Clark, 2000)

---

[56] D. Knight, *The Eschatological Economy*, 204.

[57] I take the point from D. Knight, *The Eschatological Economy*, 182.

Gutiérrez, G., *A Theology of Liberation* (Maryknoll, N.Y: Orbis Books, 1973)

_____, 'Liberation Praxis and Christian Faith' in R. Gibellini (ed.), *Frontiers of Theology in Latin America* (London: SCM Press, 1980)

Hütter, R., *Suffering Divine Things: Theology as Church Practice,* Doug Stott (tr.) (Grand Rapids: Eerdmans, 2000)

Kierkegaard, S., *Journals and Papers,* H.V. Hong and E.H. Hong (eds and trs.) (Bloomington: Indiana University Press, 1967-78)

Knight, D.H., *The Eschatological Economy: Time and the Hospitality of God* (Grand Rapids: Eerdmans, 2006)

Polanyi, M., *Personal Knowledge: Towards a Post-Critical Philosophy* (London: Routledge & Kegan Paul, 1958)

_____, *The Tacit Dimension* (Garden City, NY: Doubleday & Co., 1966)

Tarnas, R., *The Passion of the Western Mind* (New York: Ballantine Books, 1991)

Webster, J., *Confessing God* (London: T&T Clark, 2005)

CHAPTER 9

Mystery and Mastery:
Philosophical Reflections on Biblical Epistemology

D. C. Schindler

The very notion of a biblical epistemology would make many philosophers suspicious. While we intend, here, to consider the philosophical import of this project, it is good to acknowledge at the outset, if not the difficulty presented by the notion, at least the tension inherent within it. The tension resides most centrally in the complex relationship between universality and particularity in truth and knowledge as philosophy generally understands these. The Bible is the account recorded by inspired authors of the utterly unique covenant God established with Abraham and his descendants and then renewed and sealed in Christ. There are many ways in which the Bible has a singular status among written documents: it is not meant in the first place simply as a disclosure of information about God, the *principium et finis mundi*, but as an initiation into a particular and concrete mystery, namely, the spousal union between Christ and the Church. Moreover, what it does, indeed, disclose about the nature of God is not simply a reiteration of the wisdom legible, in principle, to all because it is inscribed into the natural world in which we all live and able to be inferred from the logical necessity of philosophical truth. Instead, it is a 'special' revelation, the gift of knowledge of God's inner life, made in a *particular* way to a *particular* people, which is and will remain in some decisive respect discontinuous with merely human wisdom. It is for this reason that the Bible cannot be read properly except from within a particular tradition, guided and inspired by the Holy Spirit of Christ, and unless one views what the Bible presents with the 'eyes of faith', as Pierre Rousselot describes them: the illumination that is analogous to the light of genius, but which can be possessed by even the simplest because it is precisely a gift 'from above' and so does not ultimately depend on nature.[1]

But faith's 'gift' character and the transcendence of nature it implies would seem by that very fact to place it outside of the realm of philosophy. From its beginnings, in what is generally accepted as the first strictly philosophical statement that has

---

[1] Pierre Rousselot, *The Eyes of Faith*, J. Donceel (tr.) (New York: Fordham University Press, 1990), esp. 32-35.

been recorded, namely, Thales' assertion that water is the world's principle,[2] philosophy has been essentially bound to nature: both in the sense that it aims to comprehend the essential nature of things (as opposed to describing, say, their history, be it 'literal' or mythological), and that it seeks to do so in terms of natural evidences, which are in principle universally accessible. Philosophical writings would therefore appear to be 'free' from tradition in a way that Scripture cannot be; it would also seem to have no essential need for an authority-centered hermeneutic or for a supernatural illumination. It is in fact just this freedom that has, for many philosophers, represented the appealing strength of philosophy in relation to theology and the study of Scripture.

If this is a proper characterization of philosophy, then the suspicion that some harbor about a 'biblical epistemology' – insofar as such an epistemology would claim to disclose something essential about what it means to know – would seem to be well founded. Either the Bible speaks only to the faith community and so describes not what it means to *know*, and specifically to know *God*, but only what it means to *believe* and to reflect from within belief, or one claims that it discloses something of philosophical value regarding the nature of knowledge, just like other natural evidences, and it thereby ceases to be a 'special' revelation. In either case, it would not make philosophical sense to talk about a 'biblical epistemology', if we wished to allow those terms their strong meaning. What, then, ought we to make of the contributions offered in this book?

In what follows, I hope to suggest that this characterization, as typical as it may be, fails to do justice either to the rich reality of the philosophical tradition or to the full implications of Christ's mission to the world. In the first section, I will distill what I take to be some of the significant findings presented in the essays of this book, attempting to generalize them as far as possible. Second, I will point out some similarities between these findings and various claims made in the broad philosophical tradition, especially in ancient Greek thought. And, third, I will consider what *novelty* these findings offer to thought about the nature of knowledge, a novelty that ought to be of interest even to those who do not regard the Bible as holding any special significance as a revelation of God. Needless to say, our discussion of any particular point here does not pretend to be exhaustive, but only to make some initial gestures in response to the appealing invitation to philosophy that this collection of essays represents.

Basic Features of a Biblical Epistemology

One ought to take care in speaking generally of a 'biblical epistemology', i.e., a theory of knowledge derived from the Bible, for at least two reasons. In the first place, the Bible is not a philosophical treatise on human nature in itself or even on

---

[2] Aristotle is the source of this report; the term 'principle', *archē*, is certainly Aristotle's own more technical expression of Thales' claim, which he admits is somewhat ambiguous: see *Metaphysics*, 1.9, 983b18-27.

the theoretical problems regarding the relationship between God and man. There is not a single passage from the vast text that seeks to offer anything like the definition of a technical concept. The second reason is the simple fact that the Bible collects together the texts of many authors who are writing at different time periods, out of different cultural backgrounds, and for different ends in each case.

If we nevertheless accept the basic premise of the present book, it is not only because we intend to speak at an extremely general level about the variety of perspectives offered here. We have to realize that an epistemology need not be explicit to be operative in any given case, and there is no *a priori* reason one cannot 'distill' a theory of knowledge through a careful, perceptive reading of a text that characterizes ways of knowing without making that characterization thematic in its own right.[3] More profoundly, it remains the case that, in spite of the differences among the individual books, the Bible is a unified whole. Its unity is due, first of all, to the unity of human nature within the created order – a unity that allows us in fact to read the Bible in a sort of dialogue with philosophical texts, both ancient and modern. The second and ultimately comprehensive source of the unity is the unity of God's saving plan. In this respect, the books, for all of their differences, are as it were chapters from the same story; they all recount some significant aspect of the great drama played out between God and his people in history. What Thomas Stegman writes about Luke's conviction is crucial here, however frequently it is neglected in modern Biblical exegesis: '*God* is, in the final analysis, the real author of scripture.'[4] The remarkable similarity of themes that emerge over and over in the essays of this book is therefore no accident; nor is it the result – presumably – of direct collaboration in the writing of these chapters. Rather, it bears witness to the truth of the drama of salvation and the unity of the Book that records it. In what follows, I will first paint a general picture by discussing the features that are common to most of the essays, and then I will more briefly indicate some of the significant individual insights that the authors have distilled from their particular focus in the biblical literature.

No doubt the central characteristic affirmed in some way by all of the authors is that knowledge in the Bible is essentially *relational*. As we will see, it is this feature that determines most of the other features. To say that knowledge is relational implies a number of things. To be sure, there is not an epistemology in history that is not relational in some basic sense, insofar as knowledge always entails a relationship between a subject and an object. But the term 'relationship' carries layers of meaning we do not normally associate with the simple act of knowing. Typically, we take the object of knowledge to be a thing, an abstract quality, or a concept, and we assume that the knower's 'connection' to this object is brief because it is basically instrumental. As Aquinas has explained, we can understand the nature of a thing without knowing even whether it exists in reality:[5] we register what is essential about

---

[3] See Bennema's methodological observations, 'Johannine', 107-09.

[4] Stegman, 'Luke-Acts', 95.

[5] Aquinas, *De ente et essentia*, 4.

it, and, as far as the cognitive aspect goes, our intercourse with it is apparently done. This is one of the things that distinguishes knowledge from love. The will is ordered to the good, which inheres in the actual *existence* of things, while reason is ordered to the true, which principally concerns the intelligible nature of a thing, its 'quiddity', which can be abstracted from its real existence.[6] This is no doubt why we think of love as a relationship while we tend to overlook this aspect in knowledge. By contrast, 'relationship' implies an abiding contact and calls on much more than the intellect alone; one is *engaged* in a relationship, it demands a kind of attentive receptivity, fidelity, and trust,[7] a listening and willingness to respond,[8] that involves in some fashion all of one's personal powers. Gregory Vall calls the mode of knowledge depicted in the Bible, 'whole-hearted'.[9] As Mary Healy puts it, because of its essentially relational character, biblical knowing is not impersonal and detached, but entails the 'risk of self-engagement'.[10]

Why is the form of knowledge presented in the Bible essentially relational? As we respond to this question, we will see that it opens up a way of understanding the other characteristics. The biblical form of knowing is *necessarily* relational because of the nature of the object of biblical knowing, namely, God. Impersonal knowledge is arguably adequate for an abstract quality, but knowledge has to take on a different form if it is directed at a *person*. A person has a kind of freedom and a hidden interiority that an object does not, for the most part, have,[11] which means that, for a person to be understood, he has to *offer* himself, he has to make his interiority manifest. And, because he is free, that manifestation will itself bear the marks of freedom. This requirement gives rise to an essential distinction: it is possible to know many things *about* a person who has not addressed us directly and revealed himself to us, but *personal* knowledge can occur only within a personal relation. If we grant the important qualifier that God reveals himself in an analogously personal way also in creation, this distinction would provide a basic philosophical framework for distinguishing between natural theology and theology proper, and arguably also between metaphysics/philosophy of religion and natural theology. By the same token, it also provides a ground for the affirmation of the unity of all these within their various distinctions.

But God is not simply 'a' person; he is the triune Creator and Redeemer of the world. In this sense, knowledge of God is only *analogously* relational and *analogously* personal. In other words, this knowledge has a *sui generis* character, which ought not to be generalized in a simplistic way by comparison to our relationships to other persons or things in the world. Otherwise, there would be a

---

[6] Aquinas, *De veritate*, 21.1.

[7] Martin, 'Psalms', 49-50; Healy, 'Pauline', 144, 154; Vall, 'Prophetic', 32, 39.

[8] O'Dowd, 'Deuteronomy', 10; Bennema, 'Johannine', 120-22; Stegman, 'Luke-Acts', 101.

[9] Vall, 'Prophetic', 24.

[10] Healy, 'Pauline', 144.

[11] Of course, it is possible to reconceive the being and truth of objects in analogy to persons, as for example, H.U. von Balthasar does: see *Theologik*, vol. 1: *Wahrheit der Welt* (Einsiedeln: Johannes Verlag, 1985), 80-113.

temptation to think of relation to God in the terms of liberalism, and to think of the covenant, old and new, along the lines of a contract: I am a free agent, who can and ought to commit myself to this other free being standing over against me, God, who has committed himself to me. The relationship, in this case, would be essentially the *result* of my deliberate activity; I would think of myself as the primary agent who *forms* a relationship with God. Now, while some of the essays in this book lay emphasis on the *experiential* dimension of knowledge,[12] which could lead one to think that the significance of the relationship depended in an inordinate way on my conscious and free acceptance of it (and one may wonder whether Cornelis Bennema goes a bit too far in this regard by affirming that the efficacy of the soteriological event depends on the understanding of it[13]), one finds a constant corrective in the repeated mention of the importance of fear and obedience. Fear – which, as Ryan O'Dowd describes it,[14] refers in this context not to the psychological feeling of being afraid but the more profound disposition of awe and respect – represents a radically receptive mode of being. Indeed, the ontological dimension of fear and obedience is crucial, for it expresses the *truth* of our being created: before we can *act* toward God, we are related to him in our very existence. Any claim we would wish to make on God is *always* necessarily secondary and responsive to the absolute claim he makes on us. In this respect, the importance of Ryan O'Dowd's insistence on the ontology of the divine presence as the proper ground for epistemology cannot be overstated.[15] The self-assertiveness he – and, even more forcefully, Francis Martin[16] – criticizes in Enlightenment philosophies, and paradigmatically in Kant, is therefore not simply an epistemological problem, but falsifies the truth of being and the basic nature of one's relation to God. An interesting implication is that one cannot adopt Enlightenment philosophical methods in one's study of the Bible without radically distorting precisely what it is one is studying.[17]

The *sui generis* character of the relational knowledge one may have of God has an additional implication, which is brought out by several of the authors here: God's radical transcendence of the world means that he lies in an ultimate sense beyond the human epistemological horizon, no matter how 'personally' that horizon is understood. Therefore, knowledge of God is not a potency latent within the human capacity; there must be some sense in which God not only fulfills the intentional capacity, but in fact *gives* that very capacity, so that the potential itself is received from beyond itself. Mary Healy points out that the knowledge of God will retain a dimension of mystery all the way to the end, so that even the eschatological vision is received with awe and obedience, as a gift that will not cease to surprise.[18] As

---

[12] See, for example, Healy, 'Pauline', 145-46; Martin, 'Psalms', 59; Vall, 'Prophetic', 27.

[13] Bennema, 'Johannine', 118.

[14] O'Dowd, 'Wisdom', 7-9.

[15] O'Dowd, 'Deuteronomy', 68-69.

[16] Martin, 'Psalms', 46-48.

[17] See O'Dowd's mention of a revealing remark from noted biblical scholar Michael V. Fox, 'Wisdom', 69-70.

[18] Healy, 'Pauline', 156.

several others point out, the understanding of revelation is contingent upon the gift of faith, which means the mind must be *elevated* to its object.[19] There is, of course, a connection between the necessity of faith and the centrality of the Holy Spirit, which the essays on New Testament epistemology refer to repeatedly. The Holy Spirit is the one who has, alone, sounded the depths of God. From a philosophical perspective, we might say that the Spirit is, among other things, the 'subjectivity' of the Divine Nature in *Person*. God's self-disclosure is therefore not merely the gift of a new *object* to the mind, but also the offer of the transformation of subjectivity so that that object may be properly received. Such a transformation would be unthinkable without the Holy Spirit.

While it remains the case that the relationship to God enabled by and in the Spirit is essentially discontinuous with the normal experience of knowing, it is also true that some continuity between the two would have to exist, or else knowledge of God would be strictly irrational. It would be impossible to see why such a thing would be desirable in the first place. The essays in this book admirably take pains to show that faith, as the Bible presents it, has an essentially *rational* component, that what is, indeed, offered in faith is a particular kind of knowledge, and that the kind of knowledge of God one receives in faith bears some analogy to normal human knowing.[20] Mary Healy goes so far as to suggest, in the Pauline writings, that faith and knowledge appear to be one and the same thing, though viewed under two different aspects.[21] The unity and difference of biblical knowing and knowing understood more generally in a philosophical sense is a crucial question, which we will have to return to briefly at the end.

A further implication of relational/personal knowing, which every essay mentions in one respect or another, is that knowledge of God necessarily involves a kind of *praxis*: God is not merely an object for the mind alone, as we have said, but a personal Creator who is and remains free with respect to his creation. It is thus not merely the abstract mind that is elevated to receive God's self-communication, but the whole of one's person. In other words, it is not, in the end, the mind that knows God, but the *person* who knows God through the mind. As the authors here have observed, the language of the *heart* is central in many biblical texts, the heart being not simply an emotional center, as we might think today, but the seat of personhood more basically. In revelation, God addresses his chosen people who are distinguished for having been given his Law, and for loving this Law, meditating on it, and thus internalizing it. The New Testament's *following* of Christ (which in the early Church was referred to simply as 'the Way'), the conforming of one's *person* to the mystery of Christ's mission, is a new fulfillment of the first mission to hear and obey God's will. Thomas Stegman shows the importance of *prayer*, a listening readiness to *do* God's will, which is an indispensable part of the biblical

---

[19] See, e.g., Bennema, 'Johannine', 116; Stegman, 'Luke-Acts', 101, 104.

[20] See Bennema's especially clear insistence in this regard: 'Johannine', 122-24.

[21] Healy, 'Pauline', 154.

epistemology.[22] The knowing of God is an act that includes the whole of one's life, unto its existential extremities, and both gives and demands that this life be properly ordered. Any reflection on the epistemology presented in the Bible would be inadequate if it were to fail to recognize that obedience to the law and the active love of neighbor is not simply an external consequence of the knowledge of God, but is in fact *internal* to it. Knowing God and loving God and one's neighbor are in a certain respect one and the same thing. And knowing God is intrinsic to everything one knows, as Aquinas said.[23] There is thus an implicit obedience to God, and a call to love, required in every act of knowing.

While the foregoing attributes appear to be general traits of the biblical epistemology discussed by most, if not all, of the authors in this book, there are a few features that seem more particular to one area of the Bible or another but are nevertheless worth mentioning because of their significance. The feature that stands out especially to me is the *communal* aspect of knowing that Francis Martin develops in his reflection on the Psalms (and Gregory Vall also addresses in his study of the Prophets). The 'one' whom God addresses in the psalms, the one who 'knows' God in prayer and praise, is the people of Israel, 'personified', as it were, in the figure of David. As Francis Martin points out, we have here a powerful alternative to Enlightenment individualism: the knowing mind is not the power of an individual – which would entail a concept of knowledge structurally at odds with faith and with tradition, among other things, even if it were positively inclined toward these – but a whole that is greater than the sum of its parts, a whole in which many members share. The later view of the Church as a body, indeed, as a *person* in some profound sense, who is the primary agent in man's relationship to God, is in deep harmony with the biblical tradition.

Another unusual dimension of the Bible's epistemology is the emphasis on 'sacrament', which Gregory Vall highlights in the prophetic literature, particularly in Hosea. Such an emphasis adds a strikingly *concrete* aspect to knowledge: in Hosea, the Holy Land itself is, as it were, the *place* wherein knowledge of God resides, it is the sacrament, or physical sign and manifestation, of the covenantal relationship which *is* the knowledge of God.[24] The fruitfulness of the land is, in this sense, a sign of Israel's fidelity, which as we suggested before is intrinsic to her knowledge of God.

Further, a few of the authors draw attention to the specifically *historical* character of biblical epistemology. The knowledge relationship as recounted in its various aspects in this book is no general reality; rather, it is a relation that arises from God's calling a particular people to himself at a particular place and time. It has often been observed that the pressure of the biblical tradition is what inspired the Western mind

---

[22] Stegman, 'Luke-Acts', 101-03.

[23] Aquinas, *De veritate*, 22.2.1. See Henri de Lubac's profound meditation on the implications of this affirmation in *The Discovery of God*, A. Dru et al. (trs.) (Grand Rapids: Eerdmans, 1996), esp. 35-55.

[24] Vall, 'Prophetic', 33, 35-36.

to recognize the significance of history. If the relation between God and his people has an essentially historical dimension, then so too will the knowledge that is constitutive of – indeed, in some respect identical to – that relationship. This dimension runs quite directly against the grain of the Enlightenment epistemology which drew an absolute distinction between the historical and philosophical as between the contingent/accidental and the necessary/essential (Leibniz, Lessing, etc.). If Ryan O'Dowd can highlight the 'performative' character of knowing in Deuteronomy,[25] it is because the truth of God is a historically manifest and enacted truth, which is best re-called by being re-enacted: memory and drama are thus linked.

Finally, the *end* of knowing has a distinctive character in the Bible: as Cornelis Bennema observes, truth is not simply the object of a knowing that is its own purpose, but is instead a *saving* truth.[26] It is a truth that transforms, that sets free, that elevates and heals. Just as God is the essence and the cause of truth, so too he is its end. The final purpose of knowing, as Ryan O'Dowd affirms, echoing the Ignatian tradition, is, like all other things, the greater glory of God.[27]

Philosophical Echoes of the Biblical Epistemology

There can be no doubt that the view of knowing presented in the Bible, as our authors here have distilled it, offers something quite distinctive with respect to the philosophical tradition. Before considering this novelty and its implications, however, it is important to register the similarity between this view and perspectives one finds within the philosophical tradition. There are two reasons for this importance. In the first place, facile contrasts often fail to bear much fruit in the long term because of the oversimplifications they imply. Second, and more importantly, viewing the biblical epistemology simply in its *difference* from the philosophical tradition paradoxically undermines its significance. As we suggested at the beginning, if the Bible does not reveal something about the true nature of knowledge in a general way that therefore finds some resonance in philosophy, then it is not offering an epistemology but rather an alternative to epistemology. In other words, such a view of the matter would foster an opposition between faith and reason, grace and nature, that effectively distorts and trivializes both sides of the opposition. The project of 'de-Hellenizing' Christianity, however understandable it may have been in light of the rationalizing that took the sting out of the gospel, has been disastrous for Christian thinking. Ryan O'Dowd's introductory observations on the separation of wisdom, theology, and philosophy in this regard are helpful.[28]

If we were to describe a perfect contrast with the epistemology drawn from the present essays which we have just generalized above, that epistemology would have the following features: knowledge would be thoroughly conceptual in an abstract

---

[25] O'Dowd, 'Deuteronomy', 18-20.
[26] Bennema, 'Johannine', 114, 125.
[27] O'Dowd, 'Deuteronomy', 19.
[28] O'Dowd, 'Wisdom', 65-66.

sense, which would thus be purified, on the one hand, of any personal or effective elements, and on the other hand it would be indifferent to the sphere of praxis and thus to the range of behaviors and dispositions described at length in these essays – things like ethics, humility, obedience, prayer and repentance – however much personal significance such things might have. Reason would be understood as *mastering* its object, which would mean that any resistance on the part of the object to intellectual assimilation, any residue of mystery, would represent reason's failure to achieve its proper end. Inasmuch as the objects of reason are by definition necessary and universal, the 'contingency' of faith, whatever significance it might hold for religion, compromises reason's integrity; its 'from above' character runs precisely contrary to the 'from below' *autonomy* we associate with the proper activity of the intelligence; and its historical character sets it in opposition to thought's natural aspiration to generality. And because of the autonomy just mentioned, it is the essence of reason to 'see for itself', to trust its own powers rather than depend on another, and therefore to operate individualistically when it operates most perfectly. Finally, reason, so conceived, can have its end only in itself: to subordinate knowing to a foreign end such as the greater glory of God, however laudable in itself, is to divert it from its natural course.

Such a description is, of course, a caricature, though it is not for all that very distant from the philosophical ideal pursued during the Enlightenment. This ideal has widely come under attack in postmodern philosophy, primarily because of the tyranny of the (Western male) subject it seems to imply.[29] One may argue that postmodern epistemology fails to get at the root presuppositions behind this notion and so simply repeats some of the most problematic features of the modern view,[30] or one may observe that the criticisms of this philosophical style have generally been received, in any event, by only a small, closed circle of so-called Continental philosophers, while modern presuppositions still uncritically govern, not only the larger part of philosophy in the English speaking world, but also the methods considered normative in most other academic disciplines (including, paradoxically enough, biblical exegesis), and indeed the popular understanding of the way the mind works. However that may be, it remains the case that the Enlightenment epistemology is a stark impoverishment of the Western philosophical tradition, and that the original sources of that tradition have more in common in the biblical epistemology we have sketched than with the Enlightenment caricature.

It was in the light of the modern ideal that the first Greek philosophers were thought of as warranting that name for turning *away* from religious interpretations of the world and *toward* a more scientific approach, a turn represented in the shift from *mythos* to *logos*. While one still encounters interpretations of this sort, it is more

---

[29] A 'classic' text for this critique is J. Derrida, *Grammatology*, Spivak (tr.) (Baltimore: Johns Hopkins University Press, 1976); see also his *Margins of Philosophy*, A. Bass (tr.) (Chicago: University of Chicago Press, 1982).

[30] See K. Schmitz, 'Postmodern or Modern-Plus?' *Communio* 17 (Summer 1990), 152-66.

generally accepted now that reason is not *essentially* non-religious.[31] Indeed, the great early philosophers were often at least as critical of what we might refer to as scientific positivism, naturalism, and rationalism, as they were of the mindless superstition into which religion can degenerate. It is crucial to see that their criticism of the naturalistic reduction often arose not from a desire to protect and defend religion in the face of the growing power of reason, but because such a rationalism paradoxically betrays reason itself. Reason itself, in other words, has a 'from above' aspect. We see this, for example, quite clearly in Parmenides, who receives his epoch-making insight into Being as the fruit of a divine inspiration, an insight he received, incidentally, by following his *heart*'s (*thumos*) desire to the heavens.[32] Parmenides understands his insight to have universal significance, and yet it arises as an utterly unique event, which had never been granted to any before him. The elevation of the mind that we ascribe to faith, and indeed the knowledge granted as a particular gift of the Holy Spirit, bears a distinct analogy to reason as Parmenides, one of the most rigorously 'philosophical' thinkers in ancient Greece, presented it. When Plato describes the *eros* necessary for genuine philosophical rationality as a 'divine madness' because it is called forth precisely by what lies beyond normal human capacities, he is in fact drawing on a long tradition.[33]

As we saw in the first section above, the authors highlighted the significance of fear, humility, and obedience in one's reception of God's revelation. Similarly, what Socrates asserts in Plato's dialogue on knowledge, the *Theaetetus*, articulates a general principle of ancient Greek thought: philosophy begins in wonder 'and nowhere else'.[34] As Heidegger has famously insisted, wonder is not merely the 'efficient cause', so to speak, of philosophizing – as for example taught by Descartes, who interpreted the experience of wonder as a negative impetus, like an itch, which provokes philosophical reflection precisely to overcome it.[35] Instead, Heidegger claims, wonder, as *archē*, is the *abiding*, governing principle of philosophical thought, and thus of reason itself.[36] Implicit in this affirmation is that reason is *not* essentially autonomous: if wonder represents a kind of openness to what is astonishing, what is alien and surprising – in short, what is *other* – then to say that reason is properly *governed* by wonder means that the openness to the other

---

[31] One of the first major reconsiderations of the modern interpretation of the ancient Greek thinkers is W. Jaeger's 1936 Gifford lectures, published as *The Theology of the Early Greeks* (Oxford: Clarendon, 1947); for a complementary argument, see also F.M. Cornford's, *From Religion to Philosophy: A Study in the Origins of Western Speculation* (New York: Harper, 1957).

[32] H. Diels, *Die Fragmente der Vorsokratiker* (Berlin: Weidmannsche Buchhandlung, 1912³), Parmenides fragment B1.

[33] Plato, *Phaedrus*, 244a-245b, 249c-250a.

[34] Plato, *Theaetetus*, 155d.

[35] See Descartes, *The Passions of the Soul*, 2.76 in *The Philosophical Works of Descartes*, vol. 1, Haldane and Ross (trs.) (Cambridge: Cambridge University Press, 1973), 365

[36] M. Heidegger, *What is Philosophy?*, Wilde and Kluback (trs.) (Albany, NY: NCUP, 1956), 83.

is essential to the structure of reason. In this case, reason is most truly itself when it is dependent (in a proper way, of course) on what is other than itself. The human being exists within a whole that exceeds him on all sides, a whole that provides the context *within* which his life has meaning. He is genuinely human to the extent that he embraces this position 'inside' the whole; his reason is genuinely rational to the extent that it does the same.

If this is true, we would have to revisit the normal conception of the relationship between *mythos* and *logos*. One often hears that Plato draws a clear line between the two, and that he just as clearly accords primacy to *logos*, which thus ultimately provides the measure for myth. It is for this achievement that he is often taken to be the founder of rationalism. But while it is true that Plato praises the clarity of *logos*, and insists that one cannot claim to know something unless one can give a discursive account of it (which, quite significantly, Plato himself never seems able to do), Plato's attitude toward myth is in reality far more complex. He criticizes, in fact, the rationalistic reduction that we would call 'demythologizing' in the *Phaedrus*,[37] and regularly introduces a myth, an inspiration, a prophetic vision, a daimonic sign, or a traditional story, at the most crucial junctures of nearly every major argument. Aristotle, too, says that myth-lovers *are* philosophers precisely because both have 'wonder' in common.[38] It is more adequate, in the end, to say that Plato regards the *transcendent* dimension of myth, and related figures and resources, as essentially fruitful components of proper reasoning.[39]

Along the same lines, we must observe that Platonic rationality is *essentially* pious: it is deeply respectful of tradition, of divine mystery, of its own roots, even if it is scathingly critical of conventional pieties and attachments. If he has Socrates criticize piety, in other words, it is because what pretends to be piety isn't in fact genuinely pious at all: this is quite clear for example in the *Apology*[40] and above all in the *Euthyphro*.[41] To say it again, what characterizes reason, not only in Plato, but also in the Pre-Socratic thinkers, in Aristotle, and in many of the schools in the period, is a profoundly 'other-centered' form. Reason is not 'self-productive', but inserted into a whole that remains larger than it. Though ordered to that whole, it is not ordered to the *mastery* of it, but rather to the grateful receptivity of its ever greater truth. In this sense, philosophical reason in its primary sense has the 'hermeneutical' character that Ryan O'Dowd ascribes to reason in the Wisdom literature of the Bible.[42] The decidedly 'mystical' and indeed even liturgical turn that reason took in the neoplatonic thinkers such as Plotinus and Proclus, therefore, was not a decadent departure from the original healthy movement of reason in philosophy's prime (as, for example, modern philosophers have thought for a time),

---

[37] Plato, *Phaedrus*, 229c-e.

[38] Aristotle, *Metaphysics*, I.II.9-10.

[39] See J.-F. Mattei, 'The Theater of Myth in Plato', in *Platonic Writings, Platonic Readings*, C. Griswold, Jr. (ed.) (New York: Routledge, 1988).

[40] Plato, *Apology*, 26d-28d.

[41] Plato, *Euthyphro*, 5c-6a.

[42] O'Dowd, 'Wisdom', 67, 73-74.

but a deepening continuation of these original thinkers. The encounter between philosophy and Christianity in the Fathers and the Medieval Schoolmen acquires a different character when viewed from this perspective: it represents, not the substitute of religion for thought, but the deepening, in thought, of a religious dimension that was virtually always present in ancient philosophy. And, of course, the way we interpret this encounter would have immediate implications for our reception of a 'biblical epistemology'.

It is not uncommon to distinguish between Christian/biblical thought and Greek thought as between a 'praxis'-oriented thinking ordered to love and more theoretical view of the mind oriented to the contemplation of truth. Indeed, with some important qualifications, a couple of the present authors referenced this distinction. While there is, to be sure, a different emphasis in the Greek world, it is important to recognize that the earliest Greeks made little distinction between knowing and acting. The primary verbs used for knowing in Homer, for example, had an immediate association with movement.[43] In fact, there was a basic unity between perceiving, feeling, judging, and acting: all were facets of one and the same event, and were only later conceptually distinguished from one another. Thus, it was natural, for example, for Anaxagoras to conceive of mind, *nous*, as the almost 'physical' force that sets the cosmos in order,[44] and for Heraclitus to speak of 'doing and saying the truth'.[45] Aristotle uses the word 'truth' in Greek as a verb (*alethuein*)[46] – a usage we discover again in St Paul.[47] While a differentiation between the theoretical and the practical does occur in later thinkers like Plato and Aristotle, the aspects bear, even here, the trace of their original unity. For Plato, truth is rooted in *goodness*, and goodness clearly has, for him, a practical, ethical character.[48] As many commentators on the *Republic* have noticed, there is an essential connection between the active and the contemplative life in Plato's view of the philosopher.[49] One must be good to know

---

[43] See J. Boehme, *Die Seele und das Ich im homerischen Epos* (Leipzig: Teubner, 1929); B. Snell, *Die Ausdrücke für den Begriff des Wissens in der vorplatonischen Philosophie* (Berlin: Weidmannsche Buchhandlung, 1924); P. Vivante, *The Homeric Imagination: A Study of Homer's Poetic Perception of Reality* (Bloomington: Indiana University Press, 1970).

[44] See Diels, Anaxagoras Fragments B12-B14.

[45] Diels, Heraclitus fragment B112.

[46] Aristotle, *Nichomachean Ethics*, 6.3.1.

[47] See Eph 4:15, and Gal 4:16. Cf. Jn 3:21.

[48] The Good, by which the soul and the city are virtuously ordered, is for Plato the 'cause of knowledge and truth' (*Republic*, 508e).

[49] See, for example, A.J. Festugière, *Contemplation et Vie Contemplative selon Platon* (Paris: Vrin, 1967), 454; W. Jaeger, *Paideia*, vol. 2 (Oxford: Oxford University Press, 1986), 300; P. Friedlaender, *Plato: An Introduction* (New York: Pantheon, 1958), 104. J. Annas acknowledges that Plato insists on the philosopher being *both* contemplative and active, but, presumably because she assumes the modern dualism of intellect and will, believes Plato is contradicting himself: *An Introduction to Plato's* Republic (Oxford: Clarendon, 1981), 260ff. On knowledge of the Good, the intellect's highest object, as an essentially 'practical' form of knowledge, see Wieland, *Platon und die Formen des Wissens* (Goettingen: Vandenhock und

the good, and in fact to know properly anything caused by the good (which is the source, in the end, of all being[50]); knowledge of the good leads in turn to good action, to generous work in the 'cave' of the public order. Similarly, for Aristotle, knowledge of the highest things always requires a proper love.[51] While eclectic thinkers in the late Hellenistic period – for example, the Epicureans or the Stoics – may have oversimplified the relation between the inner life and the 'outside' world, we can say that there is no simple dichotomy in ancient philosophy between praxis and theory. Again, early Greek thought and the Bible are in agreement here.

Finally, it is worth drawing attention, in this very brief sketch, to the *communal* character of reason in its original philosophical form. The tendency to privatize reason has apparently been a perennial temptation. The clearest example in the ancient world is no doubt the phenomenon of sophistry, which viewed philosophy essentially as a battle between individual positions, the point of which was, of course, victory, and the spoils of which was individual benefit.[52] But, once again, the major figures have affirmed the universal, communal aspect of reason, not merely in its content (i.e., reason aims at universal objects) but much more subtly and profoundly in its form (i.e., the proper act of reason requires a unity of minds, a *'homonoia'*). The dialogue form in Plato, after all, displays reason as a public act, so to speak, that always involves more than one person. Ryan O'Dowd speaks of the 'performative' character of the memorial recorded in Deuteronomy:[53] perhaps it is not too much of a stretch to see the dialogue form in analogous terms, inasmuch as, according to Plato, it betrays itself when it is taken simply as a self-standing thing in its own right, rather than as an *aide-mémoire* that is meant to be 'ensouled' in the actual dialogue of a living community.[54] But the thinker who reveals the communal character of reason most centrally is Heraclitus, for whom a private *logos* was the very expression of ignorance.[55] Reason, for Heraclitus, is community or *koinōnia*,[56] the communal character is one of its most basic and important features. It is quite significant that 'the common' is the central theme in the first philosophical reflection on the meaning of *logos* that we have in history.

Ruprecht, 1982), and W. Kerstin, *Platons 'Staat'* (Darmstadt: Wissenschaftliche Buchgeselschaft, 1999), 239.

[50] Plato, *Republic*, 509b.

[51] See Aristotle, *Nichomachean Ethics*, 3.4.

[52] Plato's *Gorgias*, a dialogue (named after one of the most successful Sophists) that begins with the words 'war and battle', offers a dramatic expression of the conflict between reason as ordered to universal truth in philosophy, and reason as instrument for private gain in sophistry.

[53] O'Dowd, 'Deuteronomy', 18-20.

[54] See Plato, *Phaedrus*, 275c-278d.

[55] Diels, Heraclitus fragment B2.

[56] Diels, Heraclitus fragment B113. For an interpretation of this fragment, see D.C. Schindler, 'The Community of the One and the Many: Heraclitus on Reason', *Inquiry* 46 (2003), 413-48.

Finally, if we think of knowledge as concerning propositions and abstract concepts above all, we will be inclined to think of intelligence and truth as possessing a merely relative importance, as a necessary instrument for the achieving of some additional good. In this case, we would for example draw a sharp contrast between philosophy's view of reason ordered to truth for its own sake, and the Bible's view that subordinates this end to the more comprehensive good of salvation. Philosophy's truth is just an idea; the Bible's truth is, by contrast, something more: a saving idea. But while Christianity does indeed propose a radically different notion of truth as *a person*, it is not the case that philosophical truth is merely 'an idea'. Philosophy, in the ancient world, was never simply an intellectual pursuit, but always a way of life – the *good* life.[57] It is such precisely because the truth that it pursues is a comprehensive whole that includes within itself the well-ordered soul. Plato, for example, characterizes the *true* sophist or teacher (i.e., the philosopher) as a cleanser of souls.[58] Though philosophical truth is not *effectively* soteriological, as biblical truth is, nevertheless it is concerned above all with redemption. It is for this reason that a dialogue is possible between the biblical tradition and the philosophical tradition on the meaning of truth.

The Novelty of the Bible

A more thorough investigation would of course be required to come to any definitive conclusions about the nature of reason in the ancient world in comparison to the biblical epistemology. We have had space, here, only for a mention of immediate connections and general similarities. One of the outcomes of this initial look at the matter is a discovery that, as a pre-modern epistemology arising within a traditional culture in which the human found its proper place within an order that transcended man and therefore meaningfully situated reason, the biblical view of knowing has more in common with the pagan philosophical view than either has with the modern view of knowing, however putatively 'Christian' it may be. If this judgment is true – though, again, a good deal more evidence would have to be investigated to justify it – we are faced with an interesting set of questions. What would the historical fact that a biblical view had more in common with ancient philosophy than with much of modern Christian thought imply for the relationship between nature and grace, on the one hand, and for the meaning of Modernity in relation to Christianity on the other? Unfortunately, we cannot pursue these questions here; nevertheless, we can address a more directly pertinent question: if there is so much in common between the ancient and the biblical epistemology, does the Bible in fact have anything novel to contribute to our understanding of the nature of knowledge?

If it is indeed the case that the Bible is ultimately God's self-revelation, and it is also true that God is the principle and end of the world, then we can anticipate with confidence that the view of knowledge that comes to light in Scripture will

---

[57] Pierre Hadot, *Philosophy as a Way of Life* (Oxford: Blackwell, 1995).

[58] See Plato, *Sophist*, 226c-231b.

contribute something of decisive significance regarding the nature of knowing more generally. It will cast an essentially new light on this universal reality. As Mary Healy observes, the Spirit's elevation of the mind in faith institutes 'a new hermeneutic that influences one's perception of all reality'.[59] But we must immediately recognize that the very *significance* of the Bible's status complicates its novelty: if it reveals what is essential, then the truth it discloses will be found also in some respect already in the natural order. Christian novelty, in other words, is always of a dramatic sort, in which the surprise turns out to be the solution that was demanded, a solution that sets everything in the place it was clearly meant to have all along. It shows us for the first time what was in some respect always already the case, even if aspects that had been assumed to be marginal, like the stone rejected by the builders, turn out to represent the cornerstone. In this sense, we should not look for Christian novelty simply by seeking those discrete things that were not present in the pre-Christian world, but were brought into existence with the coming of Christ. Rather, we should strive to see the more subtle change of hue that dramatically alters a landscape we have always known and shows us what we may have never noticed before.

That having been said, the change of hue in this case appears to turn most directly on the *personal* presence of God, which transforms the act of knowing into the event of an encounter in a way that one does not frequently find in the Greek world. While it is true that, in pagan philosophy, reason's relationship to God arguably set the horizon for its relation to all of its objects, God is just that, namely, the ultimate object of reason, rather than a *subject* who intervenes personally in the world. But recognizing the object as, not just a subject, but the transcendent and originating Subject of all other subjectivities reverses the relationship and makes human reason *God's own* object: not that we have known God, but that he has known us first. What emerges here is a much more dramatic view of knowing – or as Mary Healy has described it, a view of knowing as 'spousal'[60] – that is, knowledge as the asymmetric union of acts, rather than as the unilateral act of a faculty on an object. Now, this latter characterization, as we have seen, is a caricature, even if it is a familiar interpretation of knowing, which became standardized in Enlightenment thought. The moral, affective, praxis-oriented, and wonder-based aspects of knowledge in the classical epistemology get recast in the biblical epistemology in a way that makes them arguably more thematically central and integral to even the essentially conceptual aspect of knowing. If truth is not a mere quality, but is a *person*, then the love in and by which one comes to know the truth is not merely a means to one's intellectual grasp of that truth, but an intrinsic part of that very comprehension. In this case, we don't simply come to *know* the truth (and then, say, put it into practice), but we *conform* ourselves to truth, which is already itself a praxis. The following of Christ is a *philosophical* act, as the Church Fathers clearly saw. Moreover, it is a *liturgical* act – a work of the people (*leit-urgos*) – and therefore essentially

---

[59] Healy, 'Pauline', 151.
[60] Healy, 'Pauline', 142, 144.

communal. When Heraclitus wrote that *logos* is communion, he revealed much more than he could have realized.

One of the implications of this more personal, 'dramatic' view of knowing as encounter, such as the essays in this book present it, is the increased epistemological significance of the unique, the historical, and the particular. The problem of integrating the historical and particular into knowing is one of the most difficult and recurring in philosophy. Knowing in its strictest sense – as *scientia* or *epistemē* – has always been understood to be of *universal* objects.[61] The attempt to think through knowledge directly in relation to concrete individuals has notoriously spawned further problems of its own. For examples of thinkers who made such an attempt, for very good reasons but with problematic consequences, we need only think of Duns Scotus and Hegel. Both, significantly, were inspired in their efforts by Christian revelation. Scotus developed a notion of '*haecceitas*', or 'this-ness', for the purpose of giving singularity an absolute character. But the absolutizing of the singular leads to nominalism on the one hand, and total abstraction on the other, insofar as, now, even 'this-ness' becomes a quality that can be known in abstraction from the concrete. What, then, is left for the *real*? Hegel famously relativized the significance of the abstract concept and required it to undergo the 'labor of the negative', the differentiation of history, in order to become a truly rational notion: the mind's or spirit's proper object is neither the abstract universal nor the concrete particular, but their synthesis in the *concrete universal*. But the result of Hegel's identifying the real and the ideal in the utterly concrete science of the spirit is a notorious totalizing rationalism that has no room for love, for freedom and indeed for the genuinely *Holy* Spirit. These attempts ought to keep us from uniting reason and the concrete and historical individual too quickly. Privileging familiar acquaintance (*gignōskō/connaître*) over scientific knowledge (*epistamai/savoir*), though illuminating, does not yet solve the problem of how to elevate the importance of the particular and historical without relativizing the significance of the universal or even simply substituting for it; if we do not carefully qualify the elevation of familiar acquaintance, this move can lead to a fairly banal and fruitless empiricism on the one hand or a sterile rationalism on the other. It may be that an adequate epistemology which does full justice to both universality and particularity has yet to be worked out. This is not altogether unchartered territory – in addition to the thinkers just mentioned, one finds rich philosophical reflection on this problem, for example, in Schelling's positive philosophy, Kierkegaard's philosophy of the individual, Schopenhauer's and Nietzsche's revaluation of the aesthetic, Gilson's existential Thomism, Marcel's philosophy of the concrete, Gadamer's hermeneutics, and Balthasar's 'meta-anthropology' of the world's truth – but there is clearly room for deepening and development. One may hope that studies of the Bible's epistemology, such as the essays collected here, may inspire more work in this direction.

Resolving this problem, or at any rate inquiring fruitfully into it, will require not only developing a notion of reason in philosophy that is centered on the singular

---

[61] See Aquinas, *ST* 1.86.1; cf. Aristotle, *Physics*, 1.5. 189a5-10.

without compromising the universal and that opens to the religious and traditional dimension of thought without surrendering its integrity. At the same time, it requires a more profound reflection on the nature of particularity within theology.[62] To be sure, the scandal of particularity lies at the heart of the Bible, but it is a scandal precisely because it claims definitive significance for the whole world and for all of history. While it is true that God made a covenant with a particular people singled out (*ek-klesia*) from among the many peoples on earth, it is also true that the blood that sealed the new covenant was shed in principle *for all*. The particular mission of Christ has been universalized in his Spirit, and aims to bring the whole of creation back to the Father. In this respect, the spousal knowing that occurs between Christ and the Church is meant to embrace all nature and, therefore, all natural knowing. One of the implications would seem to be that theology, to be true to itself *in* its particularity, is obliged to develop its general worldly dimension: not simply to present the necessity of a discontinuous rebirth 'from above', but at the same time to share in creation's groanings, to attend to the aspirations 'from below' to meaning and value, to love the world – in Christ and as he does – as in some sense an end in itself, insofar as love cannot simply instrumentalize. In short, just as philosophy needs to open to the particular and historical, as well as to the transcendent, theology needs to open to the universal and to the natural and worldly. The project of a biblical epistemology, we might say, stands at the intersection of these two needs. And because these needs are fundamental needs of our age, this project is a timely one indeed.

Bibliography

Annas, J., *An Introduction to Plato's* Republic (Oxford: Clarendon, 1981)

Aquinas, T., *De ente et essentia*

_____, *De veritate*

_____, *Summa Theologiae*

Aristotle, *The Basic Works of Aristotle*, R. McKeon (ed.) (New York: Random House, 1941)

Balthasar, H.U. von, *Theologik*, vol. 1: *Wahrheit der Welt* (Einsiedeln: Johannes Verlag, 1985)

Boehme, J., *Die Seele und das Ich im homerischen Epos* (Leipzig: Teubner, 1929)

Cornford, F.M., *From Religion to Philosophy: A Study in the Origins of Western Speculation* (New York: Harper, 1957)

De Lubac, H., *The Discovery of God*. A. Dru et al. (trs.) (Grand Rapids, Mich.: Eerdmans, 1996)

---

[62] Cardinal Joseph Ratzinger shows that the narrative of revelation itself in the Old Testament includes an expansion from particularity to universality (without losing the particularity) in *Truth and Tolerance: Christian Belief and World Religions* (San Francisco: Ignatius Press, 2004).

Derrida, J., *Grammatology*. Spivak (tr.) (Baltimore: Johns Hopkins University Press, 1976)

_____, *Margins of Philosophy*, A. Bass (tr.) (Chicago: University of Chicago Press, 1982)

Descartes, R., *The Passions of the Soul* in *The Philosophical Works of Descartes*, vol. 1. Haldane and Ross (trs.) (Cambridge: Cambridge University Press, 1973)

Diels, H., *Die Fragmente der Vorsokratiker* (Berlin: Weidmannsche Buchhandlung, 1912^3)

Festugière, A.J., *Contemplation et Vie Contemplative selon Platon* (Paris: Vrin, 1967)

Friedlaender, P., *Plato: An Introduction* (New York: Pantheon, 1958)

Hadot, P., *Philosophy as a Way of Life* (Oxford: Blackwell, 1995)

Heidegger, M., *What is Philosophy?*, Wilde and Kluback (trs.) (Albany, N.Y.: NCUP, 1956)

Jaeger, W., *The Theology of the Early Greeks* (Oxford: Clarendon, 1947)

_____, *Paideia*, vol. 2 (Oxford: Oxford University Press, 1986)

Kerstin, W., *Platons 'Staat'* (Darmstadt: Wissenschaftliche Buchgeselschaft, 1999)

Mattei, J.-F., 'The Theater of Myth in Plato', in C. Griswold, Jr. (ed.), *Platonic Writings, Platonic Readings* (New York: Routledge, 1988)

Plato, *Complete Works*. John Cooper (ed.) (Indianapolis: Hackett, 1997)

Ratzinger, J., *Truth and Tolerance: Christian Belief and World Religions* (San Francisco: Ignatius Press, 2004)

Rousselot, P., *The Eyes of Faith*. Joseph Donceel, S.J. (tr.), New York: Fordham University Press, 1990

Schindler, D.C., 'The Community of the One and the Many: Heraclitus on Reason', *Inquiry* 46 (2003), 413-48

Schmitz, K., 'Postmodern or Modern-Plus?' *Communio* 17 (Summer 1990), 152-66

Snell, B., *Die Ausdrücke für den Begriff des Wissens in der vorplatonischen Philosophie* (Berlin: Weidmannsche Buchhandlung, 1924)

Vivante, P., *The Homeric Imagination: A Study of Homer's Poetic Perception of Reality* (Bloomington: Indiana University Press, 1970)

Wieland, W., *Platon und die Formen des Wissens* (Goettingen: Vandenhock and Ruprecht, 1982)^2

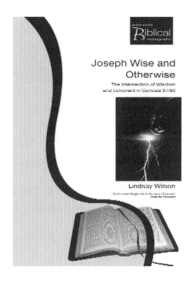

Joseph Wise and Otherwise

The intersection of Wisdom and Covenant in Genesis 37 – 50

Lindsay Wilson

This book studies how wisdom ideas in Genesis 37 – 50 relate to the themes and motifs that emerge from the Abrahamic promises. While the Joseph narrative is not simply a wisdom tale, there appear to be many features that are suggestive of wisdom. A literary reading of the chapters examines how these 'wisdom-like elements' relate to the story as a whole. Chapter 37 establishes that God will cause Joseph to rise to prominence. The intriguing story of Tamar in chapter 38 is seen as a kind of microcosm of the entire Joseph story, with Tamar securing life, justice and reconciliation through her wise initiatives, leading ultimately to the preservation of the line of promise. Joseph's public use of wisdom is considered in chapters 39 – 41, where he uses power successfully and with discernment. Joseph's private use of wisdom occupies chapters 42 – 45, as Joseph brings about change in his brothers and extends forgiveness to them. Chapters 46 – 50 complete the story by weaving the concerns of the previous chapters into the fabric of God's purposes for his covenant people. In the final form of the narrative, both the wisdom and the covenant strands are seen to be prominent. The covenant strand is reflected in the connections forged with the rest of Genesis, and the wider Pentateuch. The wisdom strand is evident in the public and private arenas, as well as in Joseph's tested character. God's behind-the-scenes activity, coupled with human initiatives, emerges as another 'wisdom-like element'. Both covenant and wisdom retain their distinctive contributions, and are complementary ways of God establishing his active rule. God uses wise human initiatives to accomplish his overarching purposes

978-1-84227-140-7

The Comical Doctrine

An Epistemology of New Testament Hermeneutics

Rosalind Selby

In this wide-ranging study Rosalind Selby explores the hermeneutical impli-cations of a Barthian epistemology in which 'givenness' (of knowledge, talk of God and Scripture, and the Church) is paramount. From this she seeks to develop a 'hermeneutics of service' that challenges both liberal and funda-mentalist approaches to theological language and biblical interpretation. Selby tackles the issues of knowledge, and especially knowledge of God, the language used to communicate that knowledge and that language as Scriptural textuality. Barth wrote of 'the comical doctrine that the true exegete has no presuppositions'. In fact, he said, 'no one reads the Bible directly – we all read it through spectacles.' In the train of his insight, Selby examines the role of community as a prerequisite for knowledge and truth claims before examining the different ways that various 'communities' inter-pret Scripture (focusing on Mark's Gospel). The presuppositions of the dif-ferent starting places are revealed and the appropriateness of various methodologies discussed. The Quest for the Historical Jesus and its struggles to handle the resurrection are used as a 'test case' to show the impact of dif-ferent hermeneutical strategies. The insights in this thought-provoking study have implications for issues as wide ranging as the genre 'gospel', the authority of Scripture, the Church as a 'reading community', the plurality of interpretations and the possibility of controlling them, the relationship between general and special theological hermeneutics, as well as epistemo-logical foundationalism and its alternatives.

978-1-84227-212-1

Alvin Plantinga and Christian Apologetics

Keith A. Mascord

The distinguished American philosopher, Alvin Plantinga, has had a career-long interest in the defence of Christian belief. There hasn't been a major contemporary challenge to such belief that Plantinga has not, in some way, addressed. This book draws together those contributions, highlighting particularly Plantinga's ground-breaking work in the areas of epistemology and the problem of evil. Historical and biographical background information is included to give perspective to Plantinga's work. His theory that both theistic and Christian belief is warrantedly basic is explored and critiqued, and an assessment offered as to the significance of Plantinga's work for apologetic theory and practice.

> 'Keith Mascord's book is a genuine achievement; wide-ranging, massively thorough, judicious, and critically penetrating.' – **Alvin Plantinga**, University of Notre Dame, USA

> 'This is an important work on one of the most important philosophers of our time. Keith Mascord has not merely written an excellent account of Alvin Plantinga's philosophy but also shown us how Plantinga has contributed to a much broader field of inquiry than academic philosophy. In addition, in the last three chapters Mascord provides his own critical and original response to Plantinga.' – **Peter Forrest**, University of New England, USA

978-1-84227-256-5

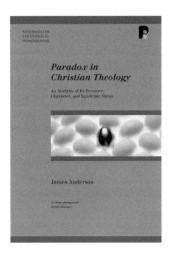

Paradox in Christian Theology

An Analysis of Its Presence, Character, and Epistemic Status

James Anderson

Does traditional creedal Christianity involve paradoxical doctrines, that is, doctrines which present the appearance (at least) of logical inconsistency? If so, what is the nature of these paradoxes and why do they arise? What is the relationship between 'paradox' and, 'mystery' in theological theorizing? And what are the implications for the rationality, or otherwise, of orthodox Christian beliefs? In *Paradox in Christian Theology*, James Anderson argues that the doctrines of the Trinity and the Incarnation, as derived from Scripture and formulated in the ecumenical creeds, are indeed paradoxical. But this conclusion, he contends, need not imply that Christians who believe these doctrines are irrational in doing so. In support of this claim, Anderson develops and defends a model of understanding paradoxical Christian doctrines according to which the presence of such doctrines is unsurprising and adherence to paradoxical doctrines can be entirely reasonable. As such, the phenomenon of theological paradox cannot be considered as a serious intellectual obstacle to belief in Christianity. The case presented in this book has significant implications for the practice of systematic theology, biblical exegesis, and Christian apologetics.

> 'In defending the ineluctable presence of paradox in theology, James Anderson argues that attempts to avoid this will result in formulations that are inadequate to the articulation of core Christian doctrines. What is particularly striking about this study is its accomplished engagement of important recent work in analytic philosophy of religion.' – **David Fergusson**, University of Edinburgh

978-1-84227-462-0

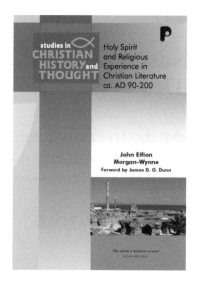

Holy Spirit and Religious Experience in Christian Literature, ca. AD 90-200

John Eifion Morgan-Wynne

Holy Spirit and Religious Experience seeks to find out how far the centrality of the Holy Spirit in Christian experience during the earliest period of the church was maintained or diminished in the third to the fifth generations (ca. AD 90-200). Three themes are explored. First, the sense of encounter with the divine presence, the numinous, a sense of being caught up into the divine being or being overwhelmed by the One who is beyond us. Secondly, a sense of being illuminated in respect to the truth, given deeper understanding of God's purpose, whether for the individual or the congregation, or guided in decision-making. Thirdly, a sense of ethical empowerment, an awareness of being helped by divine power, assisted in a course of action or development of character, in grappling with temptation, or in the ultimate test of loyalty, martyrdom. The book is arranged geographically, from Syria and Asia Minor in the East to Rome and Gaul in the West, including North Africa and Egypt.

'This will be a standard resource for its topic.' – **Richard Bauckham**, University of St Andrews

'Dr Morgan-Wynne is ideally placed to fill this gap in scholarship on the Holy Spirit in the early patristic church.' – **James D.G. Dunn**, University of Durham

'Since there has been no book like this since 1899, this indispensable guide to a vital topic is even more to be welcomed.' – **Paul Trebilco**, University of Otago, New Zealand

978-1-84227-319-7

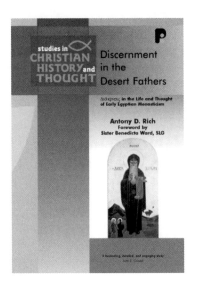

Discernment of the Desert Fathers

Διακρισις in the life and Thought of Early Egyptian Monasticism

Antony D. Rich

Discernment in the Desert Fathers is a study of discernment διακρισις in the life and thought of the fourth and fifth century Egyptian Desert Fathers. Rich argues that their understanding of διακρισις was based upon a practical application of biblical διακρισις in general and not, as has been argued, primarily a development of the gift of 'discernment of spirits'. He begins with an examination of Scripture and goes on to consider the philosophical and theological background of the period as represented by Plotinus and Origen respectively. An examination of the works of the first 'theologians of the desert', Evagrius and Cassian who lived among these first Christian monks and nuns, provides an early interpretation of the sayings of the Desert Fathers or *Apophthegmata Patrum*. The Greek, Latin and Coptic sayings that survive are then examined in detail, some of them translated into English for the first time. This in-depth analysis provides many insights into the lives of these early Christians and demonstrates how διακρισις touched on every aspect of their inward and outward lives. Rich concludes that διακρισις was a critical faculty and charism central to the spiritual and practical life of these early monks and nuns in their mystical search for God, for purity of life and knowledge of him.

> 'In this book, Dr Rich has explored with exemplary thoroughness the place of discretion in the early Christian monastic world, showing how it was understood and applied, by detailed reference to early monastic texts . . . He has given an illuminating picture of the content and the outworking of discretion, which can be as useful today as it was in the fourth century.' – **Bendicta Ward**, SLG, University of Oxford

978-1-84227-431-6

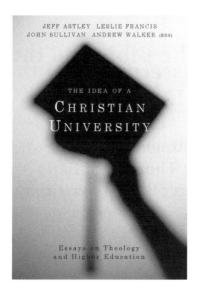

The Idea of a Christian University

Essays on Theology and Higher Education

Jeff Astley, Leslie Francis, John Sullivan, Andrew Walker (editors)

Today the academy is in a state of turmoil, torn apart by market-driven pressures, systematic under funding by central government, over worked and highly stressed staff, increased student numbers and an ever widening division between research-led and teaching-led institutions. This is a far cry from the religiously inspired ideals of Christian higher education which underpinned the foundations of so many centres of learning across Europe, North America and Australasia.

In this timely and provocative collection of essays, scholars from across the world re-examine the idea of a Christian University and offer a radical alternative vision for the future of the academy. Theologians from Anglican, Orthodox, Catholic and Protestant traditions engage both with the historic roots from which the idea of a Christian University emerges and with the contemporary challenges faced by higher education today.

Contributors include: Sam Berry, John Sullivan, Andrew Walker, Andrew Wright, Denis Robinson, Murray Rae, David Carr, Gavin D'Costa, Jeff Astley, Leslie Francis, Nicholas Rengger, William Kay, Gerard Loughlin, Patricia Malone, Ian Markham, Adrian Thatcher and Elmer Thiessen.

'A compelling read!' – **Stephen Sykes**, St John's College, Durham

'A splendid collection of essays in the spirit of Cardinal Newman and Jaraslov Pelikan.' – **Martyn Percy**, Rippon College Cuddesdon, Oxford

978-1-84227-260-2

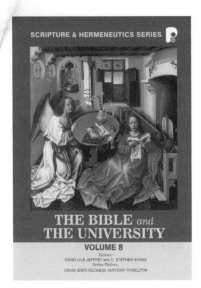

The Bible and the University

(Scripture and Hermeneutics Vol. 8)

David Lyle Jeffrey and C. Stephen Evans (editors)

It is becoming apparent that the secularized modern university that descended from the Christian universities of the past is having an identity crisis. The reason most often given is our failure to produce a morally or spiritually persuasive substitute for the authority that undergirded the intellectual culture of our predecessors. In this final volume of the Scripture and Hermeneutic Series, a group of distinguished scholars have sought to understand the role of the Bible in relation to the academic disciplines in a fresh way. Offered in a spirit of humility and experimentally, the essays here consider the historic role of the Bible in the university, the status of theological reflection regarding Scripture among the disciplines today, the special role of Scripture in the development of law, the humanities, and social sciences, and finally, some consideration for the way the Bible speaks to issues of academic freedom, intellectual tolerance and religious liberty. Contributors include: Dallas Willard, William Abraham, Al Wolters, Scott Hahn, Glenn Olsen, Robert C. Roberts, Byron Johnson, Robert Cochran, Jr., David I. Smith, John Sullivan, Roger Lundin, C. Stephen Evans, David Lyle Jeffrey.

> 'This superb collection provides first-rate engagement with a complex, but also supremely important subject.' – **Mark Noll**, University of Notre Dame, USA

> 'This important book reclaims the Bible from its Babylonian captivity to narrow academic standards and by doing so serves the university by restoring its heart; that is, any knowledge worth pursuing is the knowledge of God.' – **Stanley Hauerwas**, Duke University, USA

978-1-84227-072-1 (available from January 2008)